Growin

Lydia Jay Mason

GUS
Fitzgerald, Georgia

The material presented in this memoir was framed by old documents, letters, and recollections. I have attempted to recreate as closely as possible what actually occurred, knowing that exact details of specific events and conversations are impossible to recall.

Book Design by Sagaponack Books & Design
Paintings on cover and title page by Laura Beth Mason
Photographs collection of the author

ISBN: 978-0-578-50457-5

Summary: An autobiography of a woman growing up in the South from childhood until present day and what it means to be Southern. Recipes and photographs are included.

BIO026000 Biography & Autobiography / Personal Memoirs
CKB002060 Cooking / Regional / Southern States
FAM046000 Family and Relationships / Life Stages

www.gusmason.com

GUS
Fitzgerald, Georgia

Printed and bound in the United States of America
First Edition

Acknowledgments

This book is dedicated to my husband, Gene Mason, who encouraged me to write it even though I felt somewhat inadequate; to my children Rob and Amy Sherrell, Jay and Jaye Mason; and to my precious grandchildren Whit, Laura Beth, and Robert.

A special thanks goes to Ed Grisamore, who met with me and read several chapters, offered suggestions, and wrote my exemplary foreword; to Edna Lu Dorminy, a nurturing reader who encouraged me and supported the idea of a published book; Beth McIntyre, for proofreading and sharing her insights; and Frances Keiser for her expertise in book design and production. Let me also thank my precious granddaughter, Laura Beth Mason, for her artwork.

Last but certainly not least, I dedicate this book to the legacy that earlier generations bestowed upon me. Without them, there would be no book.

Family Tree of Lydia E. Jay Mason

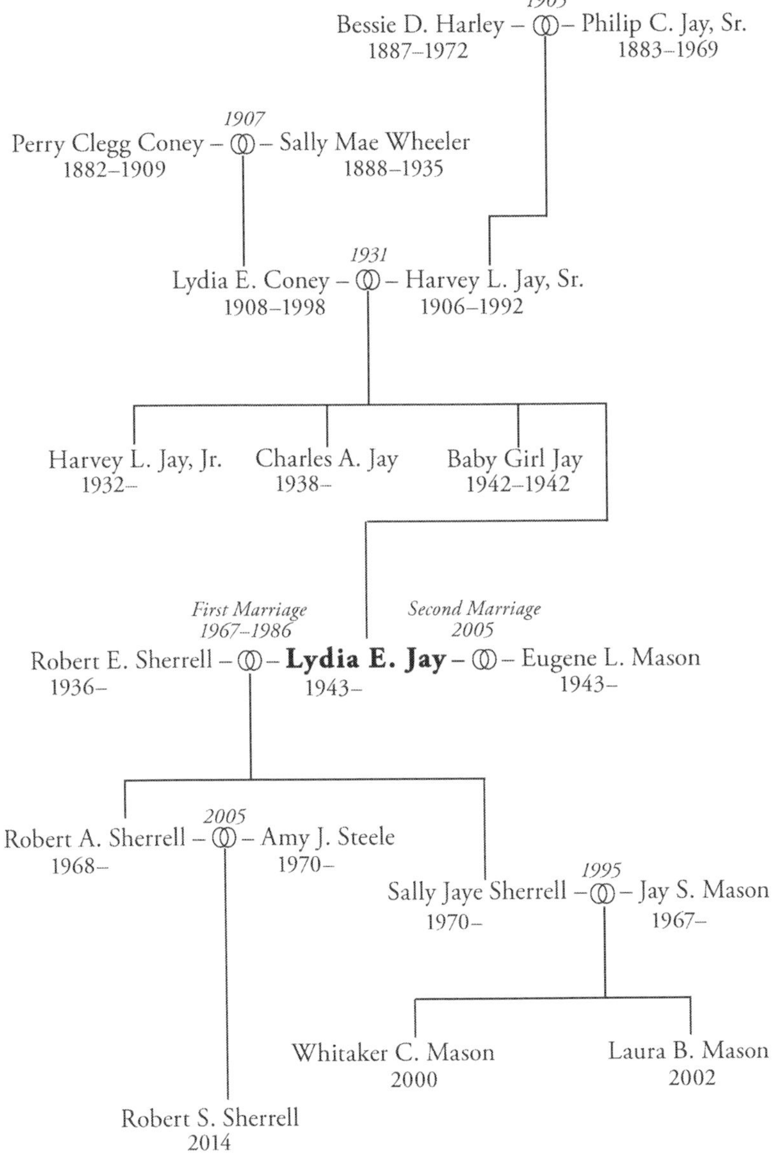

Stories have to be told or they die, and when they die,
We can't remember who we are or why we're here.
—Sue Kidd Monk, *The Secret Lives of Bees*

Contents

Foreword

Before I met Lydia Jay Mason, we shared a special kinship.

We were related, not by blood, but by roots that run deep through South Georgia like kudzu vines. We are kindred spirits, two people bonded by love of family, faith, communities and allegiance to all things Southern.

I have known Lydia's brother, Charles Jay, for more than 30 years and consider him one of the finest Southern gentlemen I know. He always is dressed impeccably, tells every lady how sweet and pretty she is and ministers to senior citizens and shut-ins.

Her mother and namesake, the late Lydia Jay, was my mother's high school Sunday School teacher at the First Baptist Church in Fitzgerald in the 1940s. Mama, now in her 90s, recalls how Mrs. Jay came to visit her parents when the family moved to Fitzgerald in 1942. She became one of the guiding influences in her life.

"She was a beautiful woman who reminded me of Grace Kelly," Mama said. "She always was immaculately dressed. Her hair was perfect, and she had a sparkle in her eyes."

Fitzgerald has long been one of my favorite places. It is one of the most unique small towns in a state that has plenty of them. Being an old newspaper guy, of course I would be drawn to a city founded by a former newspaper editor from Indiana.

It is known as the Colony City, with a rich heritage of settlers from both sides of the War Between the States. For the most part, folks have gotten along in a place where the downtown streets are named after both Unions and Confederate generals. (The town has a sense of humor, too. The fire department was once located on Sherman Street.)

Not to be outdone, the local high school mascot is the Purple Hurricanes. It's rare for hurricanes to venture that far inland, and I'm pretty sure a purple one has never shown up on the weather radar.

Fitzgerald has become known in recent years for its free-range chickens long before they became trendy. Red Jungle fowl have been running loose in yards and neighborhoods for years, and the national media has flocked to Fitzgerald to report on it.

Of course, life in the South is like that. We balance our bedrock values and unchained eccentricities.

Lydia's roots have given rise to her voice, and she writes with grace, wit, and humor. About the only time you'll be able to put this book down is when you tie your apron strings and head to the kitchen to try out one of her fabulous recipes.

If you are one of the chosen ones—Southern born and Southern-bred—you will see a lot of yourself on these pages. I know I did.

They say every creative person has a book inside them waiting to come out. We should be grateful Lydia found the angel in the marble and set her free.

Ed Grisamore, Author and Journalist
Macon, Georgia
February 2019

Preface

I love the South, where there is a rich history of the past, indelible work ethics, strong religious beliefs, gentleness, good manners, satisfying food, and a genuine love of family and friends. I am indeed concerned, for I see our Southern way of life rapidly becoming a thing of the past.

I believe the greatest legacy I can leave my children and grandchildren, besides a Christian heritage, is a compilation of their ancestry. I have a thirst for my children and grandchildren to grow up knowing about their ancestors and the childhood experiences of their parents and grandparents. How will they ever know how to make my MeMa's Angel Food Cake or her Fudge Cake for which she was so well remembered? How will they pass these recipes down to their own children and grandchildren if I don't take the time to write them down?

I have amassed a lifetime of newfangled ideas and technology, some good and some that have greatly distracted rather than enhanced my life. My grandchildren cannot comprehend that I was a part of a generation of mothers who were advised that it was ok to smoke during pregnancy, who gently placed their newborn babies in cribs covered in lead-based paint, and who had no car seats to strap their babies into when placed inside a car. When I hear the term "gay," I think fun loving, not people of the same sex. When I hear the term "alien," I think a person from outer space, not someone who unlawfully enters the USA. Our worlds are truly different today.

I have decided I do not want to be so busy living life I cannot take the time to become the custodian of my family's memories. For years, I have felt compelled to compose a book of memories, and I am finally doing so with the birth of *Growing Up Southern*. It is a mixture of history and my memories, as well as I remember them, and I pray they are somewhat accurate. I am grateful they will not die with me.

I hope you will find this book as comforting as a biscuit dripping in Cane syrup on a cold, lazy Saturday morning. Enjoy and reminisce of days gone by!

My mother Lydia Coney, age 4 and my
grandmother Sally Wheeler Coney, age 24. (1912)

Introduction

Growing Up Southern is a book that clearly deals with a state of mind, body and soul with which I was born. It's not just about magnolias, fried chicken or Coca-Cola (pronounced "co-cola") or pop if you are from the North, but rather it is about remembering from whence you came. Being Southern is much like class, you either have it, or you don't; you are either Southern or you aren't. The South has a distinct cadence similar to a nearby river that slows the mind and the soul as it alters our perception of time and daily living. Many non-Southerners do not understand this, bless their hearts, but it serves as a barometer to let us know that everything is going to be all right with the world.

I believe Southerners are gentler people because we are taught from an early age by our demanding Southern matriarchs that it is important to say and do the right thing, to always remember life is worth celebrating and to never (pronounced "ne-vuh") be rude or confrontational to anyone. We might disagree with one another at times, but we are always taught to play nicely together and to help one another.

From the earliest age, Southerners are taught to befriend others, be gracious, and as women, to understand that it is easier to ask forgiveness than to seek permission. We are instructed to refer to others as "Honey" or "Miss" (first name) and "Mr." (first name), regardless of their age or station in life. One's station in life is assigned at birth, has little to do with monetary status, and is based mostly upon your family name and lineage of a family who did volunteer work, church work, or held an elected office. Regardless of who you are, parents want their children to know that their hearts should always be open to everyone they meet, and they are to leave this place better than they found it, bless their precious little hearts.

In essence, the South is a beloved place to all of us who were born below the Mason-Dixon line. Evidently, it is to those born other places as well because they are coming south "a mile a minute." I believe they are coming south because once they visit, they are drawn into our slower pace of life and our true Southern hospitality. It could even be the sounds of crickets or the rhythmic flow of streams or red dirt roads that makes other folks want to experience the jubilation that we enjoy daily in this idyllic place. Down South, we love to smile, be friendly and throw up a hand (maybe it's a 'wave' to you) to everyone we pass, whether walking or driving or whether we know them or not, purely as a sign of human kindness.

This book is not just about being Southern, but it is also about growing up Southern in a sleepy, little Georgia town called Fitzgerald. It is a unique city sired by veterans and born of the virgin pines. Mr. P. H. Fitzgerald, an attorney and publisher of an Indiana newspaper, was most interested in Union veterans. His dream in 1894 was to establish a colony in the South where aging veterans of the War Between the States could escape the rigors of the cold Northern winters.

Mr. Fitzgerald's dream caught on and veterans, along with their families, fled to an uncharted forest, located in the center of south Georgia. He purchased over 50,000 acres, but selected 1,000 acres, shaped in a square to comprise the city of Fitzgerald. Now comes the most interesting part of his design. The four boundaries of the square were named for Northern and Southern warships. The two major thoroughfares are Central Avenue, which runs east and west, along with Main Street, which runs north and south. The streets east of Main Street are named for Confederate generals while those west of Main Street are named for Northern generals. Mr. Fitzgerald named the streets north of Central Avenue for Georgia rivers while those to the south are named for native Georgia trees.

These facts are based upon "The Unique Story of a Unique City," a speech given to the Fitzgerald Rotary Club by my daddy. The uniqueness is both sides of the War came together and shared with one another in peace, prosperity, and food. Today, that story has been reprinted numerous times and has been used for a pamphlet given to tourists who pass through our community.

I am thankful I grew up in Fitzgerald, where you knew everybody, and everybody knew you. It was a harmonious town where a handshake and a man's word was all that was needed to seal a deal, and local homegrown stores took IOUs from individuals who were down on their luck.

Professionals, such as doctors and lawyers, often took turnip greens, eggs or peanuts as collateral for their services because that was all that some farmers could provide during a bad crop year. When I was young, it was a time of small farmers who didn't comprehend the value of their land. It did not take long for them to be gobbled up by conglomerates, real estate investors, and big-time farmers who were involved in the Ecosystem, forest management, and cattle.

I love the South and am thankful for the sweet childhood memories I can share with you, along with other precious memories which include my mother telling me to "be sweet" and/or "mind your manners." Oh, and the games such as Hide-n-seek, Red Rover, Red Light/Green Light, Old Maids cards or Monopoly, that we played long after our Tea Party era had ended.

I can still envision the monkey bars and the merry-go-round on the corner of Pine Street and Lee Street in Fitzgerald, where a public parking lot is today. These are the things that pierce my heart and make me want a return to those glory days where we played hard until dusk, and then came inside for supper, which in the South, is our night meal. After supper, we would bathe, so tired that we needed toothpicks to hold up our heavy eyelids. We would then get into bed to be serenaded to sleep by the chirps of the birds, the frogs, or maybe the crickets. These are precious memories to me and have helped to mold me into the person that I am today.

My dear friend, Susan Johnson Hogan, described what being Southern truly meant when she wrote this note to me about my mother, years after my mother had died.

> *Miss Lydia was a little bundle of Southern charm, elegance, graciousness and was always fun to be around. She adored her family, her community, and her church. She was the biggest cheerleader for our dear First Baptist Preschool Center as well as for others. She had a true loving servant-focused heart for everyone she met. I so enjoyed visiting with Mr. Harvey and her in their cozy and inviting den. Love abound in that house. Thank you, Lydia, for sharing your special mama with me.*

So now, Honey Child, just sit back with a glass of sweet tea or Co-Cola, both referred to as the quintessentially "Wines of the South," and sit a spell while you enjoy this book about the South and how it made me who I am today. When you are finished, with a walk down memory lane, I hope you are as "happy as a pig in the sunshine" and not "too tuckered out" from deciphering our Southern vernacular. Oh, for all of you having difficulty from understanding it, just hang on for I hear Webster is "fixin" to define Southerness as a second language!

Chapter 1

It's a Southern Thing

Growing up Southern is all about family, friends and religion. Have you ever wondered if other parts of America have a history as rich as ours? Are you old enough to have said, "I wish I had asked my grandmother or mother about this or that?" Will you become the custodian of your memories or will someone else have to occupy that space in time? As a child, it was usually all about me and my little corner of the world, but now I realize there is so much more to life. Have you ever wished for the simpler days of life or that your grandchildren could have had a life much like you experienced?

Southerners are taught from the cradle that good manners, an attribute deeply ingrained in almost everyone in the South, will open many doors for you. From the earliest age, we are taught that the two most important words to learn, and yes they are magical, are "Please" and "Thank you." It really doesn't matter if you are unsure of the correct use of either word, just make an effort to always use them!

I also must mention the most important "pair" of words to learn early on, because they are just as innate to our upbringing, are "ma'am" and "sir." All of the above show respect and consideration of other people by placing them in high regard. I understand that these gestures, in the North, are not necessary and might even sound disrespectful, but folks, I am here to tell you that just "ain't" so in the South!

Southern mothers want their children to behave and to speak properly; therefore, if possible, they enroll them in dance and piano, and more often than not, they send them to charm school. Charm school is where they are taught self confidence, discipline, etiquette, and even how to dance. In small towns, boys and girls take these classes around the age of 11. In metropolitan areas like Atlanta, children take Cotillion classes instead as an introduction to their debut into society.

It doesn't matter if you have money, or if you live in the city or the country, if you have class that is of utmost importance to Southern girls. It appears however, that you either have class or you don't, regardless of what kind of classes you attend. It's kind of like you either know when to wear pearls or you don't. Neither one is taught but rather learned and perpetuated through osmosis.

You will often hear Southerners refer to their loving mothers as "Southern matriarchs" who are filled with euphemisms and instruct their children to say "they will" rather than "they can." As mothers, we don't always know why we do things the way we do, but we do understand that if it was done by our mother and/or by her mother before her, then we are to do the same.

Have you ever said, "Oh, my gosh, I sound just like my mother?" If you haven't, then get ready because I believe every Southern woman will experience such an epiphany at some stage of her life. It is most definitely a never-ending cycle. A prime example is when my grandson asked me one day why I thought the word "stink" was unacceptable, and my answer was, "It just doesn't sound very nice." Then, I realized I was repeating exactly what my mother had said to me as a child. Another friend of mine said she wasn't allowed to say "belly," and nor was I, for the very same reason.

If you are from the South, what are some of the first questions you ask someone you have just met? Where are you from? Who was your mother (mo-thuh or mutha) or daddy (da-dee)? Who are your kin or where did you go to school? You may wonder why we do this, but the answer is simple. We do this because we all appear to be related and who knows, the person you just met might be a first cousin "four times removed." I have always heard we are all just one inch from being kin to one another, so I guess inquiring about family is just a "Southern" thing.

Southerners are related to one another by blood, marriage, companionship, or just downright convenience. We adore our heritage and genealogy so much we often keep it in the family. Sometimes, cousins even marry cousins or sisters marry brothers from another mother. Since the founding of our nation, families have become intertwined through marriage, other families, or because of a tight-knitted community. This appears to have been more prevalent in the isolated south because there was less available transportation for so many years.

My mother was an only child but she had a double first cousin. You might just ask what in "tarnation" is a double first cousin? Why, honey, that is simple: when sisters from one family marry brothers from another family or vice versa, you could say it is an intermarriage of two families. Now, it isn't politically correct to marry first or second cousins but otherwise, on up the ladder, it is totally acceptable according to Southern standards.

Southerners might seem to have an obsession with their illustrious ancestors and genealogy. Not saying in a boastful way, Southern mothers constantly remind you to "remember who you are" or "did you tell them who your daddy was?" From the earliest age, children hear their mothers and grandmothers discuss what occurred at the DAR (Daughters of the American Revolution) or UDC (United Daughters of the Confederacy) meetings. I never desired to belong to either group.

Later in life, I did join the DAR ,but only to help them with their membership numbers so they would not have to disband. My mother was proud her great-grandparents had fought for honorable causes they believed in like the American Revolution or the War Between the States. Patriotism and the love of country was instilled in me by both of my parents, and I strived to instill the same values in my children and grandchildren as well.

We love Southern names such as Rhett, Bonnie, Scarlett, etc. Do you think I am kidding? Of course not! I have dear friends in Macon, Georgia, who named their daughter Bonnie Blue Butler! Now, if you are from the North, that might not ring a bell, but if you are Southern, it most definitely does for Bonnie Blue Butler was a character in the most famous Southern movie of all time, *Gone With the Wind.*

I grew up believing every newborn child should have a true Southern name or a family surname bestowed upon him or her at birth. Now, I am sure if your name is not a family name or a double name, there is someone in your Southern family that has such a name. In fact, I am the ninth Lydia in my family. At one time, there were actually three Lydia Jays, all living in Fitzgerald.

In my immediate family, we had Big Harvey, Little Harvey, Big Lydia, Little Lydia and poor little Charles Allan, who was named for my step-grandfather and my daddy's law partner. I also cherish the use of variants of family names and double names such as Whitaker Clayton, Robert Steele, or Laura Beth, which are the names of my three grandchildren. Southerners love their family, their legacy and the utilization of family names that we cherish to be passed on from generation to generation, even if the deceased has been long gone.

It has often been said that the entire south must be married to one another and I sometimes I believe that statement. Yes, we do pass surnames on to one another and it can become rather confusing at times. A prime example is my own daughter was named Sally Jaye Sherrell before she was married. Sally was my grandmother's name, Jay was my maiden name and Sherrell was my married name. I added an "e" to my maiden name so that the name Jaye would become more feminine and she would not receive a military draft card.

When Jaye married, she married none other than a boy named Jay Scott Mason. So, they became Jaye and Jay Mason, and they both even have the same three initials. When I mentioned to my Jaye that it might be a good time for her to use her given name, Sally Jaye, her husband responded that with both of them having the same name and living in a new community, it would be a definite advantage and that folks would certainly remember their names. And, guess what, he was right!

Confusing names do not apply only to people ,but also to animals. I remember well, one of my best friends, Pat Puckett, had a dog named "Hey You" and did we ever have fun with that name! We would walk down the street and call out his name as loudly as we possibly could. You should have seen people turn around and stare at us, as if we were referring to them. Animals are also often named from terms of endearment, initials, color, or remembrances.

We once had a dog named "Bo Daddy" because we bought him from someone that lived on Bo Daddy Road in Yulee, Florida. Bo Daddy was a funny little Peek-A-Poo and my children adored him. As was often the fate of our dogs, Bo Daddy got hit by a car. He ran off afterward and hid for almost a day. When we finally found him, his body was literally torn apart. My daddy was at our house when all of us hurried to take Bo Daddy to the best vet ever, Dr. Dwain Smith. All the way to the vet, my daddy kept trying to let my children know Bo Daddy probably would not make it. After spending a few days at the vet, we were able to bring him home. When my daddy came over and saw that Bo Daddy was going to survive, he said to me, "If I ever get as bad off as Bo Daddy, please take me to Dr. Smith."

Not only do we love our Southern names, we also like to wear them proudly by monogramming every thing we own, beginning at birth. Some babies in the South will never reach their first month birthday without owning a smocked outfit and/or a piece of monogrammed clothing. There will be numerous babies who will even have a monogrammed piece of sterling silver or monogrammed letter of their first name somewhere in their room decor.

The adulation with monograms continues throughout one's life, even if the initials don't flow or spell as well as you would like. An example of that is Amy, my precious daughter-in-law, whose initials before marrying my son were "AJS." After their marriage, her initials became "ASS." Did that stop her from monogramming items she purchased? Absolutely not, but she did prefer using the first initial of her middle name which then became "JSS" instead.

We love to entertain in the South, regardless of the occasion or even if there is no occasion. There have been numerous parties in my lifetime, but growing up, most of my childhood parties were birthday parties. Later, as an adult, the parties became Coke parties, brunches, and teas which were held for newcomers, visitors, friends and/or brides.

If you weren't reared down south, you might wonder about the term "Coke parties" but don't think for a minute that I am referring to a drug. I am referring to the "Wine of the South," Co-Cola. For you see, Coke parties are merely get-together parties with friends. At these celebrations, the hostess serves open-face sandwiches, cheese straws, desserts, and Co-Colas wrapped in hand crocheted covers to keep one's hands from getting cold. And, if there are no upcoming brides or newcomers to welcome, we still have Coke parties just so we can socialize with one another. In recent years, we enjoy having Wine and Cheese parties since wine has become permissible in most religions.

Speaking of Coke parties reminds me that the South is as hot as blue blazes in the summer and mild in most winters; therefore, we spend a lot of time being thirsty. Are we really that thirsty or could it just be in our genes since Coca Cola, as well as Nehi Grape or Orange, RC Cola and Sprite, all originated in the great state of Georgia? I am not sure of the answer to that one, but I must add that there is also another drink or "Wine of the South," known as sweet tea.

Last year, a transplanted friend of mine from Illinois told me he had brought his mom down to live in a retirement home, and the one thing she seemed to enjoy the most was her indoctrination to sweet tea. We aren't "big" on green tea or hot tea, but give us a glass of homemade iced tea with a little lemon, ice and lots of sugar and we are just fine and dandy. Have you ever been in a restaurant, outside the South, and they didn't have iced tea, or if they did, there was very little ice in the glass? I haven't ever been able to figure that one out, but talking about it makes me have a hankerin for some good ole sweet tea!

Southern women have always been recognized as great cooks. We have been taught to cook in black iron skillets, whether it is cooking frog legs, quail or plain ole fried chicken. My mother taught others through the years that the best fried chicken must be cooked in a black skillet. It must work because I do not believe that there was ever a piece of chicken left on her platter. I can't go any further without discussing black skillets, in case you belong to the new generation or aren't familiar with them.

Heavy, black cast iron skillets are often purchased, not at Walmart, as one might think, but rather at a local hardware store. These skillets are so precious to true Southerners that they are bequeathed at death or even requested by close friends. These kinds of skillets absorb flavor each time they are used and will often impart memories to others. If you weren't blessed to have a family who possessed sterling silver, having this family heirloom was the next best gift. If you did not inherit one, then you must learn how to season the skillet once you have bought it before you can actually use it.

In order to season a black iron skillet, you first wash it with a mild soap (the only time you wash it with soap ever), rinse it well and dry it off. Next, you take oil, any kind will do, and lathe it generously before placing it in a 200 degree oven. Leave the skillet in the oven for approximately eight hours before removing it, and then wipe it out. It is now ready to use and will allow one to fry and enjoy the best fried chicken ever. Even though fried chicken originated in the South, today it has definitely become an American dish, rather than just a Southern one.

With much emphasis on healthy living today, we are being told to no longer fry food or cook anything the old way. We are being instructed or taught what is best for our digestive systems or medically sound. For the past 20 years, we have been told not to use pork in our veggies as well, but instead to use a bouillon cube. I understand that might be passable, for some foods, but there are certain things that just taste better seasoned with a big ole' ham hock.

It is interesting also that we are now being taught about organic food and home grown food. To me, that's pretty interesting because farming has always been a part of the South. Our region was once known for its farm to table food. Today, we have come full circle, where farming and farm to table food is now in vogue. As I watch cooking shows, it doesn't take me long to realize how many of the great American chefs were taught by their mothers or grandmothers who were from the South.

I cannot speak about Southern food without mentioning the Southern comfort food, BBQ (Bar-B-Q) or to those not Southern, barbecue. We serve it at picnics, backyard gatherings, family reunions, tailgating, pit masters contests or any kind of a social gathering. However, when I was a child, BBQ was not acceptable as a funeral food, as it is today. That is a prime example of one of the numerous questions I regret not asking my mother.

Cooking good barbecue pork is a passionate art that must be done slowly, over a period of multiple hours, and even sometimes overnight. It occurs around a pit filled with hot, slow coals, entertaining stories, and a few good friends. Once it is cooked, it becomes known as BBQ, and is not to be sliced, but rather it is to be "pulled" away from the bone. The secret to good BBQ is not necessarily the pork but rather the kind of firewood, the rub, and the sauce used.

There are so many varieties of BBQ sauces, some that are handed down through generations and are kept as a family secret. Some sauces are made with ketchup, some with mustard, some with vinegar while others might be an original concoction. I hate to admit this, but I was actually 50 years old before I indulged in anything other than homemade mustard and vinegar based BBQ sauce. As human beings, we are somewhat limited by only the things of which we are exposed.

Southerners honestly believe that the best form of grief therapy is food. I have never completely understood it, but there is a distinct correlation between death and food. Death cannot occur when within minutes, there are people arriving at the back door with food to console the bereaved and wanting to know their exact needs.

The mourners are usually members of one's Sunday School class, garden club, bridge club, or tennis club. Sometimes, there will be a handful of folks who just come out of curiosity rather than concern. When my parents died, I will never forget that I had a local bank representative call to see if I needed an additional refrigerator or freezer at my house, and if so, he would have it delivered and set up for me. This is nother prime example of how things are done in the South, especially in small towns.

Even, in this day and time, friends in small communities still arrive, after the loss of a loved one with mostly homemade food. I learned recently, that is not true everywhere in the South. I was at a relative's home in another state before the loved one's funeral where there was plenty of food for the family. However, only two dishes were actually homemade. Friends came by, but they came with fried chicken from KFC, potato salad from Publix, pies from the local bakery, and green beans from the nearest restaurant. This almost blew my mind because in my community, this is unacceptable. I just hope that this is not a sign of new times in the South.

Sometimes the grieving family might even share a memento with those who drop by the house for visitation. My dear friend, Bill Hammond, a beloved doctor in my hometown, loved Moon Pies, and folks that knew him well were aware of this craving. In preparation for visitation at his home, a family member went out and bought small moon pies which were distributed to anyone who wished to take home a memento of their friend, Bill. This is another example of how loving and generous Southerners are, for even in their time of grief, they still manage to think of others.

In the South, we are always ready to help our neighbors and friends in times of trouble. Honestly, I doubt that there is a pantry in my neck of the woods that doesn't have at least one can of Campbell's Cream Soup. Please understand it can be cream of mushroom, cream of chicken or cream of celery soup. When you get up to cream of asparagus or a little fancier soup, it doesn't hold a candle to the savoriness of the basic Campbell soups.

Funerals or church socials are one of the few times we don't do fresh foods, but rather fill the dishes with lots of salty soups and carbohydrates. Southerners have been taught that the ingredients in these soups seem to soothe the soul. Of course, don't forget to add the can of onion rings, crushed potato chips or cheddar cheese to the top of the casserole to dress it up when using it strictly for therapy.

Usually at a funeral or social gathering, someone will always appear with a deli tray from Walmart or the grocery store. I understand that it is always delicious, but the tray must be rearranged a little so that it doesn't appear to be "store bought tacky," a term often used in the South. One idea is to place a few open-faced sandwiches intermittently on a pretty tray. You must be sure that you cut the bread crusts off the sandwiches, a lesson that we learn at an early age from our Southern matriarchs. Now, don't forget to add a few deviled eggs to the tray, or if there is not enough space, you can serve the deviled eggs on your own special egg dish.

Every cook in the South has at least one extra special deviled egg dish that they received as a wedding or a birthday present. Southerners enjoy deviled eggs and must understand how to boil a good egg. A tip I was taught for boiling eggs was to only cook them for a few minutes, then cover the pot, remove it from heat and let the eggs cool before peeling. It is incredible how easily they will peel.

Lastly, when taking food to the family of a deceased, you can never go wrong with homemade pimiento cheese sandwiches. An effective trick my mother taught me many years ago was to always place a damp tea towel or cheese cloth over the sandwiches to keep them fresh and presentable. This tip only applies if your family or you do not plan to gobble them up immediately.

Did you realize pimento cheese is not a part of northern cuisine? I honestly thought that people everywhere ate pimiento cheese! Another food I did not realize was regional was cream cheese. In the South, we put it on a dish with pepper jelly on top and serve it with crackers. I understand in the North, cream cheese is mostly used on bagels. Isn't that interesting?

Southerners know instinctively that solace for a friend in need is a bowl of chicken salad, a casserole (probably made with cream of mushroom soup), or maybe a fresh, homemade peach pie. As parents, we pass on these acts of kindness and encourage our children to show respect, love, and warm hospitality to everyone, wherever they go in life. I have often wondered if we do this because we were reared in the Bible belt, or is it because we are just remembering the golden rule, "Do unto others as you would have them do unto you."

Speaking of funerals in the South, there is definitely correct etiquette in regard to funerals. We teach our children how to behave at a funeral, and when to visit the funeral home, and not the deceased's residence. They are taught as well what kind of food is appropriate and how to order flowers from the florist, or on-line today.

In small communities, policemen stand in significant intersections to stop traffic with their hat over their heart. Spectators or vehicles on the side of the road, stop while the slow-paced procession, led by the long, black hearse, respectfully goes through the intersection. I understood that this was the proper thing to do and just assumed everyone did so in honor of those bereaved until my college roommate from Pennsylvania taught me differently. She was indeed puzzled when she saw me pull over to the side of the road when a procession came by because she had never heard of that before.

In the South, it is seen as a display of respect and compassion for the grieving family as they make their way to the cemetery. It warmed my heart when I saw the processional of our late U. S. President George H. W. Bush as cars pulled over in respect of this man. Once again, this was exhibited by true Southerners in the great state of Texas. When you are part of the grieving family in a processional, you truly understand how much this act of kindness means. Another act of kindness is for others to have an extra handkerchief or tissue to share. Neither of these expressions costs much, but it is the act of being thoughtful that is long lasting and memorable to those in need.

People often say sports are akin to religion in the South, and they are close to being right. We like basketball; we like baseball; but we love our football. Not necessarily pro football, but our high school and college football teams we follow ardently. In Southern small towns, it is the only place where people go on Friday nights from August through November. It is also a place where our local heroes become legends. For instance, a famed high school football coach, Wright Bazemore, grew up right here in Fitzgerald. Coach Bazemore is in "Ripley's Believe or Not" for scoring 10 touchdowns in a game twice while playing for the Fitzgerald Purple Hurricanes. He went on to compile a record at Valdosta High School as a coach of 30 years with a 268-51-7 record, 14 state titles and three national championships.

College football in the South, led by the SEC (Southeastern Conference) teams which have dominated football for the last century, are revered by true Southerners. I never see a red-and-black shirt that I don't think of the Georgia Bulldogs or see an orange-and-blue shirt that I am not reminded of the Florida Gators. Why, recently, my husband and I bought new beach chairs, and I became somewhat distressed.

When he inquired about my long face, I asked him if they only came in blue-and-orange. Inquisitively, he looked askance as I told him that orange-and-blue chairs were totally unacceptable to a UGA fan.

Every August, we begin to ready ourselves for the first game of the season. The butterflies in our stomach begin as we ponder whether or not we will be ranked again this year. I grew up with three men in my house, all having been football stars, so I virtually grew up thinking that everybody loved football like I did. It was amazing to me that some people don't even see Fall as the best season of the year, as we get fired up for football games, whether they are high school or college games.

The love of your special college team doesn't end once you graduate from said college. Just a few months ago, a friend reminded me of something that my daddy wrote to him many years ago. This local pharmacist and dear friend, Jerry Dixon, said that he sent a statement to my daddy, and at the bottom of the bill, it stated "Go Dawgs." When Jerry received the payment in the mail, my daddy wrote that he might just have to change pharmacies. You see, my daddy being a Georgia Tech fan, the "Go Dawgs" on his bill, significantly offended him. When Jerry told me that he knew my daddy was kidding, I looked at him and thought to myself, I am not so sure he was.

I must admit that growing up, my daddy made me a Georgia Tech fan. Later when I married and had children, I switched allegiance to the University of Georgia. My ex-husband played football at Presbyterian College but went on to play in the South Professional League. His team was located in Atlanta and preceded to the arrival of the Atlanta Falcons the following year. Some of you might even remember this Atlanta minor league team was called the "Mustangs." While the team was playing in Jacksonville, Florida, they were paid off that night in counterfeit money. Thus, ended the league, and led to the emergence of the professional team the Atlanta Falcons!

I almost found myself not wanting to type the words "Atlanta Falcons" because I am still not completely over their loss in the 2017 Super Bowl. Even my best friend said to me that she had never seen me so devastated after a football loss. She was right, and I responded that I just couldn't help having a broken heart over the loss. Football has always been instilled in me, and it is a sport I love. In fact, I am such a football addict that I will cancel out a glorious night at the country club or the Ritz to watch college football!

Did I ever play sports? Absolutely not because I was not athletically endowed. I just cheered the team on and tried to look as attractive as I possibly could. My parents sent me to an all-girls college, but I still participated in the football games and parties at the University of Georgia and Georgia Tech on the weekends. In that era, we wore our Sunday best, like a Kimberley Knit or a Tahari suit, with gloves and hats. Then on to the fraternity house and the college football games. Today, people wear very little and most definitely not their Sunday best. All they seem to care about is that they don their team's colors.

Southerners still tailgate at football games and continue to schedule all social affairs around the football schedule, even though it doesn't always work out. I have a dear friend, Patricia Waters, whose daughter, Shaw, and her future son in law, Gill Braddy, scheduled their wedding in December. Knowing that by that certain date, the UGA season would be over, and it would be convenient for everyone to attend. After all, what kind of woman would ask her friends to choose between football and her wedding?

After the wedding was scheduled, the local high school team made the state playoff. That particular year, the state playoff was held at the high school rather than at the dome as it is today. The high school football field was located across from their church. Everyone, including the bride and groom, hurried over to the stadium to catch the ending of the game, after the wedding. To some of us, yes, you could say that football is much like religion, and I could easily be one of those folks.

Entertaining is so much fun in the South, and Southern women learn at an early age how to do it up right. I remember on birthdays or other milestones in my life, my mother or her friends would have parties in my honor, thereby teaching me that life is filled with times of joy and celebrations, as well as sorrow. Entertaining is not necessarily about the decor or the food. Instead, it is about inviting others into your home for a relaxed time.

No matter what the occasion, happy or sad, Southerners can always throw a party, and enjoy being with one another. It doesn't have to be an extravagant menu. Instead, have a party, and make it about the foods you cook best and the particular dishes for which you are known. Being together should be the theme of any party of which you are a part.

I have also learned that if you are going to the trouble to clean and decorate your house, you might as well have two parties just as well as one party. Everything is pristine, and the flowers are still beautiful, so why not have another party for the next day or night? Yes, you are tired but what a great way to kill two birds with one stone and mark it off your calendar.

My dear friend, Danna Smith, still reminds me of the time that she and I had a party for our friends one summer. After the party, my mother suggested that we have a party at my house the next day for her friends, and that we did. However, when it was time to clean up, Danna and I soon realized that my mom was nowhere to be found because she had left with the guests. She was right; it was a great idea for her!

As Southerners, we love to decorate or have a party for every event that occurs. I must admit some of us are worse than others. My husband has told me on numerous occasions that he loves to see what decorations or favors I have scheduled for the upcoming holiday. Even though he laments that he hates to see me work so hard, he thoroughly enjoys the celebration.

If you went into my daughter's home in Dublin, you would see that the trait of having a party for every season or event has been passed on to her. In fact, it is now in the hands of my granddaughter, Laura Beth. Last year, when Thanksgiving was on the horizon, a new student at her school inquired as to when her Thanksgiving party was going to be. She looked puzzled when he said, "Well, you had a back to school party, an after the game party, and then a Halloween party. I just assumed that you would be having a Thanksgiving party." The fact that it is now in the hands of another generation tickles me to no end.

Of all the times to entertain, springtime must be the best time for partying: Easter, St. Patrick's Day, the Masters week, and then topping it off, the Kentucky Derby. When I entertain, I always have a theme to decorate my table. For instance, on St. Patrick's Day, I still use my St. Patrick's Day china, with leprechauns dancing around the table amidst an arrangement of greenery. Then, I use green tulle and wrap up miniature bottles of Irish liqueur for my guests to take home as a remembrance. If I have a Kentucky Derby party, I use my brown china, my collectible Derby glasses, and the favor becomes a wrapped miniature bottle of Kentucky Bourbon.

You might be wondering what I would do for favors of "booze" if I were entertaining the Baptist preacher. The very same thing as above because the preacher could use the "flavoring" on his ice cream, his cake or give it to a friend. Believe me, it probably will stay at his house, and he will be thankful he received it! Yes, there was a time that Baptist preachers, as well as many Baptists, did not partake of spirits. It appears that day and time is long gone in most congregations.

After springtime comes the "Big Three" celebrations which are Memorial Day, Fourth of July and Labor Day. This an easier time because the napkins, drinking straws and star-shaped plates are all in red, white and blue. Normally, these three celebrations are hosted at our lake house where we place American Flags everywhere. On our front door is a wreath that I made out of red, white, and blue flip-flops. There are flowers as well to welcome our guests as they enter our lakeside home. We eat boiled peanuts and BBQ throughout the day. The patriotic celebration always ends with homemade peach ice cream and pound cake. Afterwards, we all head out onto the lake to see the spectacular fire-works display.

Isn't life grand now that there are electric ice cream churns, and we no longer have to take turns at churning the ice cream? Yes, I said "churn" which I am sure that most of you cannot comprehend. Even though it sounds horrendous, and we often complained, it was really fun times. Truly, the South is all about entertaining, and making your guests feel comfortable, whether it is a big "whoop di do" or just a small, unpretentious gathering.

Religion is deeply engrained in the life of Southerners. Even in my small community of 16,000, there are more than 100 churches and a synagogue. The purpose and belief of religion and faith are important to us. Our lives have always revolved around our church and its beliefs.

In the region known as the Bible Belt, it is common to hear the name of God used in conversations without any apologies. Our social events such as sporting games, schools and clubs all begin with a prayer. It is still something that occurs today in most rural southern communities.

I have heard others, not from the South, discuss how we offer to pray for someone we barely know if prayers are needed for that person. Well, folks, I can't explain it except that it's just something we feel compelled to do for one another. We also believe that our strong religious beliefs help to ease the pain and the journey for those who are hurting as well as for ourselves.

Southern girls grow into beautiful Southern women, and the following is a true Christian testimony of receiving others into your heart. I grew up with this childhood friend who was several years younger, Lou Williams. Lou related the following splendid encounter she had with a beggar on Sunset Boulevard in California during this past year.

The beggar had his hand outstretched and begged, "Please, ma'am." She had left her wallet at home and was walking back to the bakery to place an order when she was approached by him. In haste, she shook her head to imply "no" and then realized that he wasn't asking for money; instead, he was asking for a dance. She grabbed his hand and the two of them did a jitterbug on the sidewalk. She turned him, he turned her, and soon time resumed its rightful place. She went on with her errands. The beggar thanked her profusely as she left, but little did he realize that the pleasure had been all hers.

Only a Southern girl would have taken the time to dance on the streets of LA with a toothless old man, but just think of the love and gratification they shared with one another. It was just the natural thing for Lou to do. We Southern girls have been taught that when we give to others, our gain is actually much greater! It doesn't matter whether you are dancing with the CFO of a large conglomerate or a toothless old man. What really matters most is that you approach both with the same degree of warmth and respect that your parents taught you.

Southern women firmly believe they cornered the market on being original or different. We like to believe we are "steel magnolias" and can weather any hurt or loss with dignity and faith. After all, we learned from our forebearers, like Scarlett O'Hara. Need I say more?

It is quite obvious that we must be different women because how many times has someone said "Please talk for me. I just love to hear you talk." Have you ever heard of someone asking a northern woman to speak because they liked the way she spoke? In fact, the next time you are with one, ask her just how often that has happen in her life. You can also quote Winston Churchill, who once said: "The most beautiful voice in the world is that of an educated Southern woman."

I heard a transplanted Southerner say she had no desire to move back South because she never got the attention down here that she does in the North due to her southern dialect. Some Southern girls' accents actually get "thicker" once they have lived in the North. Evidently, there must be something soothing to a thick as molasses Southern drawl. In addition to our drawl, we also have certain sayings that are passed down through generations. Some of them that might be recognizable to you are as follows:

- Oh, this is good a sight.
- This will make your mama proud.
- Cattywampus or crank sided.
- I swanee, and I don't mean the river.
- If you can't say something nice, don't say anything.
- I don't know diddly squat about that.
- I think I have died and gone to heaven.
- Poor as Job's turkey.
- I use a buggy not a shopping cart.

There are people who want to believe that our sayings, drawl, and speech imply that we are hillbillies or rednecks, which is a total misconception. My grandson went off to an exclusive summer camp in North Carolina one summer. A boy in his cabin was from Florida. When he learned Whit was from Georgia, he asked him if he was a "redneck." What a misconception that young man had of the great state of Georgia and true Southerners. Yes, I understand Florida is in the South, but it is not occupied mostly by southerners.

I began to wonder exactly what is a redneck, so I decided to look it up in Wikipedia. It defines a redneck as a word chiefly used for a rural poor white person of the Southern United States. It is a derogatory slang, similar in meaning to cracker, hillbilly, and/or white trash. It is a stereotype often synonymous with one who lives in the South. In the early pioneer days, it referred to those who settled America and in later generations as the "illiterate, toothless, good ole boys." Just because we speak slowly doesn't mean that we are slow mentally. Please understand that we definitely take offense to others calling us by such names. I guess only a real Southerner knows and understands the difference in the meaning of a cracker, hillbilly, white trash or a redneck.

Like every part of the world, there are literate and illiterate people that occupy space on God's green earth. The movies portrayed the South for numerous years as being occupied by uneducated, poor, whiskey-toting men, and unattractive women. You either saw the beautiful sloping green grass of the plantations or the rocky, dirt front yards with mamas sweeping or raking the dirt daily.

When the movie producers constructed the homes, they always placed inside the houses, pictures of Jesus everywhere. They would even use babies, who had succumbed to snake bites or typhoid fever, as part of southern decor. In these make believe homes, rarely were there patriotic symbols which have always been a part of the home. Southerners had more men in the military than any other section of the country; therefore, one could say that loyalty to one's country or to one's family ranks very high in the South.

I am thankful I am "Southern born and Southern bred." Yes, we might be curious or persnickety to others, but we are who we are. There are those who believe that we are conscious of how we present ourselves to others because we are still hurting from losing "the war," but that is hogwash. Southerns love their past and want to cling to it as well as share it with others. Why? Of that, I am not quite sure. All I know is that we just want those from other parts of the world to see us as resourceful, hard working, unabashed Southerners. Truthfully, we love our way of life, along with all its nostalgia and want others to love it as well.

SOUTHERN RECIPES

In the South, food is a distinctive characteristic of who we are and what our heritage is as we gather around a table with friends and family. It is a tradition that when we are invited to someone's home, we are to take a gift which usually is some homemade jam or jelly or maybe just a paper bag of tomatoes or whatever is growing at that time. In the earliest of times in the South, it was necessary to have an abundance of food in order to nourish the hardworking field hands and families. You will note that many of the ingredients in the recipes below are items that could be found on a farm in the earliest days. These recipes are some that are impossible to forget because they have always been a part of our life. Enjoy these truly Southern delights!

ICED TEA

6 tea bags
2 cups boiling water
1 ¾-2 cups sugar
6 cups cold water

Pour boiling water over tea bags. Cover and let steep for about 15 minutes. Take out tea bags and pour mixture into a pitcher. Add sugar and stir until it is dissolved. Pour in cold water and let cool. Optional: Squeeze a fresh lemon and add for flavoring.

PEACH ICE CREAM

6 eggs
3 ½ cups sugar
10 peaches, pitted and chopped
4 cups whipping cream
2 cups half and half cream
2 tsp vanilla
¾ tsp salt

On stove top, cook eggs and sugar together until a light yellow. In another pan, heat milk over medium to low heat until it begins to simmer. Gradually add milk to egg and sugar mix, stirring constantly. Return to heat but do not allow it to boil and then place in refrigerator until it is chilled. Puree peaches in a food processor. Once the refrigerated mixture is ready, stir in cream, peaches and vanilla. Put into an ice cream freezer canister and freeze.

Deviled Eggs

6 eggs
¼ cup mayonnaise
1 tsp white vinegar
1 tsp yellow mustard
⅛ tsp salt

Optional: paprika for garnish, sweet pickles to mixture or caviar on the top.

Put eggs into a pan and cover eggs with 1 1/2 inches of water above the eggs. Heat on high until water boils, cover, turn heat off and leave for about 15 minutes. Remove from pan and rinse under cold water for a few minutes and peel eggs. Slice them in half, remove yolks to a bowl and put egg whites on a plate. Mash the yolks into a fine crumb and then add ingredients.

BBQ Sauce

⅔ cup butter
2 Tbs sugar
1 tsp salt
2 Tbs flour
⅔ cup water
2 Tbs worcestershire sauce
1 ½ Tbs lemon juice
½ cup vinegar
¼ tsp tabasco

Melt butter, combine dry ingredients and add melted butter. Stir until well blended and remove from heat. Combine remaining ingredients and gradually stir into butter mixture. Return to heat and cook, stirring constantly, until thick.

Cheese Straws

1 lb sharp cheese, grated
1 stick butter
2 cups flour

Dash of salt, sugar and red pepper. Cream cheese and butter until well blended. Blend flour, salt, sugar and pepper and add to mixture, mixing until a smooth dough. Put the dough into a cookie press or roll very thin and cut into strips. Place on an ungreased cookie sheet and bake at 400 degrees for 10-15 minutes.

Open Face Sandwiches

2 oz cream cheese, room temperature
¼ tsp onion powder
½ tsp dill weed
4 slices of bread, cut in rounds
1 cucumber

Mix first three ingredients together until blended. Using a cookie cutter or small glass that is a little larger than your cucumber, cut them out. Spread cream cheese mixture on bread. Cut thin slices. Top bread with cream cheese, add cucumber slice and garnish with Dill sprig. Options are unlimited.

Chapter 2

Back to My Roots

As one who has reached the senior years of her life, I have begun to reflect on my ancestry and from whence I came. Very few days pass that I do not thank God for giving me the wonderful heritage that He did. My parents and grandparents taught me to believe that with the grace of God, I could accomplish anything in life that I so desired, as well as that family and God were first and foremost.

I was not blessed to know my maternal grandparents but oh, how well I knew my paternal grandparents. I lived across the street from them in a house that my parents built in 1934 when my oldest brother was only two years old. Yes, there were times I wished my grandparents lived "far away" so I could go for weekend jaunts to visit them. All in all, I was contented to have them right next door to me.

My paternal grandfather, Philip Clayton Jay, Sr., affectionately known as Two-Dads to his grandchildren, was the embodiment of a Southern gentleman. He taught his children well because all four of them placed family above everything else and were among the finest men and women that I have ever known. Of all his children, I guess my dad and he were the most alike, in that they were both quiet and soft-spoken. Let me give you a little background on this fine gentleman.

In 1896, David Belton Jay, affectionately known as D. B., moved his family to Fitzgerald, Georgia from Morgan, Georgia, which is located in southwest Georgia. Later, that same year, his parents, James Lemuel and Priscilla Jay, followed them to Fitzgerald and were two of the thirty-four charter members of the First Baptist Church in Fitzgerald. Sin was prolific, liquor was sold in quantities, saloons were plentiful, gun-toting men were everywhere, and this challenge provided a beautiful opportunity for others to begin churches and introduce Christ in this flourishing new city.

In 1902, Two-Dads had an article featured in *The Atlanta Constitution*, for which he was paid $5.00, on how Fitzgerald was transformed from a wilderness into a booming town. He loved to tell me the story of how his family, in 1896, came to "Shacktown" from Calhoun County in a horse and buggy. He reminisced that as they slowly crept across the Alapaha River on a shaky, wooden trestle, that his father's words to his mother were "You are now leaving civilization behind you." As they approached the small colony city, my grandfather told me that the sky was filled with bright lights which he thought to be electric lights. As they got closer to the city, he realized that the lights were actually coming from hundreds of "Stump fires" where people had cleared land to build homes and businesses.

Two-Dads explained to me how he saw people sleeping in tents, wagons and shacks as they entered the town that would become their new home. His father, David Belton Jay, purchased three of these wooden shacks and moved them to South Lee Street, making them into a rather lovely home. Later, when Two-Dad's mom died, his father remarried and built a house outside of the city limits. Today that house is owned by Lois Epps and is located on Wheeler Avenue. The last house that my great-grandfather built was a brick two-story house on West Pine Street where David Jay and his family lived for many years.

Two-Dads also told me that he would spend hours cutting wood, and his father paid him a dime for every stump that he cut up. He was one of only a few Southerners in the public schools since most families here had moved from Indiana to escape the winters. The following year, the colony city was given the name of Fitzgerald, after Mr. P. H. Fitzgerald, editor of the *Indianapolis Tribute*, who led the humanitarian efforts to move Union veterans to a warmer climate. During the first year of existence, Fitzgerald grew to 12,000 residents as they came by wagon, rail, and horseback.

Two-Dads developed his love of trees when he was only a young boy. He had not been in the colony city long when he met a man who brought in small magnolia transplants from the river to sell to the new colony city settlers. He had very little money but when he did, he said, "I always would spend my 25 cents and buy a tree from the old man."

One tree he planted, according to an article in the January 21, 1955 edition of the *Fitzgerald Leader*, is the tree that sits in the yard of the old J. H. Mayes home, on South Lee Street, next to the house where he grew up. Today, the tree still stands on the corner and is mentioned in the book *Under Magnolia* by the highly acclaimed Fitzgerald author, Frances Mayes.

My great-grandfather, D.B. was a graduate of Howard College, in Marion Alabama, which is known today as Samford University. There he was a member of Sigma Chi fraternity. He was a former Judge of Calhoun County, an ordained Baptist minister, instrumental in the establishment of the First Baptist Church of Fitzgerald, Solicitor General of Irwin County, and a Fitzgerald school board member. He practiced law in Fitzgerald with his son, Clayton Jay, Sr., and their office was located for numerous years in the Five-Story Building.

D.B. was instrumental in 1905, in leading the drive for Fitzgerald to leave Irwin County and form its own county, Ben Hill. The new county would be named for Benjamin Harvey Hill. It was a shrewd choice because Hill opposed secession, supported the Confederacy and was an apologist for Reconstruction.

There is a story of how several men from Irwin County wanted to meet D.B. Jay in a duel because of his desire for Fitzgerald to become a new county. The men knew that would lead to the taking of revenues from their county. A letter to our local newspaper in August 17, 1943, from Jesse Mercer, who later became the Director of the Georgia Literacy Crusade, was as follows:

> *Soon after the colony had been established and before I moved to Fitzgerald an effort had been made to move the country seat to the city from remote Irwinville, a very difficult thing to do in Georgia. Of course, Belton Jay was a prime mover in the undertaking, as in everything for the community advancement. Returning from a remote district in the then large county, he met in the road a party of active*

> *and violent opponents to removal. Then and there, during the inevitable controversy that ensued, an attempt was made to assassinate him; and it was his single-handed, manly and courageous stand that saved his life.*

Governor Northern of Georgia worked with my great-grandfather in this effort. D. B.'s son, Clayton Jay, Sr., actually hand drew the map for the establishment of Ben Hill County in 1906. A few years later, D.B. Jay was running for the Georgia House of Representatives. According to the local newspaper, he was selected to win when he became gravely ill and died. The editor of the Fitzgerald newspaper wrote the following when he learned of his death in 1910.

> *His moral life is unexceptionable, his record is clear and as far as Fitzgerald and Ben Hill County is concerned, he stands right at the head of the list and conspicuous among the men who have always been ready and taken an active part in the creation of the new county... With almost a life-time acquaintance we have never known of his doing or heard of his saying anything that he would not be willing for his parents to know or hear. With a little more selfishness he might have had quite a great deal more of this world's goods but he is not a selfish man, capable and fitted in every respect to represent the county in the Georgia legislature. If we had been asked to designate the man in Fitzgerald who was farthest from mistakes, truest to his friends, kindest to his family, and fairest to his neighbors, we would have said Belton Jay. His death was a cruel blow to the writer.*

D.B. was married first to Annie M. Clayton, who bore him two children, Dixie and Clayton, Jr. Annie died in 1900 and he then married Carrie Jean Goebler, from Indiana, in 1902. Together, they had one son, David B. Jay, Jr. D.B. Jay is buried at Evergreen Cemetery in Fitzgerald, Ga. On his grave is a poem, *The Hills of Rest*, by Albert Paine, Mark Twain's biographer. Again, I am reminded of my grandfather's love of Mark Twain and wonder if his father requested this verse or if Two-Dads desired to put this quote on his father's headstone.

Two-Dads planted trees for their beauty and his love, but he also planted them so that others would one day see their ultimate beauty, and reap the rewards of them. He desired to instill in his children a tradition of planting trees so that future generations would pass on this same tradition.

When Two-Dads was mayor, he planted trees throughout the city as well as at the Evergreen cemetery. This was a tradition that my daddy kept when he became Mayor of Fitzgerald. The beautiful Crepe Myrtle trees along Grant Street were planted by him, but when they widened Grant Street, they cut down all the trees. Today the city has begun to replant Crepe Myrtles on Sherman Street, and how exquisite their blossoms and foliage.

Two-Dads' love of reading, writing, and art went back to his childhood days. I have in my possession a delightful book of writings and art that he compiled during his high school years. His father spent two summers in the legislature trying to secure the creation of Ben Hill County, but the person who drew up the map for the new county was my Two-Dads. The map that he drew up in 1906 was accepted as the boundary lines for the new proposed county, Ben Hill, and he received $3.50 for the drawing.

Two-Dads had one of the most prolific personal libraries in the early 1900s in his house on South Lee Street. He told me that he would loan his books to those who could not afford such a library since there was not a community library at that time. When he built his new home in 1923 on South Main Street, he had a beautiful, large library upstairs. It had approximately 20 glass encased oak barrister bookcases filled with books of all kinds. After his home was put up for sale, I selected a few of his treasures. I acquired a beautifully leather bound set of Mark Twain books that are autographed and also a complete set of Charles Dickens novels.

Having a servant heart instilled in him by his father, my grandfather was first elected Mayor of Fitzgerald in 1917 and served three terms. While mayor, he designed the city parks down Main Street and Central Avenue, paved the city's first streets with beautiful red bricks, purchased the land for Evergreen Cemetery and later planted the Magnolia trees along its entrance. Also, he drew up the map for the establishment of Ben Hill County, Fitzgerald's County seat, when the county split from Irwin County.

Two-Dads related to me that his first year as Mayor was a year of a multitude of local sacrifices similar to the austerity programs implemented in Europe. He said that was the year he learned to eat breakfast cereal without sugar. With a ration on sugar, Two-Dads was not allowed to use it on his cereal. Soon, he was taught to use karo syrup on his cereal or eat it unsweetened. "Those were difficult times," Two-Dads would often remind me.

During that same year, Two-Dads left his office of mayor and became a full time partner in the law firm of Jay and Garden. The firm was originally in the Five Story Building, but that year they purchased the Ben Hill National Bank building. It was 1933 and the building was located at 101 East Pine Street. Today, the law firm is in the same location.

As I mentioned earlier, Two-Dads loved trees and owned a farm which was composed of nothing but pine trees and pecan trees. As a child, almost every Sunday afternoon in the fall and winter, I rode with Two-Moms and him to the farm. Two-Dads loved to peruse his "little piece of heaven on earth," as he liked to call it.

I can still visualize, my grandparents in the front seat of their big blue Buick, always blue, and me in the big backseat all alone. If it were fall, we would still have the windows down, and I could always see Two-Mom's arm hanging out the window. I never did understand why she liked to ride that away. Maybe it was like the way that I wanted to put my head out the car window and feel the breeze rustle through my hair. Who knows the answer?

My grandparents would always inquire about my plans for the upcoming week. When we finished talking, Two-Dads would turn on the radio, and the three of us would listen intently. When we would arrive at his farm, off the Evergreen Road, Two-Dads felt he was in his earthly heaven. He would ride us up and down the dirt road, the lanes of his pine trees and also through his pecan orchard. As I reflect, I am reminded of all the children who never had the opportunity to make such treasured memories with their grandparents.

Clayton Jay, Sr., my Two-Dads, was a quiet man of few words. I only remember seeing him perturbed once, which was not part of his normal personality. He was relaying to my daddy a story about Franklin D. Roosevelt, and something he had done that was inconsistent with Two-Dads' point of view. He ended the story with "I'm not sure that was his own viewpoint. I just think he listened to Miss Eleanor one time too many!" Through the years, he would often give reference to that story concerning a local situation.

There appeared an article, written by Irene Paulk Royal, in The *Fitzgerald Leader* in 1955, that concluded with the following about my grandfather;

His exceptional legal talents are accompanied by a sincere desire for service far beyond professional requirements. He had an enviable record as a citizen, attorney, husband, father and friend which bespeaks his desire to contribute his finest and best to his professional work as a lawyer and also to all worthwhile phases of his life.

What a beautiful tribute but probably the nicest tribute was the one from my grandfather's 50+ years secretary, Teresa Griffin, who once told me that she had never heard him say an unkind word about anyone. Can you imagine? What a legacy to leave to others!

The quiet, unobtrusive gentleman, Clayton Jay, who practiced law for 60 years, died at the age of 86, in the wilderness he moved to and so dearly loved, called Fitzgerald. My sweet Two-Dads has left a legacy that now has spanned several generations.

My paternal grandmother was born Bessie Louise Harley to James Hugh Harley, son of James F. Harley and Mary Louise Harley of Thomasville, Georgia. She had two sisters, Ruth Harley Young and Margaret Harley Campbell, and two brothers, Lamar Harley and Emory Harley. I knew my grandmother's two sisters but not two brothers. I remember her telling me that her baby brother, Emory, died when he was only one year old.

Bessie Harley Jay married my grandfather in October 1905 and moved to Fitzgerald, Georgia where they both lived to the ripe old age of 86. My grandmother Bessie, better known to my brothers and me as "Two-Moms," was the epitome of a true Southern lady. She was a stay at home mother, much like most women of that generation, whose primary concern was only for family.

Having been taught the importance of helping others by her parents, Two-Moms gathered all the neighborhood children under ten together to aid in assisting those who were fighting overseas during World War I. How you might be wondering did she accomplish this task? It was simple. All the children would bring their old cotton scraps and scissors to her house on a particular day, and they would make comfort pillows for soldiers who were in the military hospitals. This was just one of many ways she taught her children and their friends how God had blessed them, and in turn, they were to be a blessing to others. This is definitely a trait which has also been passed down through several generations of Jay descendants.

My grandmother and grandfather were very active in the religious community during this wartime era. They helped, along with several others to bring the eminent revivalist, Bob Jones, to Fitzgerald where he preached in a tent to over 3000 people in 1917. Can you imagine that occurring today in a small community?

Later, several couples and my grandparents took a group to Atlanta to hear the acclaimed Billy Sunday preach to an even larger congregation. My grandparents saw these outreach services as a way to help bring peace and comfort to those who were hurting at home while others were away serving their country.

My grandparents continued to support their local church which was Central Methodist Church, located on West Central Avenue. Recently, I had a friend who reminded me that the two of them always sat four rows from the back of the church. She told me what puzzled her the most was how my small, but stout, arthritic grandmother made it up those many steps that did not have hand rails in those days. I believe it is called desire and dedication to something that you deem important in your life.

On the corner of my grandparents' front lot was a beautiful palm tree. The elegant fronds would catch a breeze as it waved its arms, reminding our neighbors to look westward, to the front porch. My grandfather purchased this Palm tree, located next to Palm Street, when he purchased several to plant downtown by his law office. Today, the tree by the house is gone but the trees downtown are over fifty feet tall.

Growing up, I adored sitting on the front porch of my grandparent's home and visiting with Two-Moms. You noticed I said front porch because Southerners put their porches for sitting on the front of the house, not on the back or side. Yes, we have back and side porches in the South but they are off of the kitchen area, and serve only as exits to the side or back yard.

On my front porch visits with Two-Moms, she would always call Lula, her devoted friend, to bring us her reputable Iced Tea. Lula made this tea, usually spiced with lemonade, but sometimes orange juice. Today, we know this as an "Arnold Palmer" drink. People would walk by Two-Moms' house which was two blocks from town, and always veer towards it to see if anyone was on the porch so they could stop while.

Two-Moms loved her front porch and spent a great deal of time enjoying it. She had slipcovers that were seasonally changed for summer and fall for her beautiful white wicker furniture, and straw back rockers with turned posts. Two-Moms' porch ceiling was painted "haint blue." This was a common color throughout the South, but do you know why? Think about the adjective for a second, and you might come up with the real reason. It was painted that blue to keep the "haints" away. This is attributed to an old folk tale which originated in Louisiana.

There was a myriad of people who walked daily by Two-Moms' house. There was Mr. Bradshaw, who owned a music store downtown. His mentally challenged and friendly son Oscar accompanied him to and from work daily. There were others such as Mr. Bankston, who was always dressed to a tee; Mrs. Pauline Bush, the largest woman I ever knew; and my favorite of all, Mrs. Spell, our seamstress. Mrs. Spell lived across the street and was always the one person I couldn't wait to see.

I must admit, however, that there was one neighbor that I did not like to see approach Two-Moms's porch. Her name was Mrs. Ella Mae McCarthy, and I must admit that I would often hide from her. She was so loud and boisterous, and always wanted to talk about other women in the neighborhood which I did not like. Later in life, I learned her nickname, " Mrs. Busybody," which was indeed appropriate.

When our neighbors saw us on the porch, they would wave and call out, and Two-Moms would invite them to come over and "sit a spell." If for some unknown reason, they couldn't stop for long, there were still greetings and conversations carried on across the front yard. I can still hear the echoes of "Hello" vibrating in my head, as friends walked by and offered us their salutations, as we sat on the comfortable front porch. These enjoyable events happened before air conditioning came into our lives, and people no longer took the time to stop and enjoy one another.

During this era, some houses had a "sleeping porch" but Two-Moms' house did not have one, nor did mine. I guess her sunroom was the closest thing to a sleeping porch that she had and my screened porch was similar. You might be wondering, what is a sleeping porch? It is a place where family members would sleep when the house was too hot or stuffy on warm nights, and the breeze would float through the screens or multi opened windows. I am sure that sounds strange to this generation who never open their windows and have been taught to deadbolt all of their doors at night!

If it was an early fall or a winter morning, you could find my Two-Moms in her overstuffed blue chair by the fire, in the sitting area of her bedroom. She was known throughout the community for a true Southern trait which is seldom used today, the gracious art of letter writing. Two-Moms's chair was situated next to her French Provincial desk that stored all her tools for making notes and clipping out newspaper articles. As a child, when I inquired why she enjoyed cutting up her newspaper, she always told me that she enjoyed sending notes to people. She liked to include the newspaper clippings about their accomplishments, their joys and/or their sorrows, in the letters that she wrote.

Two-Moms had a beautiful way with words, and throughout my life, it has amazed me how many people, from all walks of life, have often reminded me of the letters and notes that she had shared with them. I rarely see Nan Lee when she comes back home that she doesn't remind of the lovely note that she still has today from Two-Moms. Yes, most definitely, the art of letter writing today is viewed by many as being antiquated or archaic, but how nice it is to receive an uplifting note from a friend. Can you even remember the last time that you received a letter from someone, especially now since emails and texting have become so rampant?

Another remembrance for me is my grandmother's famous Rock Cream or as Edna Lu Dorminy called it "snow cream" and her ice box cookies. As a child, my favorite treat was her Ice Box Cookies while my brothers adored her Rock Cream. When I left home for camp and later for college, Two-Moms always had Lula to fill up an old empty Whitman's Candy box with her Ice Box cookies for me. Afterwards, she tied it up with a pretty little blue ribbon, or on a rare occasion, she used just an ugly rubber band.

Honestly, how insignificant and inexpensive were these two items, but fifty years later, I still have those "warm, fuzzy feelings" just thinking about that old Whitman's candy box. Both of these recipes were handed down to her by her mother, better referred to as "Grandmother Harley," whom I never really knew. Knowing that the recipes had been passed down for generations, I believe, seemed to make both desserts even more special to me, and I have included them at the end of this chapter.

My precious grandmother loved to go shopping whether it was to Atlanta, Macon or Albany. If my mother and I went to Atlanta for the day, we would have to leave home about 6:00 in the morning, so we could be at Rich's or J. P. Allen's when they opened their doors at 10:00. But, no matter what time we left, if we did not invite Two-Moms and she found out, she would pout for days with my mother. Therefore, we usually took her with us when we went shopping.

Two-Moms's favorite place to eat was the Frances Virginia Tea Room. It was located on Peachtree Street, just a few doors down from where the Downtown Ritz Carlton is today. Now, when I say a "Tea Room," the image you probably conjure in your mind is a small room where ladies go for lunch. Actually, that was not what it was in the 1950s.

The Frances Virginia Tea Room was a large restaurant where women, men, and families came together to dine on freshly ironed white tablecloths, with well-dressed waiters and waitresses assisting customers. It was somewhat formal and closely resembled a private club. The restaurant was founded in the late 1920s and survived two World Wars, but finally saw its demise in 1962. I have included at the end of this chapter several favorite recipes cherished by my grandmother, mother and me from this fine establishment where we dined for many years.

My precious Two-Moms loved babies and often referred to a baby's new teeth as "little white pearls." How many times have I heard her ask a young mother, "How many pearls does the little one have now?" Again, this term reminds me of how exquisite the pearls were that filled her beautiful blue jewelry box. Many of them were gifts from her beloved daughter, my dear Aunt Dot, who spent most of her life living in Hawaii, and traveling throughout the Pacific. Because of Two-Moms's love of the color blue, her favorite pearls were most definitely her Mikimoto blue pearls from the South Pacific, which I now have in my possession.

As I continue to reminisce about Two-Moms, and one thought leads to another, I am reminded of her giving me a beautiful strand of topaz gems that my grandfather had brought to her from New York in the 1920s. I could not believe it when she offered to give them to me. When I exclaimed that I could not take them she answered, "Where in the world would I ever wear a topaz necklace with my blue wardrobe?" Was she ever right. I would have loved to have seen the expression on her face when Two-Dads handed her the box with the yellowish brown jewels. My mother and she always said that they loved all the colors in the rainbow, as long as they were blue, and no truer words were spoken by those two ladies.

All of my childhood life, we went to my grandparent's house on Christmas Eve. We opened presents with my family, my younger cousins and their parents, as well as my grandparents. It was a tradition or a ritual to open gifts on Christmas Eve. It is something I continued with my own children long after they were gone.

Christmas was especially revered by my grandfather since that was the only time of the year that my grandmother allowed whiskey in their home. The first time I was of legal age, according to Two-Moms' philosophy you had to be 21, I was allowed to have a taste of Two-Dads Bourbon flavored Egg Nog. It was about the strongest drink I have ever tasted and was definitely not what I had expected after waiting all those years.

I only wish now that I had thought of what my sister-in-law, Kerry Jay, did one Christmas while Two-Moms was alive. She presented Two-Moms with a diary the first Christmas that she belonged in our family. Kerry asked her to write as often as possible in it, and then to give it back to her the next year as a Christmas gift. What a treasure that diary is today and how clever was Kerry to think of that?

Several months ago, Kerry shared it with me for the first time in almost 50 years. What a treasure that book is for future generations! My desire is to reproduce a portion of this inestimable handiwork for my own grandchildren since they never really knew my Two-Moms and Two-Dads. My oldest child, Rob, moved with us to Fitzgerald in July 1969, and my Two-Dads died six months later, and my Two-Moms died several years later. I had dreamed of his indescribable Egg Nog, and the Christmas celebrations with them and my children, but that wasn't to be. The following was taken from Two-Moms' diary that Kerry received, and I would like to share this entry that she wrote the day after Two-Dads's death.

> *Two-Dads would have been 85 on December 23rd but he left us on the 20th even though his living presence is still with us. After 64 years of a happy life together, his absence has left an aching void but we have so much to be grateful for that we cannot spend time in grief and sorrow. We must remember that we prayed that the good Lord in his mercy would take us to his everlasting home without a long period of helplessness so do not grieve for us.*

How blessed I was to be with my grandmother at the local hospital in April 1972, when she died. My mother did not like sad occasions, so Rosa Lee, Two-Moms's other daughter-in-law and I were at the hospital when my sweet grandmother breathed her last breath. I can see her now, all dressed in a blue gown and a little blue bed jacket. She was smiling, nodding gently at me as she lightly squeezed my hand and then passed through this life through the pearly gates of heaven.

Recently, I discovered the funeral service given for my sweet Two-Moms. The Methodist preacher described her as a "gracious Southern lady" and I feel that described her to a tee. He went on the say that she was a person of genuine christian character in everything which she did. What a beautiful tribute for a beautiful lady.

Two-Moms' legacy lives on in the hearts of many who grew up in this small community. My dear friend, Edna Lu Ward Dorminy, told me several stories recently that I did not know about my grandmother. She said that Two-Moms gave her a beautiful lace handkerchief to carry with her on her wedding day. She also related to me a story of the respect that others had for my grandmother. One day, Edna Lu's mom, Callie Sue, was telling her that there was only one person in Fitzgerald that she would not smoke in front of. When Edna Lu asked who it was and why, she said: "Miss Bessie because I had too much respect for her." It makes me wonder about what kind of legacy I am leaving for others and instills in me a desire to live a better life.

Memories of my grandparents will live forever in my heart and I pray that the stories I have passed on to my children will live with them as well. There is a precious baby stocking that my grandmother hung up before the birth of my daddy, and every year afterward in honor of him. Later, I hung it up at my house, and today it has been passed on to my daughter (pronounced "dawtah) who hangs it in a strategic spot in her home. It is a small, worn cotton stocking, not much to look at, but inside is a verse written in Two Moms' handwriting which goes like this "Hang up the baby's stocking, without even a fret, for the dear little precious darling has never seen a Christmas yet." (Emily Huntington Miller.)

My grandparents had three daughters, Louise, Dorothy and Ruth, and two sons, my daddy and Clayton. Louise died when she was only three; Ruth, who never married, returned home in her forties to care for her parents; and Dorothy, who married Quinton Adams, and lived most of her adult life in Honolulu, Hawaii. Therefore, my aunts were

Dorothy, Ruth and Rosa Lee, wife of Clayton. My uncles were Clayton and Quinton, who was the husband of Dorothy.

My Aunt Dorothy, who was a year younger than my daddy, and lovingly known to me as Aunt Dot, moved to Hawaii in the 1940s. Her husband, Uncle Quinton, a former Golden Glove Champion, graduated from Georgia Tech, and immediately went to work for Coca-Cola. His employer transferred him from Boston, Massachusetts to Hawaii at the end of World War II, when the Coca-Cola Company became committed to providing Coke to the American soldiers overseas. I understand that when my grandmother heard that her daughter was moving to Hawaii, she cried for weeks. My Uncle Quinton promised Two-Moms that he would let Aunt Dot come back to Fitzgerald for a few weeks every year, and he lived up to that promise!

I treasure the memories I have of spending adult time with them and letting my two children grow to love them, just like I did. Uncle Quinton was a large man whom I loved dearly and my son, Rob, was enthralled by his being a Golden Globe Champion. Rob was certainly impressed that he had boxed at Madison Square Garden. My precious Aunt Dot was as small as her husband was large and possessed a heart of gold. She, like her mother and my mother, thought the only color on the color wheel was blue. My heart overflows when I think of these two special people and how they enriched not only my life but my children's lives as well.

Aunt Dot and Uncle Quinton had two children, Quinton and Dotsy, who were closer in age to my brother Charles and me than any of our other cousins, so we became "bestie" cousins. How enchanting it was to have cousins that lived in Hawaii and knew how to do the hula! As a child, a puzzling memory for me was just how my cousin Quinton was able to bring his car over to the mainland, across the ocean, when he was preparing to enter college in Colorado. Oh, only the minds of little ones could think like that.

What memories my cousin Dotsy and I have made throughout our life. We spent many hours playing in Two-Dads' home library, walking to the movies, trying to put two cans together with a string so we could talk from her upstairs bedroom to my upstairs bedroom across Palm Street, performing plays in her other grandmother's garage that actually had a stage, tasting the strange Hawaiian fruit that was dried and salty to which she introduced me, and her trying to teach me the hula. The only time that I remember we had words was when

I told her that maybe one day I might move to Hawaii and become a Baptist missionary to all the island heathens! Those were just part of the wonderful memories as children when Dotsy would come every summer to visit her grandparents and me.

In her late teens, Dotsy decided to come to the "mainland" to attend college, and how excited I was when she chose Florida State University. She spent lots of weekends and holidays with us during that time, but two years later she elected to leave for school in Paris. After her junior year abroad, Dotsy headed home to graduate from the University of Hawaii. What a glamorous life she lived, traveling the world, and living directly on the beach in Honolulu!

I have never understood why people refer to others as "brother" rather than by their given name, but I have come to realize that it is truly a "Southern" thing. My daddy's brother was always referred to as "Brother" or "Uncle Bud" by his friends and family. It was only as an older adult that I begin to refer to him as "Uncle Clayton."

Nicknames appear to make Southerns feel connected, and they use them as an expression of love and affection. In our society today, because of bullying issues, few kids have or wear their nicknames proudly as people did years ago. Even in highly acclaimed Southern literature, such as *To Kill a Mockingbird,* Harper Lee had Scout and Boo as two of her most prominent characters; needless to say, they were called by their nicknames. Everyone I knew fashioned a nickname of sorts, and in fact, when I was growing up, my brothers called me "Pete." Why? I don't know, and they don't know either, but to this day, some of their friends still refer to me as "Pete."

My Uncle Clayton kept my grandmother from attending my daddy's high school graduation because she was eight months pregnant with him. During those days, it was not proper for ladies to be seen in public that late in a pregnancy. My daddy always reminded him of it, jokingly, since it was obvious that these two men definitely adored one another. Uncle Clayton and my daddy were not only 16 years apart but were as different as night and day.

Clayton was fiery, an investor in rental property, and later in life, more of a land investor. He never stopped wanting to invest in real estate, and even a few weeks before he died, he asked my husband to help him find some land to purchase. I can remember one Christmas when my daddy told us that we might have a slim Christmas that year. When I asked why he said that he was concerned that he might have to support his brother's family if Clayton didn't stop borrowing money to buy property. Later, he told me that Clayton would either end up poor or rich, and that is exactly what happened to him; he ended up richer.

On the other hand, my daddy never desired wealth or to invest in anything other than the stock market because he was financially conservative. A cute story that my dear friend, Jim Parrott, learned from his dad is as follows: A group of men were sitting around one night, just shooting the bull, and discussing all the holdings and wealth that they had accumulated. Then one of them turned to my dad and said, "Harvey, tell us what all you own." His response was "Not much, really. All my assets are tied up in cash." There was a hush among the group of men and the verbose bragging seemed to come to an end on that note.

Even though Uncle Clayton's father and brother both served as Mayors of Fitzgerald, Uncle Clayton desired to leave politics alone. He contributed as much as anyone ever has to the industrial development of Fitzgerald. The Georgia Department of Industry and Trade often sent leaders from other communities to apprentice under him so they could learn how to attract industry to their own community. In honor of his accomplishments, one of our largest industries, Shaw Industries, named their Fitzgerald plant "Plant Jay."

Uncle Clayton or Uncle Bud, as we often called him growing up, married a liberal, in the eyes of most people in our community. Rosa Lee and Clayton married during World War II, just a few days before he left for the European battlefront. Rosie, as affectionately called by those who loved her dearly, was different from most Southern women of that era.

While her husband was overseas, Rosa Lee had an article published in *The Ladies' Home Journal*, to the horror of my genteel grandmother. Rosa Lee wrote about how poor they were during the war. Two-Moms' response always was "I just wish she had told me because we didn't know they were poor." Rosa Lee was truly liberal in the eyes of our conservative family but was deeply loved.

My dear Aunt Rosa Lee, who later became Rosie to me, enjoyed marching to her own beat and doing things differently. For instance, women of that era enjoyed collecting pieces of their china and silver pattern because money had been scarce during World War II. Not so for Rosie, who loved to set her dining tables with as many different and unique patterns of sterling silver and china as she could.

I only knew Rosie as my aunt when I was a child but in my adult years we became dear friends and she was a source of inspiration to me. Her divine philosophy was not to worry about what others thought but to do exactly what you thought was right. My dear Aunt Rosie definitely practiced that up to the very end of her life.

Rosie knew that her children and I, separated by numerous years growing up, had not reaped the treasures that each of us had stored within ourselves. The last few weeks of her life, she was determined to bring us all together and she so wisely did. Her precious children and grandchildren would call me to come whenever she got "low" or when she decided it was time for a "cup of coffee." When they phoned, I could hardly get there fast enough. Rosie's last week of dying at home brought us all closer together. Once again she and I were together when God opened the gates of Heaven, but this time, it was for her entrance.

What a blessing Rosa Lee showered upon me in her final days, for as older adults, her children and I, as God's children came together as a family. After her death, her children presented me with a family heirloom that Rosie and I both loved so dearly. While the two of us were cleaning out Two-Moms and Two-Dads' home, we discovered inside a back porch cabinet, several interesting items. Our favorite was the most exquisite cut glass punch bowl set on a pedestal that you have ever seen. This is the heirloom that they presented to me and words are inadequate in expressing how special this bowl is to me. It has a designated place in my home and my heart and is only used on very special occasions.

The greatest legacy that Rosie left me was for me to understand that your body needed a time to rest, something my mother had never taught me. Today, when I want to sit around, read or do just exactly what I want to do, I refer to it as a "Rosa Lee Jay Day." Why? Because on those kinds of days, no matter what time of day it was, you could stop by to visit Rosie, and she might still be in her nightgown, or her dishes might still be in the sink, because she was doing just what she wanted to do.

Before she died, I told her that I had named a day after her. I can still see her throwing back her head and laughing uproariously. Thank you, Rosie, for teaching me that it was okay to be unindustrious sometimes and let the outside world pass by. If I had not learned that from her, this book would have never happened!

My Aunt Ruth had a much different life than my other relatives. She lost the love of her life during World War II and never married after that long engagement. She worked in Atlanta, for RCA, after her college days. Aunt Ruth was a loner, fought bouts of depression, and never found true happiness within herself or others. I truly feel that she loved me as much as she was capable of loving anyone. As I was growing up, she always wanted to visit and spend time with me on her weekends at home.

As a child, she was an aunt who was always bringing me gifts from the city, better known as Atlanta. I must admit that my favorite gift of all times had to be a live duck which we named Donald. Now wasn't that original? Donald lived for about two years in the backyard at my house, and we all adored him. He was killed by a car, crossing Palm Street, while following my mother next door.

Aunt Ruth invited me several times to Atlanta where I spent a few days with her. She also took me to the Caribbean when I graduated from high school, and what an interesting trip that was. Several years later, in her early forties, Aunt Ruth moved back to Fitzgerald to care for her parents. After their deaths, she continued to live in the family home, across from my parents, until she died of cancer.

Aunt Ruth was blessed to have been able to stay at home with two wonderful sitters, Bessie Campbell and Lula Gordon. Rosie and I alternated spending an hour every day so the sitters could go home to refresh. Once again, the two people that were joined together with her when the angel of death appeared were my Aunt Rosie and me. God was always throwing the two of us together and wanted us to gather the best qualities from one another, which I believe we did.

My daddy and uncle allowed their "Sister Ruth," as they affectionately called her, to live in the old home place until she died. After her death, the three siblings and their spouses, and me (because I had been one of her caregivers) sat around the large dining room table and discussed what to do with all the things in the house. For you see, when my grandmother died, everything was left as is, by my Aunt Ruth and her brothers.

The three siblings drew straws, and decided who would have the first choice of what they wanted. My dear Aunt Dot picked her mother's jewels which were appropriate since she was the only daughter. Next, my Aunt Rosie picked the exquisite cut glass punch bowl that we had discovered stored away in a cabinet. Lastly, my parents didn't want anything so they allowed me to choose, and I picked Two-Moms' flatware sterling, Fairfax by Gorham.

If you are from the South, you understand why I selected my grandmother's sterling flatware because it is almost viewed as a sacred gift. If there is sterling silver in a family, it is usually passed down through generations. Each generation selects the same silver pattern or one very similar so that one day, the flatware will all match or blend well together. If your family did not have sterling, then there were other items passed down that had the same meaning to you. Family and heirlooms are very important to Southerners.

My fervent wish has always been that I could have known my maternal grandfather, Perry Clegg Coney, and my maternal grandmother, Sallie Mae Wheeler. My grandfather died in 1909, and later my grandmother married Charles Whatley. They continued to live in Cordele, Georgia. Sadly, my mother was an only child, so I have no aunts or uncles on my maternal side.

My maternal grandfather, Perry Clegg Coney, was born on December 30, 1882 to Samuel Whitsett Coney and Eoline Elizabeth Hamilton. According to my research, Eoline Elizabeth was part of the lineage of Mary, daughter of King James II of Scotland, who married Lord Hamilton in the 1400s. Until the 1590s, the Hamiltons retained their position as heir to the Scottish throne.

It appears that there were many intermarriages between the Stewarts (Stuarts) and the Hamiltons, which was a common practice among nobility of that era. Eoline Hamilton's parents were Warren B Hamilton and Caledonia Baskin. An interesting note is that her uncle William Hamilton, Warren's brother, harbored Georgia Governor Joe Brown during Sherman's March to the Sea. Why one might ask? William Hamilton was married to a relative of the Georgia Governor and Milledgeville was Georgia's capital at that time. The Governor feared for his life because Sherman was heading that way. William and Elizabeth Warren invited him to come stay with them in Cordele, Georgia. Some people from there like to say that Cordele served as the capital of Georgia at one time, but that is an unofficial statement, according to history.

My maternal grandfather, Perry Coney, was only seven years old when his mother died. His father, Samuel Whitsett Coney later married Leolone Barfield, and together they had numerous children. My paternal great-grandfather, Sam Whitsett Coney, was born in Lee

County, Georgia to Susan Whitsett and Charles Culpepper Coney. Sam Coney was a farmer, who lived in Coney Grove, a few miles outside of Cordele. The run-down house has now been restored to its magnificence and is across from the old Coney, Georgia depot. Sam Coney was also the organizer of the first train but sold it to Sam Hawkins for whom the SAM train line is named.

In researching my ancestry, I have discovered that Sam Coney was one of a committee, along with my maternal great-grandfather, John J. Wheeler, who drew up a bill providing for the creation of Crisp County. Sam Coney was also the first Ordinary of the newly created county which had split from Dooly County, Georgia. Interestingly, both of my great-grandfathers played a significant role in the establishment of their newly designed counties, Ben Hill and Crisp counties.

As I mentioned earlier, my grandfather Perry Coney, was an only child and a cotton buyer when he married my grandmother, Sallie Mae Wheeler. Together they had only one child, my mother. The year after my mother was born, her father died of influenza, and my maternal grandmother became a widow.

Sally Mae Wheeler, according to my great aunts, was an adventurous woman always looking for excitement. She was the first woman in Crisp County to ride in an airplane and died in her early forties due to an injury while riding her beloved horse, Smoky. The story goes that my grandmother's horse was spooked by something, reared up, threw her off, and the horse landed on top of her. By so doing, it ruptured her spleen, which led to her death.

My mother spent a lot of her childhood with her maternal grandparents, John and Lydia Wheeler, rather than her paternal grandparents because of her paternal grandfather's marriage. Grandpapa Wheeler was at the Appomattox Court House, on April 9, 1865, when the surrender documents were signed by Lee and Grant.

Grandpapa Wheeler was the son of Josiah Wheeler. He was a successful developer of farming interests, ran the Wheeler warehouse, and had a keen sense of business. His wife, Lydia Williams Wheeler, was the daughter of Captain Hiram Williams and married him on March 11, 1870.

At the death of Grandpapa Wheeler, he left a thousand acres of farmland to each of his seven children's children. He was known to be one of the largest landowners in Crisp County. These farms consisted mostly of cotton early on because "Cotton was King" in the South. The cotton crop was transported on approximately 40 wagons to a nearby town, Hawkinsville, Georgia where it was loaded on an Ocmulgee River barge and floated up to the Macon cotton market.

My dignified mother never told me this story but I discovered it in an article written by Mary Fitzgibbons Williams, a cousin of mine. According to my great grandfather's daughter Alma, my great aunt, whom I referred to as "Big Mama" the story about Grandpapa Wheeler goes as follows:

> *He was known as making the best corn whiskey in the county, possibly learning how to make it when he served in the Confederacy. His wife, Lydia, was mortified when her younger brother, Dr. John Williams, and he were 'excommunicated' from the Baptist Church but they were later reinstated when the collections went down.*

My mother went to Cordele, at least once a month, to visit with her family and friends. Mother, being an only child and having no living parents except for a stepfather, stayed connected with her Cordele friends. It is unique she had eight of her kindergarten friends who, in their late eighties, were still active and visiting one another. These friends were Sally Mae Slade Brannon, Sarah Wheeler Lee, Emma Lee Sheppard Fitzgibbons, Lula Mae Fenn, Earlene McKenzie Smith, Mary Strozier Ferguson, Elizabeth Slade Williamns, and Alma Whatley Adkins.

I was always wishing for a grandmother that lived out of town, so my mother's Aunt Alma instructed me to call her "Big Mama." Aunt Alma was entirely different from the other Wheeler women which made her even more attractive to a young child. Whenever, I went to Cordele to visit friends such as Molly Turner, Nancy Cannon, and Marsha Ann Smith, I always wanted to stay with this intriguing relative.

Aunt Alma was indeed independent for she ran her own 1000 acre farm with the help of Really Lawson (Loss) Morgan. She also carried a gun in the glove compartment of her car, something few women of that era did. I spent many nights during the summer, listening to her stories, walking with her down to visit her sister, Aunt Lydia, and accompanying her to her farm. Mother and I always made sure that we arrived at her house in time for lunch because her friend, Ida Mae, had prepared a meal "fit for a queen." This precious "Big Mama," at the age of 96, pushed a couple of intruders down her back doorsteps as they tried to rob her. She was an inspiration to a me throughout her lifetime.

Today, if you go to the old section of Sunnyside Cemetery in Cordele, you immediately see an immense mausoleum that has the name "Wheeler" on it. This is where Grandpapa Wheeler, Grandmama Wheeler, and a cousin they took in, Martha Jones, are all buried. Surrounding it, all of Grandpapa's seven children, their spouses and some of their children, are buried.

The past year, I have been blessed to reconnect with some of my mother's Cordele family. Several of the grandchildren of mother's Aunt Lydia and I have reacquainted ourselves with one another. Jeannie Barkuloo Brown, Nancy Barkuloo Futch, Judy Barkuloo Branch, Jan Grimsely Smithey, and Pat Fitzgibbons and I are presently enjoying our new found family. On several occasions, we have visited and discovered informative facts about our heritage. Pat is the elder, in his late 80s, but I must admit his mind is better than all of ours put together. I am sure our mothers and grandmothers are ecstatic that we are spending time together.

Of all the legacies left to me, besides my Christian background, probably the most significant is the value that my ancestors placed on education. It never dawned on me that everyone's grandparents or great grandparents were not college graduates until I went off to college.

My maternal grandparents were educated at Lucy Cobb Institute, a girl's college in Athens, Georgia, and at Georgia Military and Agricultural College, a boy's college in Milledgeville, Georgia. My Paternal grandparents were educated at Georgia State College for Women in Milledgeville, Georgia, and Mercer University in Macon, Georgia. My paternal great-grandfather was a graduate of Howard College, known as Samford University today, and my maternal great-grandfather was a graduate of Riverside Military College, in Gainesville, Georgia.

What a vital impact education has had on my life, for it helped to shape me from a young homemaker into a middle-aged woman who obtained several masters degrees and a doctoral degree late in life. Of this legacy and accomplishment, I am indeed proud.

My Grandparents' Recipes

Christmas is all about family, friends and good cheer. This was the only time I ever saw my grandfather in the kitchen or with any liquor but oh, how he loved his eggnog. My grandparent's rule was that you must be over 21 before you were allowed Two-Dads' Egg Nog and I now know why! A question to ponder though is "What happened to the liquor that was left over after the Egg Nog was made each year?"

Two-Dads' Egg Nog

1 dozen eggs, separated
½ lb 10X sugar
1 cup bourbon
½ cup brandy
1 quart whipped cream
1 quart half and half
¼ tsp nutmeg

Beat the egg yolks, gradually adding the sugar. Add the two liquors a little at a time. Refrigerate overnight. Fold in the whipped cream and then add the half and half. Beat the egg whites until stiff and fold into the mixture. Top with nutmeg.

Salads

These salads were favorites of Two-Moms' children and her grandchildren. The first one was our favorite salads but the aspics were what she always got Lula, her helper, to make for grieving families. I doubt there have been many Southerners buried without a congealed salad being served in their honor.

Grapefruit Aspic

1 envelope gelatin
¼ cold water
3 lemons
1 can grapefruit
1 can pineapple, small
2 cups fruit juices from cans
½ cup sugar
1 tsp salt

Dissolve 1 pkg gelatin in cold water. Heat juices and mix.

SOUTHERN BELLE SALAD

1 can bing cherries
1 pkg cherry jello
1 bottle Coca Cola, small
3 Tbs lemon juice, fresh
1 pkg cream cheese, small
½ cup nuts, cut very fine

Drain and pit cherries. Measure juice from cherries and add water to make a cup. Bring to a boil and add jello. Stir until dissolved. Add the Coca Cola and lemon juice. Chill until it partly congeals. Mash up cheese until smooth and fold in cherries and nuts. Chill.

TOMATO ASPIC

6 lemon slices
3 onion slices
2 bay leaves
3 whole cloves
4 cups tomato juice
3 Tbs horseradish
2 Tbs salt
1 Tbs pepper
1 Tbs worchestershire
1 Tbs lemon juice
4 Knox gelatin envelops
½ cup apple cider vinegar

Simmer the first four ingredients for 15-20 minutes. Mix gelatin and vinegar together and add to the tomato juice, stirring until gelatin dissolves. Add all other ingredients and pour into lightly oiled mold. Chill overnight.

CASSEROLES

Casseroles, whether round, square, rectangular or oval, and covered dishes are the theme of the South. You have probably noticed that many of them have masking tape remnants on the bottom where your mother or grandmother took them to someone and wanted to be sure their dishes were returned!

When our friends are sick or grieving, we adore taking them any kind of food, but especially casseroles that they can enjoy then or freeze later. I have always tried to keep an extra one in the freezer to send to someone in an emergency.

I once heard someone lament that folks will put down small southern towns until a funeral or illness comes, and then the smaller the town, the larger number of dishes that arrive at the back door. I must add that most of the casseroles have Campbell's Cream of Mushroom or Cream of Chicken soup, and this new generation hasn't a clue what we did before either arrived on the scene. I am sure you know and so do I! (We spend a significant amount of time making a white sauce.) The first recipe doesn't have the Campbell's soup in it and I truthfully like it much better.

Squash Souffle

2 cups yellow squash
3 Tbs onion, grated
3 Tbs butter
2 eggs
1 cup sweet milk
1 cup bread crumbs,
salt and pepper

Cook squash and press through sieve. Melt butter in hot milk and pour over bread crumbs. Add squash, well beaten eggs and seasonings. Pour into a butter dish, top with buttered crumbs. Bake at 300 until firm.

Chicken Mornay

1 chicken
1 ½ cups cheese, grated
1 can cream of chicken soup
1 pkg broccoli or asparagus

Boil chicken until tender and keep stock hot. Make your favorite cream sauce or cream of chicken soup, add chicken stock to taste and grated cheese. Bake 40 minutes at 350.

Sweets

Sweets are probably one of the first foods that we give babies in the South. Certainly, that must be true because I have few Southern friends who don't have a "sweet tooth." However, this first sweet is not as sweet as most. Whenever I came home from college for the weekend, Two-Moms always had me a Whitman's candy box filled with these cookies, and I adored them. She even tied them up with a pretty blue ribbon for my journey north.

Icebox Cookies

3 eggs
½ tsp salt
1 cup butter
1 Tbs cinnamon
1 cup sugar
2 tsp baking powder
1 cup brown sugar
1 cup nuts
4 cups flour, sifted
1 Tbs baking soda

Cream butter and sugar. Add eggs, one at a time. Mix baking powder, salt, soda, and cinnamon to the flour mixture. Mix 1 cup flour at a time to the first mixture and then add the nuts. Make into 2 long pans, like old ice tray pans. Place in refrigerator for several hours. Slice and cook them at 350 for 10 to 15 minutes.

Miscellaneous

When someone sends you a deli tray from the grocery store, which is always a hit, don't forget to add a few pimento cheese sandwiches, pronounced "puhmenna cheese" among the store bought tray to make it appear "homey." Pimento cheese is definitely a Southern comfort food, and I was astounded that folks in other parts of the country don't consider it a staple in the refrigerator. It is soothing and so easy to make. Just for your information, rat cheese is another name for hoop cheese.

Pimento Cheese

1 8 oz sharp or rat cheese
1 8 oz mild cheddar cheese
1 jar, small, diced and drained pimentos
4 Tbs homemade or Hellman's mayonnaise
1 tsp tabasco
1 tsp worcestershire
½ tsp garlic powder
½ tsp onion powder
1 Tbs sugar

Grate your cheeses and mix together. Add the other ingredients, adding mayo and pimentos last, blend well.

Salted Pecans

½ stick butter
4 cups pecans
1 Tbs salt

Preheat oven to 325 degrees. Melt butter in pan, add pecans and sprinkle with salt. Place one level of pecans and toss nuts several times within 30 minutes, making sure they are coated with the salt and don't burn. Let cool.

Sugar Nuts

1 cup brown sugar
½ cup white sugar
½ cup sour cream
1 tsp vanilla
2 cups walnut halves

Combine sugars and cream and cook over medium heat, stirring until dissolved. Cook until a soft ball is formed in cold water. Remove from heat and add vanilla and walnuts. Stir until well coated.

TuTu's Pickles (My Aunt Dot)*

2 quarts dill pickles
4 cups sugar
1 cup vinegar
¾ oz mixed pickling spices

Drain pickles and cut in 1 inch pieces. Cover with water and soak over night. Drain water off and combine sugar, vinegar, spice and cook 5 minutes. Pour over pickles and place in jars. Refrigerate 4-5 days before use. Must be kept refrigerated.

*This recipe was given to my grandmother, Two-Moms, by her daughter, Dorothy, whose husband always helped her make them. They are delicious!

SALLIE MAE WHEELER CONEY RECIPES (MY MOTHER'S MOTHER)

These recipes are from the grandmother that I never met but mother always talked about her as if her death occurred only yesterday. I could not imagine why mother constantly talked about missing her until I lost my own mother. No other love is like that of a mother. The third recipe, Candy Kisses, was the first recipe that I was taught to ever cook, and oh what memories I have of them.

TEA CAKES

Whisk:
3 ¼ cups flour
1 ½ tsp baking powder
½ tsp salt
Beat on medium speed:
2 ½ sticks butter, soften
1 cup sugar
Then, add and beat:
1 egg
1 Tbs milk
2 ½ tsp vanilla

Stir flour into butter mix and blend. Place half of dough between waxed paper and roll out or place in refrigerator. Bake at 350 on greased baking sheet about 6 minutes.

CANDY KISSES

6 Egg whites
1 box powdered sugar
1 tsp cream of tartar
2 tsp vanilla
2 cups nuts

Beat the egg whites until stiff. Slowly add the sugar in and beat for 15 minutes. Add the cream of tartar and beat 15 more minutes. Add vanilla and fold in the nuts. Line a pan with waxed paper and place the kisses on it by the spoonful. Put in a cold oven and cook on 250 for 30 minutes.

Date Nut Candy

4 Tbs butter
2 cups sugar
4 eggs
1 cup chopped dates
4 cups rice cereal
1 cup chopped walnuts
2 cans (4 oz) shredded coconut

Melt butter and remove from heat. Stir in sugar, eggs and dates. Cook over low heat, stirring until mixture leaves side of pot (about 20 minutes). Remove from heat and add cereal, nuts and vanilla and blend well. Cool and shape into a roll. Last, roll in coconut and store in refrigerator.

Frances Virginia Tea Room Recipes*

The following recipes are from the famous Frances Virginia Tea Room, that once stood on the famous Peachtree Street, in Atlanta, Georgia. It was my grandmother's favorite place to eat on our shopping ventures to the city.

Lemon Chess Pie

1 ½ cups sugar
1 Tbs flour
1 Tbs cornmeal
pinch of salt
4 eggs, beaten slightly
¼ cup milk
½ cup lemon juice
1 tsp grated lemon rind
1 tsp vanilla
¼ cup melted butter
1 9' unbaked pie shell

Mix dry ingredients. Add remaining ingredients. Mix well. Pour into pie shell. Bake until set.

**The South's Legendary Frances Virginia Tea Room Cookbook*, Mildred H. Coleman, Favorite Recipes(r) Press, Nashville, Tennessee.

CREAMED CHICKEN WITH CELERY AND ALMONDS

1 cup celery cut diagonally
¼ cup sliced almonds
2 Tbs butter or oleo
2 cups diced, cooked chicken
3 cups medium white Sauce, using part stock, part milk (see recipe)
3-4 cups chow mein noodles

Steam celery until slightly tender and crisp. Sauté almonds in butter. Mix chicken, celery, and almonds with hot White Sauce. Add few drops yellow color. Serve over chow mien noodles. Garnish with parsley. Serve immediately or noodles will be soggy. 6 servings

Tea Room Note: This was a "party dish" often served at special luncheons and bridal showers.

WHITE SAUCE—MEDIUM

2 Tbs butter, fat or oleo melted
2 Tbs flour
1 cup milk
½ tsp. salt

Melt fat in heavy saucepan. Slowly add flour. Do not brown. Add milk and salt. Stir constantly until thick.

Chapter 3

My Parents

My parents, Harvey Lamar Jay and Lydia Elizabeth Coney were born in the early 1900s and married on February 21, 1931. I truly believe that I could not have had two better Christian parents, and I thank God daily that He chose them for me.

My daddy was born on August 12, 1906, in Fitzgerald, Georgia, and was christened Harvey Lamar Jay. His parents were Philip Clayton Jay and Bessie Harley Jay. My daddy's paternal grandfather was David Belton Jay, who was the son of James Lemuel Jay and Priscilla Aisley Price Jay of Edgefield and Abbeville, South Carolina respectively. D. B. Jay was married to Annie Mae Clayton, daughter of Philip and Jane Moore Clayton of Calhoun County, Georgia.

My daddy, attended Third Ward School, and graduated from Fitzgerald High School at the age of sixteen. His childhood friends were Will Ed Smith, Paul Stone, Mark Mayes, Garbutt Mayes, and Raymond Rodgers. My daddy's first home in Fitzgerald was at 810 South Lee Street, next door to the two Mayes boys and their sister Hazel. There were few houses "that far out" from downtown, so the Mayes boys and he hunted rabbits and squirrels behind the Old Hopkins house on the corner of Lee Street and Roanoke Drive.

My daddy's house had a large area under it where they would often play. They even dug a tunnel from the Jay House to the Mayes house so that they could be entertained, and sometimes they would go there to smoke rabbit tobacco. Daddy often reminisced about climbing out of the window of the second floor of his house, sliding down the cedar shake shingles to the roof of the first floor porch, and ending up in the bushes.

Whenever he would tell me these stories he would always end with, "We were truly a mess," and somehow I believe it. He lived on South Lee Street his entire life until he left for college, and his parents built a house at 415 South Main Street, across the street from where he later built his own house at 501 South Main Street.

In June 1923, my daddy graduated from Fitzgerald High School where he received numerous accolades in academics and sports. The fall following graduation his best friend Paul Stone and he attended Georgia Tech, where my daddy became a member of Alpha Tau Omega fraternity. After two years at Tech and two summers interning in the mills in Hawkinsville, Georgia, he decided against an engineering degree. He left Georgia Tech to attend Mercer University, from which he graduated, and later earned his law degree from Mercer University School of Law, magna cum laude in 1929. Daddy entered the law practice with his father, Clayton Jay Sr., and Allan Garden. This practice was started by his grandfather, D. B. Jay in 1896.

My daddy and mother met in 1931 after she had graduated from Martha Washington College in Abingdon, Virginia, at a dance in Fitzgerald, Georgia. Mother had a childhood friend from Cordele, Georgia, Frankye Mayes, who had married and invited her, and another friend, to ride the train over to Fitzgerald for a dance at the illustrious Lee-Grant Hotel. Mother said that when she walked into the ballroom and saw this handsome man in a blue and white seersucker suit, she thought to herself, "That is the best looking man I have ever seen."

Now, you did notice the word "seersucker," didn't you? Summer suits for men of that era were made from seersucker, a lightweight, puckered, all-cotton fabric. This particular fabric stands away from the skin to aid in air circulation in order to help them stay cool. If you still are wondering what seersucker is, just picture Atticus Finch, Mark Twain or Andy Griffith, whom became known for seersucker suits, as well as many other Southern gentlemen.

My mother, spying my handsome daddy at the dance, was introduced to him, by Garrett Mayes, Frankye's husband, and it was love at first sight, according to my mother. My daddy had just finished law school, and was practicing law in Fitzgerald with his father. My parents courted less than a year and were married in a small family wedding at her home. My mother's mother had just been diagnosed with a terminal illness. Mother often lamented what a disappointment it was that she could not have a large wedding like her cousins, but she was most grateful that her mother was able to be there. Her mother, due to a trial study, lived a few years longer than expected and was alive to see my oldest brother, Harvey, the only grandchild she ever knew.

My daddy was appointed by Governor Eugene Talmadge to the office of Solicitor General, which today is called District Attorney. Allan Garden, his law partner, was called back into the military in 1941 which opened this position. In my daddy's 25 years as District Attorney, he never experienced political opposition, and he was blessed to spend more than 50 of his 86 years practicing law. His peers referred to him as a "gentleman's gentleman and a lawyer's lawyer." A local attorney, John Croley, wrote the following on my daddy's 80th birthday:

> *The name 'Harvey Jay' will always stand for so much in my mind. It stands, for above all, honesty and integrity. It stands for intelligence, fairness, compassion, and wit. It stands for attainment of the goals for which we all strive but of which few are attained.*

Ten years after the death of my daddy, Norman Fletcher, Chief Justice of the Supreme Court of Georgia, stated in the *Georgia Bar Journal, February 2002, Volume 7, Number 4,* that he was attracted to the profession because of two lawyers from Fitzgerald, Caryle McDonald and Harvey Jay. Chief Justice Fletcher stated that what he admired most about the two gentlemen was that they were also community leaders, something that needs to be ongoing today in our world. He further stated that the men were highly respected in their community. How proud those comments make me today. Even though my daddy is no longer here, I feel blessed that his legacy lives on in the minds and hearts of others.

One of many lessons that my daddy taught me was his appreciation and love of God's earth and nature. As a young mayor, he planted crepe myrtles on Grant Street. In addition, he replaced some of the magnolia trees at the entrance of Evergreen Cemetery that were planted when his father was mayor. Under my daddy's leadership, his administration received a donation of 4,000 dogwood trees from two prominent citizens, B. H. Dorminy and J. H. Dorminy. Every single tree was given out to local residents who had agreed to plant and water them during the upcoming sweltering summer months.

For my daddy's love of trees, my brothers and I donated Bradford pear trees, along with several other trees to First Baptist Church in honor of his 85th birthday. Our original desire was to plant them in the city parks and throughout the community. However, that did not work out, because the city felt they did not have the available workers to plant them. We were granted permission to plant two of the Bradford Pear trees in the park directly across from Two-Dads' house on South Main Street.

The successes in my daddy's life was based upon his philosophy that everything you do, you do through your love of Christ and your family. I remember that someone described him to me as "a man of great empathy for all people." They went on to express that they viewed him as a trustworthy individual whose sense of fair play was excelled only by his love, interest, and concern for his church and his family. These are all lessons well learned by us from a Godly daddy.

My daddy was a man of many loves. He loved his wife, his children, his church and his community. John Burch, his pastor at First Baptist Church, always said when Daddy spoke at church conference or Deacon's Meeting, it was like E. F. Hutton…the room got quiet. My daddy informed me early in life, but it obviously didn't take, that the most intelligent people he knew, were people of few words. If you knew my mother and me well, you will definitely know that left both of us out of the loop!

It all but took "an act of Congress" to get my daddy to attend the Fitzgerald Chamber of Commerce's annual meeting in January 1986. It was not that he didn't wish to attend but because of his declining health, he did not go out at night. Daddy finally relented if his grandson Rob would help him to the podium to receive the prestigious Citizen of the Year Award.

I remember when my daddy received the award that night, he told the audience that when he was a small boy, so many of his friends talked about wanting to run away from Fitzgerald but he never did. He had always loved his hometown and had no desire to leave here. He reminded the audience that he was so thankful that when his parents had the opportunity to decide whether to put Ben Hill County or

Irwin County on his birth certificate, they chose Ben Hill. Daddy was born the month that his father had drawn up the map dividing Ben Hill County from Irwin County. The map was presented by his grandfather to the General Assembly during that time. Therefore, in August 1906, his parents had the option of listing his birth in either county.

Southern culture is filled with a good work ethic, religion and loyalty to one's family and hometown. Daddy was always humbled by his accolades, another Southern trait that can be learned if you don't naturally "come by" it. Wherever he was, he repeatedly had to mention his love for his hometown of Fitzgerald especially whenever he received an award.

My daddy believed that one of the best educations came from travel and people being exposed to the arts. During my senior year in high school, my mother and he took me to Atlanta to see the opera, La Boheme. Afterward, I informed him that I hadn't really enjoyed it and certainly felt discombobulated trying to dissect it. His response to me was "Neither did I, but now you know what you don't like."

Regarding travel, my mother and he traveled around the world numerous times. Upon their return, they always enjoyed regaling their adventures with us children in hopes of creating a thirst for travel. Neither of my brothers had traveled that much but my parents' fabulous trips certainly whet my appetite for travel.

When the federal savings institutions began to be bought out by larger ones, my daddy was put on the Atlanta Board of Fulton Federal Savings. Mother and I loved that because he had to go to Atlanta for a meeting once a month. These meetings provided us an excuse to go shopping in the city. I was living in Fitzgerald at that time and would drive them to Atlanta for his meetings.

Daddy always dressed nicely but never knew what his clothes cost and didn't want to know. Mother used to buy him Hickey Freeman suits and Countess Mara ties which were very expensive. Often, especially at the Fulton Federal Savings meeting, other men would comment on them. Having no idea what he was wearing, Daddy would just say, "Thank you. I think my wife bought them at Halperin's or Gottlieb's" which were our local stores. He never bragged about anything that he had and actually had no idea what his clothes cost.

Rarely did I hear my daddy be critical of anyone. The only pet peeve that I was aware of was when he would see women downtown in hair curlers. He used to say to me, "I wonder where they are going that they will see more people than they will downtown." You must remember that was an era when our downtown was still bustling.

There was every imaginable shop, many owned by Russian Jewish immigrants. There were ladies' dress shops, men's shops, shoe stores, furniture stores, jewelry stores and even a few department stores. Today, there are few stores left, especially small homegrown businesses due to the influx of Walmart and other large conglomerates.

On my daddy's 80th birthday, my brothers and I decided to have a big celebration. When we mentioned it to him, it did not take him long to tell us "absolutely not." The three of us acquiesced, followed his wishes, and had only a small family affair. We did invite others to share their tributes with him through letters and notes which we shared with him in a bound book. I am thankful that my brother Charles had this idea.

The celebration was more than we had ever conjured in our wildest minds with the mayor declaring it "Harvey Jay Day." There were newspaper articles, editorials, banners, and even the American Flag, which he dearly loved, was flown over the White House in his honor. There were over 150 congratulatory letters and notes from friends and associates. *The Macon Telegraph and News* sent a columnist, Audrey Post, down to interview him and here follows some of her comments.

> *Harvey Jay has had 80 years' worth of birthday greeting and he accepts it all graciously, a little humbled and awed by all the fuss. 'I left town this week because I didn't want a big to do over my birthday and besides, I've been feeling 80 for several years now,' said Jay. " Colonel Jay served as major and district attorney but higher political office never appealed to him. He was encouraged to run at one time or another for the Legislature, Congress, US Senate and even for governor. His response was 'I've been in Fitzgerald all my life. I've traveled all over the world numerous times and I've never seen a place liked better. Why would I want to live anywhere else?' Emphysema has taken a toll on him and his frequent coughing made a birthday bash impossible. If Fitzgerald had an aristocracy, the Jays would be at the top of the social register. D.B. Jay, his grandfather came for Fitzgerald when it was first settled and became the city's judge. His son and*

> *grandsons followed in his footsteps into public service. Jay is a sentimental patriot, too. His children say he gets choked up when the national anthem is played, the sound of his sniffles, betraying his emotions. There is an old saying that there is a 'certain spirit of Godlihood when you can look upon your work and find it good.' You can certainly look upon yours and find them good, as the writer ends the interview.*

Let me take this time to share with you a few of my daddy's other accolades. He served as mayor of Fitzgerald at the age of 33, from 1939-43, one of the two youngest mayors in the history of our town. He was a charter member of the Fitzgerald Country Club. He was a charter director of the Abbeville State Bank, now known as Wilcox County State Bank, and the first Director Emeritus of that fine institution. My daddy was a charter member of Fitzgerald Federal Savings and Loan Association, and was president of it at the time they merged with Fulton Federal Savings and Loan Association. He was appointed to served as a director on the main Fulton Federal Savings and Loan Board. He was a director of the National Bank of Fitzgerald, and was a director when it merged with The C & S Bank. Later the bank became known as Bank of America and is now Ameris.

As I reflect upon my daddy's faith and his teaching Sunday School on the radio for thirty-five years, I am amazed at the number of lessons he must have prepared. It also reminds me of how many lives he touched and how he shared his dry sense of humor with others.

Several years before Daddy died, he got a call from C.C. Hall, a well-known African-American undertaker in our community. I happened to be there and handed him the phone, and told him it was Mr. Hall. When he took the phone from me, he said, "Now, C.C., I know you've called me to solicit business because you heard I had been mighty sick. I'm sorry but I have already told Mickey Paulk, of Paulk Funeral Home, that he could have my body when the time came for burial." I thought Mr. Hall was going to "bust a gut" for I could hear him laughing all the way through the phone.

In actuality, Mr. Hall had called my daddy, as often was the case, regardless of color, to let him know how much he enjoyed listening to him "preach" during Sunday School on the Sunday morning radio. Very few weeks escaped him that someone did not call to let Daddy know how much they gathered from his teaching the Baracca Class.

Daddy was not only a friend to everyone, but he was often their attorney or even their Sunday School teacher if they could not attend church. He often told the story of how people would say that he was a contradiction, for he was teaching them Sunday School on Sunday, and trying to prosecute them on Monday. His response was, "I was trying to get through to them on Sunday so I wouldn't have to prosecute them on Monday." I have known few people that were as extraordinary a Biblical scholar as he was, and later when I taught Sunday School, the only commentary I needed was him!

If only everyone could pass from this earth into "old glory land" like my daddy. On a Thursday, October 8, 1994, I went with him to our beloved doctor, Dr. Bill Hammond. Bill told him that his lungs were filling up with fluid and that he needed to be hospitalized. He asked Bill if he thought the end was near, and Bill answered, "Yes." My daddy then told me he did not want to go to the hospital, but instead he wanted to go home to die. I agreed with him, and took him home.

When I got him home to my mother, and our dear friend Helen, I took both of them into the living room. I told them what had transpired at the doctor's office. Afterward, I stayed in the living room, and had my crying spell. In only a few minutes, Daddy told Helen to tell me that crying wasn't allowed but celebrating was, and he was ready for me to come sit with him in the den.

On Saturday morning, two days later, I went over to visit Pa, as the grandchildren called him. As I entered, I asked him how he felt. His response was, "With my fingers, how do you feel?" His dry sense of humor was insatiable. With a smile on his face he told me that he had visited earlier that morning with two of his best friends, J. Paul Stone and John Ed Smith. Both friends had died several years earlier, so I asked him what they said. Immediately, he told me that they said the fish were biting, they were tired of waiting on him, and for him to come on up.

The next day, the interim preacher came by after church, and prayed with us. After he left, Daddy asked my mother to call everyone so he could pray with his family privately before he left us. He prayed out loud that he had always tried to live a good life for others, to do his best, to take care of his family, and that he was ready to get to heaven. He insisted several times during the prayer that he wanted God to take care of all of us who were left behind and help us each day.

On that Sunday morning, he refused pain medication saying that he wanted nothing to slow down the process. This truly grieved my son, Rob, who begged us to make him take his medicines. When I told my son that we needed to obey his wishes, he went outside, wearing his grandfather's cashmere overcoat, and sat on the curb waiting on my daddy's devoted helper, Helen Wenze, to arrive. Rob prayed that she could change his grandfather's decision.

The few next hours, Daddy lay in bed, alternating between chest pain and smiles. I firmly believe that he was visiting with his loved ones who were welcoming him to the pearly gates of heaven. What a beautiful legacy daddy left all of us! He not only showed us how to live, but also he taught us how to die. My fervent prayer is that when my time comes, I, too, can face death as graciously as he did.

At my daddy's funeral, his long time friend and pastor, John Burch delivered a beautiful eulogy with adulations and comments such as "He was a wise counselor, a man of sterling character, a scholarly teacher, a well-serving deacon, a dedicated Christian, and a wonderful friend." How many people would be honored to have such declarations about them?

Our pastor's eulogy led to an editorial in our local newspaper, *The Herald*. The editor, Jerry Pryor, spoke of my daddy's service. Jerry wrote of how often he had watched my daddy tee off at the golf course, and how much my daddy loved his weekly games of golf. He further noted the following:

> *Harvey Jay never swung a wood but instead, he played the game only with irons. I'm not much of a student of the game, but as I understand it, woods are made for long drives. Irons do not usually produce the longest drives but offer more accuracy and better control. Colonel Harvey didn't have any long drives to boast about, but he wasted little or no time wandering around in the rough. His golf game was also the kind of life he lived. He had no hooks or slices. He was satisfied with a straight game, never missing and never veering off to the side. And, when it was over, even those who could brag about their long drives, couldn't match his score.*

That was my daddy… a man who rarely hooked to the right or sliced in his life and rarely ended up in the rough. He was a man with a solid stroke, who always went straight down the middle, never veering or having to get himself out of a rut. I know of very few individuals who could have that comment made about him.

My mother was born to Perry Clegg Coney and Sallie Mae Wheeler in 1908. Her maternal grandfather was John J. Wheeler of Dooly County, and her maternal grandmother was Lydia Williams of Dooly County. Her paternal grandparents was Sam Whitsett Coney of Dooly County, and Eola Elizabeth Hamilton of Dooly County.

No one loves you like a mother, and no one is more demanding of you because of the belief that what you do and say is a direct reflection upon them. I had a male friend once tell me that the most influential person in his life was his mother. Indeed, that was interesting to me since his father was one of the wealthiest, and most influential men in our community. My husband, Gene, strongly agreed with him. Gene said that mothers teach tender love, and fathers teach tough love. Reflecting, that is probably true, especially for men. I affirm that a mother gives a daughter tough love as she constantly reminds her daughter that one day she will understand why she did what she did. I do not believe that is something a daddy would ever say to a daughter.

My mother was the voice of cultivation, class and poise. She was a beautiful woman, inside and out, but she never told any of her children how beautiful they were. Now, I don't mean that negatively, but mother felt that beauty was strictly from within. Beauty within was much more important to her than the genes that we inherited from my daddy and her. I must agree that beauty comes from within. When someone radiates love, compassion, happiness and virtue, it shines through regardless of their genetic history.

My mother was born to be a Southern aristocrat from "the get go." She idolized my daddy, and always said that he was her everything. Daddy was her mother, her father and her best friend. Mother's generation still went by their husband's name, and she honestly thought that being Mrs. Harvey L. Jay was the most glorious title in the world. I know of no stronger love between two people than the love that they shared with one another for 62 years. Having lost her parents so young, he was indeed all she ever had and, she adored him as much as he adored her. Mother waited on him with her entire being and he, in return, gave her his all, whether it be attention, love, faithfulness, or monetary gifts.

My parents had two sons, Harvey and Charles, six years apart. Then, they had a little girl who lived only a few hours. The baby was born with the umbilical cord wrapped around her neck, which is known as a "blue baby." A year and a half later, mother gave birth to me.

I often asked my mother wasn't it awful losing a child, and she responded in a positive manner, as always. She would say, "Yes, after carrying a baby nine months, and the expectations of it, it was truly awful. It is something you never get over, but you just learn to live with." She lamented how she cried for weeks. Then, finally one day, my daddy walked in and said how crushed he felt each day. He also told her that having to leave her at home crying when he went to work was almost devastating for him. After that conversation, mother said that she put on "her big girl panties." According to her, if she had not experienced that tragedy, she felt that she would never have had me.

My mother was what we referred to as a homemaker. She always liked to remind people that her college degree was in Home Economics. She must have listened intently because there was never a better cook than my mother. She loved to stand at her kitchen window with her eyes on the world as she prepared meals for her family. There were many times that she would see disenfranchised children walking by in the rain or cold and stop what she was doing to go offer them a ride. It always warmed her heart and even in her older age, she still wanted to do so but Helen and I would have to remind her that now it was no longer safe.

Mother was well known for her wonderful menus and entertaining others in her home. She valued her cooking skills and enjoyed passing them on to others. I have a friend, Sandra Hancock, who still likes to remind me that she learned to make a fruit cake by observing my mother many years ago. Mother had taken one to welcome Sandra and her husband Fred to Fitzgerald. Sandra loved it and asked if mother would teach her how to make a fruit cake, and mother did.

My mother made delicious Parker House rolls but she never did conquer the thin lacy cornbread. It didn't really matter because Rose Dunn, her neighbor and dear friend, definitely had conquered it. Rose loved telling mother to meet her in the park, located between the two houses, and she would give her a plate filled with cornbread. However, what I think Rose liked most was telling mother that she could cook something that mother could not. They always enjoyed teasing one another and were close friends until they died.

When I was a child, mother and daddy joined their friends often at a cabin outside of Fitzgerald. This did not last long because mother said some of their friends liked to party more than they did and they decided to refrain for a while. Later, Mother and Daddy began hosting smaller parties where everyone could be seated at the dining room or den tables. They were lavish dinner parties with beautiful china, silver dishes and sterling silver flatware. Mother would spend days polishing her silver, securing her linens, and cooking in preparation for the big night. If Mother and Daddy wanted to invite more people than they could accommodate at the tables, they would host a "drop by party" which did not require having to seat all the guest. She still enjoyed using her silver serving pieces and china, but guests were able to roam around the house as they picked up finger food. The days of silver and fine china are certainly a thing of the past.

My mother never worked outside the home, but she enjoyed the Magnolia Garden Club, the Review Club, Daughters of the American Revolution, and the Ladies Missionary Group. Mother taught a young adult Sunday School class for twenty-five years which she dearly loved. I now belong to that same Sunday School and regularly some of the members will bring up my mother's name. Just a few months ago, Melba Mitchell told me one of the things she remembers most was my mother saying, "Be careful what you pray for because it might just come true." I have often wondered what was meant by that statement, and that is another question I will ask Mother when I join her in heaven.

Another member, Joyce Vaughn, handed me a gem clipped "vitamin pack of scripture verses" from her purse. She told me that my mother gave it to her forty years ago and that she had used it through the years. Later, she decided to give the package to me. I, in turn, wrapped them up, and gave them to my daughter that Christmas. Again, my heart burst with pride at the person my mother has been to other people.

I truly believe that no one loved to shop any more than my mother. Trips to Macon and Atlanta were always fun times with her. After two days in Atlanta, we would arrive home, and she would put me out at the front door. Why? Because if she didn't, Daddy sitting in his blue chair with his smoking jacket on, would see us as we paraded past him with armloads of packages. He didn't care what mother bought, but she wanted him to think that she hadn't been spending money too foolishly. She would enter with a few bags, tell him that we had a pretty good shopping trip, and then go unlock the front door for me to bring in the rest of the packages. Mother definitely believed the old adage that men didn't need to know everything.

My mother loved beautiful clothes and shoes, and taught me to love to shop almost as much as she. Yes, it was a skill that had been passed down to her as well. Mother would share stories with me about her aunts and her mother going to Macon, via dirt roads, on monthly shopping trips. She said Aunt Lydia, Aunt Alma, and her mother, laughed and giggled all the way home about the beautiful items they had purchased. Once home, they would spend the next day, going among the three houses on the block, sharing their purchases with one another.

Mother thought nothing of driving to Atlanta for the day. My friend, Connie Parrott, reminded me recently that my mother and her mother in law, Grace Parrott, and two other friends went to Atlanta on a shopping trip. As Mother drove down Peachtree Street, her friends would comment about the clothing in the windows. In so doing, then my mother would respond, "Yes, did you see that yellow dress?" She didn't miss a thing, even though she was driving.

Yes, Mother would be proud of her precious great granddaughter, Laura Beth Mason. Once, when Laura Beth was about ten years old, I asked her what was her favorite thing to do. With a puzzled look, Laura Beth replied, "Why, you know, MeMa, shopping. I just guess I was born to shop." Another generation to help support our economy!

As a child, the only time I remember my mother being in the hospital was when she had an appendectomy. I was in the fourth grade, and she awoke with an excruciating pain that would not stop in her side. It was time for school to begin, so Daddy took me to school, a rarity, before taking Mama to the hospital. As soon as he left home, Mama called her dearest friends, Elene Dorminy to come over and help her get things together for the hospital. Elene knew precisely where to look for the beautiful gowns that mother had purchased in case of an emergency. Where does one keep their emergency suitcase or gowns for an emergency? Why, in a box, under the guest room bed, of course. Mother, not like me, would save her best lingerie for the appropriate time.

Besides loving to shop, when I was still in elementary school, Mother enjoyed going to the early movies with her dear friend, Ann Smith. Ann was the second wife of Dr. John Ed Smith, and the mother of John Ed Smith, Margie Smith Maris, and Mary Beth Smith Haase. The two of them would laugh that every time the movie changed, they were there. It took me many years before I understood that the movies were their escape from being housewives with small children.

When I reached my high school years, Mother and Ann no longer went to the movies. Ann was diagnosed with cancer in her forties, and mother wanted to make sure that she was home when I came in from school every day. Ann Shelton Smith was a beautiful woman from Atlanta and loved her family deeply. Even though I was a teenager, I will always remember how courageously she fought her cancer down to the very end. The last time that Ann was in our local hospital, she asked me to go downtown to Hybernia's to see if they had any shorts to fit her. I honored her request and returned to the hospital with them for her to see.

The next week, Mickey Paulk, our local undertaker and a family friend, drove Ann to Piedmont Hospital in Atlanta in the hearse. Uncle John was allowed to ride in the back with her because he was a physician. I venture to say that most people do not realize that there was a time that we had no emergency ambulances. The hearse was the only mode of transportation for the sick. Actually the hearse and the ambulance were the same, but when it was used for the sick, it was referred to as an ambulance. When it was used to transport the dead, it became a hearse. My brother Charles and I followed behind the ambulance so that we could leave a car for Uncle John to have in Atlanta. We then rode home with Mr. Paulk in the front seat of the ambulance/hearse. Two weeks later, there was no beach trip for our families as planned because sweet Ann died.

After I left home for college, mother began to paint china and play bridge in the afternoons. And, oh, how that lady loved to play bridge! She would play several times a week, and quite often, she took her friends to her beach condo. There, the ladies would play bridge, eat, drink, and be merry until the wee hours of the morning. Before leaving for the trip, though, mother would always have Daddy to go by the liquor store and pick her up a bottle of Vodka for their Bloody Marys. Oh, if those walls could talk!

I can honestly say that mother never went into a liquor store because she thought that would be "uncouth." It wasn't uncouth to drink the liquor, but a lady of her generation thought it uncouth to go into a liquor store. I know of some ladies who drove up to the liquor store, and blew the horn for them to come out to wait on them but not my mother. When I asked Mother if they ever gambled while playing bridge, astonished she answered, "Why no, not usually; but, we all do keep a little pouch filled with nickels, dimes and quarters, just in case someone wants to place a bet." I thought that was very interesting!

My precious mother taught me, "Courtesy is owed, respect is earned, and love is given." She was genteel, proud, smart, self-effacing, sweet, and somewhat naïve, all traits of a true Southern woman. Mother truly believed that having "class" had absolutely nothing to do with money. She would always remind me that some of the most prominent families in the South no longer had money, but they did have good breeding and good manners.

My mother was "big" on Emily Post and teaching me manners. Probably the two most important lessons that Mother taught me were good manners and the art of writing thank you notes. In society today, we are seeing that the latter is almost becoming a lost art. My late dear friend John Dorminy was well known for writing thank you notes rather than texting. At John's funeral, his youngest son Charlie, even mentioned it as an admirable trait of his father.

The most important element of writing a thank you note is that it not to sound generic or as if you are filling in the blanks. A thank you note should be personal. I remember well when my daughter in law, Amy, was beginning to write her wedding thank you notes. She didn't personally know the thoughtful people in Fitzgerald, but I went over the list with her, so that she could remember something about each giver. This allowed Amy to correctly write her note and thank each one personally.

Southern women have often been portrayed as "gushee" but when someone gives you a gift, it is definitely one time you need to gush. My feelings are if someone is kind enough to buy or made a gift for you, the least you can do is graciously thank him or her. What does writing a thank you note actually do? Personally, I believe it instills the act of gratitude, an admirable character trait, that is often seen.

I have written about mother teaching me table manners and politeness but she was also brimming with something called phone etiquette. Once upon a time, there were no cell phones, believe it or not. If we wanted to make a call, we began by picking up the phone from the receiver, and a voice referred to as "central," answered the phone. You then asked central to please call "so and so" by giving them the person's name and they connected you to that person.

Miraculously years later, you dialed three numbers, and that connected you to the person. Several years later, you were able to dial seven numbers, and then ten numbers. Today, we just speak the person's name in our cell phones, and the call goes through. During what some refer to as the "dark ages," we rarely made a long distance call. When we did call long distance, it was usually after 6:00 p.m., when the rates were lower and you could talk longer. I remember when I was in college that I would call home when I got back into the dorm. I would let the phone ring three times which told my parents that I had arrived safely at school. Doesn't that sound archaic, even to me!

Speaking of phones reminds me of the importance of phone manners to my parents. I will never forget my mother calling a friend in her Garden Club one afternoon. As I watched the grimace on my mother's face, I wondered what had just transpired on the phone. When mother hung up the phone, I inquired what had happened. She responded, "When Sue answered the phone, and I asked where her mother was, she answered 'Huh?' I was horrified, Lydia, and I just better 'ne'vre' hear you say that to anyone." I knew where this was leading and that was to another lesson on manners. Growing up Southern, we are taught at the earliest age that you always address or respond to an adult with "yes or no ma'am" or "yes or no sir." Why do we do this? Because it sounds respectful and our mothers told us to do so!

Some other civilities that my mother thought I should know were as follows:

- Ladies never sweated but rather they lightly perspired.
- Ladies never hit anyone, threw objects, cussed or expressed their true opinion.
- Ladies never show cleavage.
- Ladies never curse because cursing is for the illiterate
- Better to be underdressed rather than overdressed.
- She taught me foresight…always wear clean underwear, in case you are in an accident.
- A gentleman never went shirtless in front of a lady or kept his hat on at the dining table.

- Never light candles in the daytime but always make sure when you use candles that the wick has been lit.
- A lady never chews gum in public for chewing is for cows.
- Always put your knife on the side of your plate and never leave your spoon in a dish or bowl but always place it on a plate. Also, remember to place the knife with the sharp edge pointing inward, when setting the table.
- After using your napkin, fold it and place it next to your plate.
- Never use the term "Stuffed or full" rather "I have had a sufficient amount."
- Never use words like diarrhea, puke nor speak of any bodily functions.
- Never show PDA (Public Display of Affection) because if you would do that in public, what would you do in private.
- Men walk on the outside to protect the woman.
- Always ask others about their family, listen to them, and ask them to tell their family hello.
- Never return a dish or plate empty.
- Always take a hostess gift when invited to dine in someone's home.
- Never wear white before Easter or after Labor Day.
- Always cross your legs at the ankles rather than the knee.
- Lastly, remember your manners because if you don't, everyone else will.

My mother's Southern legacy is enduring and endearing because her name is constantly mentioned, and she is always remembered as a "refined" lady. My dear friend, Debra Brown Weil, said that to this day, her mother, sister and she still comment about certain things that my mother did.

Probably, the latest comment Debra Weil made about my mother was that whenever her mom, Betty Brown, or her sister, Deena Reese, and she go shopping, and find a great parking space, they respond "We got a Mrs. Jay's parking space." Traveling with my parents on banking conventions, they always went shopping with my mother. Mother was usually the chauffeur, and could always find a parking space right at the front door! Maybe it was reserved for her because her reputation for shopping preceded her.

I often do things a certain way just because my mama or grandmother did it like that, don't you? It might be something insignificant to most people, but it is definitely a tradition that is passed on from one generation to another. Good genes can't be bought or replaced, and I am sure that attributes to much of our behavior. As my "pretend" little sis, Margie Maris, once said, "Your mom had great genes; some of hers were just funnier than others." Mother was an engaging person to be around and always uplifting others. She made it her goal to make everyone who entered her home feel welcome by putting forth a little effort, serving the best she had, and looking on the bright side of life.

Earlier, I spoke of how much my mother idolized my daddy, but I haven't mentioned that he loved her just as much. You could be with them for only a little while and experience the love they shared with one another. Daddy always liked to tease her and would tell her that she must think money grew on trees, a source of conversation quite often.

For mother's 70th birthday, Daddy engaged our local florist, E. S. Wynn, whom we all loved, to make mother a money tree. Daddy's secretary, Ellene Echols, who had been with him for most of his career, approached E. S. about designing a money tree. She took him five hundred dollars in different denominations. He built a tree, put the money on dried branches, and then tied them with green ribbons. I only wish that I had a better picture of my mother's expression when E. S. entered our house with her "Money Tree." We all enjoyed the money tree, especially the grandchildren, who would come over to her house, and say, "I need a little money." Mother's response was always the same, "Go get it off of Pa's Money Tree." See, even then, in her mind, it was not her money tree but rather she had it because of his love and generosity.

My mother was selected, by the Fitzgerald Woman's Club, as Fitzgerald's First Mother of the Year. Many years later, the honor was changed to Woman of the Year, an honor that I was so blessed to receive as well. Mother never desired fame or glory but rather to always be the best wife, mother, and Christian that she could possibly be. When my mother was in her eighties, a sweet group of women who had her as their Sunday School teacher early in life, hosted a social, and invited mother and me to attend. After the dinner that night, they presented her with this framed poem, written by a class member, Shirley Coxen.

As young brides we were so blessed to have one
To Lead us each Lord's Day,
Dedicated in study to show us the better way.
Teaching His word so that others we might undergird.
From bride to mother, all along the way,
Serene, lovely, gracious Mrs. Jay.
You've molded us and touched our hearts
Of our lives you've been an integral part.
God bless you and keep you in His care
With hearts full of love and gratitude
This is our prayer.

What a beautiful tribute to a former Sunday School teacher. According to the ladies that night, Mother had not only impacted the lives of her own family but the lives of others as well. Oh, if people could speak so highly of me one day!

My mother, the perfect lady, never got over the fact that her son-in-law left her daughter, granddaughter, and grandson. If you really wanted to get her to have a hissy fit, just mention her ex son-in-law's name. You understand I used the term "hissy fit" and not just a conniption. What is the difference? My mother used to describe a hissy fit as being a short lived fit whereas a conniption could last all day long!

No one loves you like a mother and no one is more protective of their children. It doesn't matter if it is a female or male which inflicts hurt. I remember well my brothers never understood why Mother felt the way she did about her ex son-in-law until they had to deal with the same issue later in their lives. She would often express her feelings about him by saying, "I am so mad at Robert Sherrell, I'd like to egg his car." Now, for a fine, Christian lady, that was about the worst thing she could think to do or say about someone who had disappointed her child and grandchildren. It was rather amusing to everyone but me.

Most of my life, my mother bragged that she had never had a headache or a backache, and I know for a fact that is true. She had never been sick, and had only been in the hospital to have four children, and an appendectomy. I can honestly say that I do not ever remember seeing my mother "resting" during the day. Mother felt there were too many things she wanted to do and that it would appear that she was lazy if she did so.

People always commented on how pleasant she was and how she was always smiling. I firmly believe her secret to cheerfulness was that she only thought about the things that she wanted to think about and blocked everything else out. Plus, I must add, she always got a full ten hours sleep at night.

Good fortune finally ran out for my mother. When she was 82, she had a stroke. We took her to the hospital, where she stayed overnight, and then she went on to Macon to the hospital. After a few days, mother came home to her beautiful Biggs bed which we had positioned under her antique chandelier, in her dining room. She was horrified that we had moved her bed from upstairs and turned her dining room into a bedroom.

My Aunt Rosa Lee and I tried to explain, to little avail, that she could not go up the stairs, and that the only bedroom downstairs, was occupied by my daddy. Mother was most upset, pouted, and was unhappy until we informed her that we had positioned her favorite chair by her bed. We explained that we did that so she could look from the dining room, into the den, and there she would be able to see my daddy as clear as a picture. Because of her undying love for him, we finally brought a smile to her face and were able to leave her in the dining room for a while.

Thankfully, the stroke was not completely debilitating for mother. Being the determined woman that she was, she worked diligently to get over it, and she did. Being a typical Southern mother, she had enough pride to want to set a good example for all of us to follow, if ever we were incapacitated. The weakness from the stroke did leave Mother where she would fall and break both of her hips, in the years ahead. Realizing that her body was weaker than before and wanting Daddy to move back upstairs, she had a chair elevator installed for them.

After my mother's stroke, and my daddy was having to stay home with his emphysema, we discovered a wonderful companion for them named Helen Wenze. Mother was adamant that she did not need any help, so we informed her that Helen was not just for her but for Daddy was well.

Through the years, Helen could be seen driving Daddy around town. Sometimes, she might be driving him in his golf cart at the golf course, observing golfers, or sometimes, in his own vehicle. The two of them were seen all over town, and if mother could talk them into an out of town shopping trip, they were there as well. Daddy's vehicle was such a part of the two of them that when he died, we gave the car to Helen.

A story which describes my daddy's dry wit involves my good friend, Jim Parrott. Daddy discovered it was time to replace the slate roof on his house and asked Helen to drive him to Standard Supply. Helen went inside and asked Jim to come out to the car. When Jim appeared, Daddy told him he had just been informed that he needed a roof and that when he built the house, Lauren told him it was a life-time roof. Jim looked at him and said, "Well, Harvey. We just didn't expect you to live this long." Daddy replied, "I guess not Jim, so send out materials for a new roof."

The first time mother broke a hip, she was at my house and fell over our dog. When I tried to call 911 to get her up, she begged me not to, but rather she instructed me to call my son, Rob. She commented that Rob was strong, and she knew he could help her get up, without calling anyone else. Rob helped her up but we were able to finally convince her that we needed additional help from 911. Her only request, when she finally submitted, was that they not employ the siren, and they did not.

The next time, about five years later, Mother's other hip gave way, causing her to fall, and break it. It appeared that when the Macon doctor did surgery on this second hip, he made a mistake and severed a nerve. This made her slightly drag her left leg which was dangerous. Being concerned that she would fall if unassisted, this accident led her to use a wheelchair the last few years of her life.

Let me tell you about one of Helen and mother's capricious adventures that occurred at Macon Mall. When Helen and mother arrived, the mall entrance was surrounded by policemen. Mother told Helen to pull up and inquire as to what was going on, which she did. It appeared to be a hostage situation, and the mall was closed, according to the policeman. Mother responded to him that all they needed to do was go inside to Macy's, return a blouse, and then get a Chick-fil-A. You can imagine the look on the face of the policemen as he instructed them to turn around.

Afterward, mother asked Helen to try all three of the entrances to Macon Mall. She told Helen there might just be a kind policeman who would allow them in, but that was to no avail. How did the situation end that day? Of that, I am not sure. When Helen and mother left, there was still a hostage and a police standoff, neither of which made my mother a happy camper.

Another humorous story about Mother and Helen related to mother's 3 lb. dog, B. J. One day, Helen was in the kitchen cutting up a rutabaga, and B. J. was sitting on the floor next to her by the sink. The rutabaga slipped out of her hand, fell, and hit B. J. in the head. Helen screamed because it knocked B. J. unconscious. When the three of them arrived at the vet's office, Dr. Dwain Smith informed them that he had seen lots of animal accidents in his life. He believed though this was the first time that he had ever seen a dog knocked out by a rutabaga.

Speaking of Dr. Smith, we once had a dog named Bo Daddy. Bo Daddy was playing outside when he was attacked by a large bulldog. His body was severely torn apart, and we thought he would die from the wounds. After several days at the vet, the prominent Dr. Smith returned him to good health. When my daddy saw that the vet had saved Bo Daddy, he was amazed, so amazed that he told me that if he was dying, just to drop him off at Dr. Smith's office because he could resurrect anything or anyone.

My mother's dogs were notorious to people in our community. Her last dog, Frosty, was actually featured in the local bank advertisement, with Mother and Helen along for the ride. The bank called to asked mother's permission to put their picture in the local newspaper. She agreed after they told her to make sure that Frosty would be in the car with them for the photo session.

After the death of my daddy, my mother decided it was time for a new car. Now mind you, she was 85 years old. Mother belonged to the generation who believed when a car had close to 50,000 miles on it, the time had come to trade. I called my brothers, and told them that we either needed to buy her a new car or she was going out, and buy one by herself. The three of us decided that it was best that we bought her a new car.

My siblings and I knew how much mother loved her Cadillac. The next day, we order her a brand new blue Cadillac. When it arrived, I was out of town for a meeting. I called her that night and the first thing she told me was that her car was not blue but rather it was purple. I tried, every way I knew how, to dissuade her from thinking that it was purple. When I got home on Saturday afternoon, and saw it, she was right. Even though the color chart called it blue, it had an awful lot of purple in it.

The following Monday morning, I received a call from Tony Deese, a local friend who owned a body shop. Tony said, "Lydia, I hate to tell you, but your mother just left my shop. She wants to know how much it would cost her for me to paint her brand new car blue, since it was purple." I almost had a stroke!

I called our dear friend in Macon, Georgia, Marshall Butler, who owned multiple car dealerships. I asked him to gather every blue car he had, and that mother and I would be up there the next day. Our thoughtful friend brought every blue car that he thought she would like to one central location. The next day, off we went to Macon to trade one new car for another new car. We returned home that afternoon, with a brand new blue Lexus, the very first Lexus to arrive in our small community. Mother had no idea what a Lexus was, but she did know her colors. To her, all that mattered was that it was the right shade of blue!

When mother was 89, she went to the hospital because her doctor wasn't sure what was going on with her. After numerous tests, a surgeon came into her room and asked her if she knew that she had gallstones. Mother answered, "Of course. I've had them for thirty years but they've never bothered me until now." His answer was that she had as many gall stones as she had years. Imagine, over 89 gall stones and never complaining or telling anyone that you were uncomfortable.

As you can tell, my mother was a small, petite woman, very determined, somewhat stubborn, filled with tenacity, and giving up was not in her vocabulary. Earlier in the year, before the gall stones event, mother became confined to a wheelchair. As a result of the strokes and broken hips, her bones would give way and she would fall. After several incidents, we decided that a wheelchair was the safest avenue for her.

We continued to take mother shopping, to the beach, and anywhere else she desired, in her wheelchair. I will say she did limit her activities to out of town, because she was too proud to let people she knew see her in a wheelchair. Mother viewed this albatross as the only thing that she was not able to overcome.

When, mother turned 90, we wanted to have a 90th Birthday Bash for her, and sweet Aunt Rosie offered to have it at her house. We spent a few weeks getting ready for the celebration. I ordered 20 boxes of Godiva chocolates, a favorite of our mother. We tied them with a burgundy ribbon that read "Celebrating 90 years" to be given as favors for the party. Her close friends, and family members came, and helped her celebrate this milestone. Charles, Harvey and I presented her with a cookbook of her favorite recipes and pictures that were reminiscent of her 90 years. Mother received many tokens of love that day, but her favorite gift arrived the next day from her grandson, Rob.

Rob could never understand why his grandmother did not have a washer and dryer at her home. He could not comprehend that this "Southern belle" had lived a much different life than his own mother. My mother always had someone to wash her clothes by hand, or she sent them to the dry cleaners. Once in a blue moon, she would take them to the "washateria," not laundromat, if they were too large to fit in her kitchen sink.

Through the years, we would asked Mother if she wanted a washer and dryer, but she said no. Then, mother always added, "I don't really want them and actually, I have no place to put a washer and dryer." Now, don't forget that she lived in a 3400 square foot house so there was definitely a place for them. Regardless, Rob sent her a brand new stackable washer and dryer for her 90th birthday. I must add that it was the only gift that she certainly did not have, and suffice it to say, she was well-pleased because it came from Rob!

My precious mother died with all of us by her side when she was ninety years old. We honestly thought that she would live forever. How many times since her stroke at 82 had she overcome the odds, and always trudged on, just like a trooper? However, the last time she went to the hospital that changed. Mother had what was thought to be a sinus infection.

After a few days in the hospital, Mother improved, and came home. As I was putting her in the bed, she cried out that she felt like I had bruised her ribs. I asked her if she wanted me to take her back to the hospital, but she begged no, so I did not. The next morning, Helen and I took mother back to the hospital. After several tests, her sweet doctor, Bill Hammond told me that she had a heart attack after she left the hospital. I am not sure who was more shocked, him or me. Mother had no history of heart issues.

Two months after the death of my mother, the news media reported that pain in a woman's jaw or face had now been identified as a warning sign of a heart attack in women. What was thought to be a sinus infection turned out to be a heart attack. I had done everything that I knew to do to care for my mother during those ten years that I cared for her. My only regret is that I did not bring her back home to die in her own bed. If I had realized her condition, it might have been different.

I can reflect upon the hours afterward as we prepared for the days ahead. Mother loved life, lived it to the fullest, but loved her God, and her family above everything else. When her beloved preacher, Gene Wilder, came by to visit, and get her Bible to peruse, we shared her life as a mother with him. Our wonderful preacher conveyed to us his own love of her as his dear friend.

At her funeral, Dr. Wilder began by saying he wished that he had known her as a teenager. He just felt and knew that if he had, she would have been his girlfriend. Everyone loved my mother's spunkiness. Just the day before she died, she informed Dr. Wilder how handsome he looked in his sweater. Mother always enjoyed the company of men, but especially those men who were a part of her life.

My sister-in-law Kerry Jay and her daughters said they would help Jaye and me decide on the dress for my mother to wear one last time. Now, for some that wouldn't have been a big decision, but for my mother who adored clothes, I wanted to be sure we sent her to Heaven in style. We went through several selections, when Jaye said, "I have the perfect suit in mind." When she brought it out of the closet, we all exclaimed in unison, "Yes, that is it."

The clothing selected for my mother's departure was a royal blue St. John Knit suit with a bejeweled collar and cuffs. Most definitely, it was one of her all time favorites. To conservative me, it was a little too flashy. I said to my family members, "Y'all, please remember when I die, don't bury me in anything like that." To which my Jaye replied: "Mama, you don't have to worry because you don't own anything like that." Amen, was she ever so right because indeed I had never owned anything that flamboyant!

Wonderful Helen stayed with my parents for ten years as their sitter, driver, companion, cook, and friend. With Helen now being family, we wanted her to be with us when both of them died and she was. Yes, there were walls built by the times and society, but there was also so much respect and love among all of us for one another. How truly blessed we were to have Helen in our lives!

Reflecting on everything my parents taught me, I realize that neither taught me how to live without them. It is bittersweet to reflect on everything they did to instill their Christian values in me, but few days go by that I don't wish they were here. I can remember my mother saying to me at the age of 90, how much she missed her mother. I could hardly imagine that since her mother had been gone for more than 70 years, but now I completely understand. My fervent prayer is that I can have the influence and be an ally for my own grandchildren, as my parents were for my children. Words are truly inadequate to convey the impact that both of my parents had on Rob and Jaye, as well as the love that they, in turn, had for my parents.

My Mother's Recipes

Someone once asked me what cookbook did my mother use the most, and I was at a loss of words because Mother used numerous cookbooks. I do remember her oldest cookbook was one she had in college entitled "*Southern Cooking*" by Henrietta Dull, and she would refer to it as "Ms. Dull's Cookbook." Later, I learned why mother would tell me "Cook this dish in a slow oven" rather than at a definite 200 degrees because that is how she was taught by the prominent Ms. Dull. Along with that cookbook, which was falling to pieces, were *The Joy of Cooking* and numerous other cookbooks compiled by local groups as well as those she brought from her beloved hometown of Cordele. Mother was a wonderful cook, and on her 90th birthday, we compiled her favorite recipes, and bound them together in a cookbook for her three children and six grandchildren.

Desserts

The following was one of my mother's claim to fame recipes. Every birthday she baked us an angel food cake, and she always took one to others on their birthdays. Last year, Elaine Pust wrote me a note about the "beautiful and delicious angel food cakes with the fluffy pink icing that your mother brought to my parents' backyard parties. We usually kept it in the kitchen for ourselves until we had little choice but to bring it out." Mother's secret was two fold: (1) Let the Eggs sit at room temperature, and (2)Make sure your beaters were washed in warm water before using them again for the divinity icing. Yummy!

Angel Food Cake

12 Eggs, at room temperature
1 ½ cups cake flour
¾ cup sugar
¼ tsp salt
1 ½ tsp cream of tartar
1 tsp almond flavoring

Beat 9 egg whites on high until foamy and add salt. Add cream of tartar and beat until stiff and peaks form. Add flour and sugar gradually, and add almond. Bake in preheated oven, 45 minutes at 375°.

Icing:

3 egg whites
1 ½ cups sugar
⅔ cup water
½ tsp salt
½ cup corn syrup
1 dash of vanilla

Cook sugar, syrup and water. Cook over medium heat until it comes to a boil and spins a thread. Beat 3 egg whites, medium speed, with salt until foamy. Slowly add 1/3 of syrup to eggs. Cook 2/3 of syrup to firm ball stage and slowly pour over eggs and beat. Turn to high speed, beat until stiff peaks. Add vanilla.

Lane Cake

2 sticks of butter, softened
2 cups sugar
3 ½ cups cake flour
1 cup milk
3 tsp baking powder
1 Tbs vanilla
8 egg whites

Preheat oven to 350. Cream butter and add sugar until it is light. Mix the flour and baking powder in another bowl. Add the flour mixture to the butter and sugar, alternately with the milk, but ending with the flour mixture. Add vanilla and beat egg whites until stiff and fold them into the batter. Pour into two square pans, lined with waxed paper. Cook for 20 minutes. When completely cooled, spread the filling between the two layers and on top.

Filling: Cook the following in a double boiler over medium heat until thick. Then, add the egg yolks and let it cool before pouring over the cakes.

½ cup butter
1 cup sugar
1 cup raisins
1 cup nuts
¼ cup pineapple, crushed
¼ cup cherries
½ cup bourbon
8 egg yolks

Icing: White Divinity Icing or the following

2 ¼ cups sugar
¾ cup hot water
3 egg whites
1 Tbs vinegar

These were additional desserts of my mother's, and became her claim to fame towards the end of her life. She shared them with friends, and shut-ins, and when she was no longer able to bake, she taught her devoted companion, Helen, to make them. People all over town adored to see the two of them drive up because they knew there would be a chess pie or a peach, blackberry, or apple pie in the car. It was also a request of mother's children at any of our family gatherings.

Chocolate Chess Pie

½ cup melted butter
2 eggs
1 cup sugar
½ cup flour, sifted
1 square chocolate, dark
1 Tbs vanilla
½ cup pecans, if you like

Beat butter and sugar together and then add the eggs. Beat until mixed. Add chocolate and vanilla. You may add nuts if you like but it is just as good without them! Pour into a crust and bake at 320 for 25 minutes.

Fruit Pie

2 cups fruit (peach, blackberry apple)
¾ cup sugar
2 Tbs flour
¼ stick butter
salt, just as dash
2 frozen pie crusts

Preheat oven to 325 degrees. Lay sliced fruit in one of the crusts. Mix the other ingredients together and pour over fruit. Bake for about 30 minutes or until the filling is bubbling or crust is golden brown.

CHRISTMAS DESSERTS

Christmas never came and went without a few candies and cakes that were enjoyed by family and friends. These were always my favorite desserts during the Christmas season. When you read the fruit cake recipe, you will notice that it calls for two coconuts. As a child, I remember well, sitting on the back porch steps and watching mother take an ice pick, and poking the eyes of the coconut to drain its milk.

Then, she used a hammer to open the coconut. Last, she picked out the fresh coconut meat. (I googled, and discovered that one coconut weighs about 4 pounds.) Of these three recipes, the last one, Martha Washington Jets, is a recipe that mother brought with her from her hometown of Cordele. I have only seen this recipe one other time, and it was from a friend whose mother also grew up in Cordele. Like her mother, my mother had an exquisite china jar, which belonged to her grandmother, that she kept them in. The container of candy was always kept in our living room which was the coldest room in our house because it was seldom used.

WHITE FRUIT CAKE

1 lb butter
1 ¼ lb sugar
12 eggs
2 coconuts
1 lb flour
1 lb citron
1 lb. white raisins
1 lb cherries
1 lb pineapple
1 tsp mace
1 tsp allspice
2 tsp cinnamon
1 lb almonds
1 lb pecans
1 tsp baking powder

Toss fruit in the extra flour. Line loaf pans with waxed paper. Bake 20 minutes at 325. Decrease oven to 300 and bake for 40 more minutes. Cool. Pour whisky, as much as you like, over top of cake.

PECAN TASSES

Crust: Put in small muffin tins

1 3oz cream cheese
1 stick butter
1 cup flour

Filling:

1 egg
¾ cup brown sugar
1 Tbs butter
vanilla
⅔ cup nuts

Bake at 350 for 25 minutes. Makes 24.

Martha Washington Jets

½ cup butter, softened
1 box 10x confectioner sugar
4 Tbs cream, heavy
1 tsp vanilla
1 cup pecans, chopped

Mix butter and sugar and slowly add cream and vanilla. Last, add pecans, roll them into balls, and chill. After they are firm, you will dip them, using a toothpick, into the chocolate mixture.

Chocolate Mixture:

8 oz semi-sweet chocolate
4 Tbs butter
1 tsp vanilla
2-3 Tbs cream

Do not overcook this sauce but rather get it simmering and then remove from stove. Dip each ball into the chocolate sauce and put on waxed paper. When cooled, put them back in refrigerator to chill.

MEATS

These two chicken dishes were favorites of my mother's when she was hosting a female gathering at her house. In her earlier years, she entertained often with luncheons, dinner parties and women's church groups. The almond chicken loaf was one of her favorites to bake because few ladies made it. In later years, her chicken salad was usually requested and most often served at smaller gatherings. Today, it is a specialty of mine that I enjoy sharing with others.

MeMa's Chicken Salad

2 whole chicken breast
1 cup celery, chopped
3 tsp Hellman's mayo
1 tbsp horseradish sauce
Dash of lemon pepper

Cut up chicken and toss all ingredients together.

Almond Chicken Loaf

6 whole chicken breast or 1 hen
5 hard-boiled eggs
¾ almonds
mayo to taste

Cook chicken and cool. Put it thru the grinder. Chop almonds and grate eggs. Add enough mayo, salt and pepper to hold together. Rinse tin loaf pan in cold water and pour the mix in. Chill overnight.

ALMA'S SHRIMP ÉTOUFFÉ (MeMa's Double First Cousin)

2 lbs shrimp
1 cup onions
½ cup celery
4 garlic cloves
½ cup butter
½ cup sherry
mushrooms, small can
1 bell pepper
salt and pepper

Sauté onions, garlic, celery and shrimp in butter and sherry over medium heat. Add peppers and mushrooms. Serve over rice.

SALADS

It appears that this generation of women always felt that they must have a salad of some substance with every meal. It also appears that they preferred gelatin salads instead of fresh greens or fresh fruit salads as is the choice today.

PEACH PICKLED SALAD

1 pkg lemon jello
1 pkg orange jello
2 ½ cups water, boiled
½ cup peach juice
1 can peach pickles
½ cup celery
½ cup pecans

Drain and save peach juice. Pour boiling water over jello and add peach juice. Add peaches, celery and pecans. Refrigerate.

PINEAPPLE CUCUMBER SALAD

1 ½ cup cucumbers, diced
1 ½ cups Pineapple, tidbits
3 cups water
1 box gelatin
salt and pepper

Add gelatin to 1/2 cup of cold water. Mix other ingredients together

Asparagus Salad

¾ cup sugar
½ cup vinegar
2 envelopes gelatin
1 cup water
½ tsp salt
1 cup celery
½ cup nuts
2 pimentos, small jars
1 asparagus tips, small jar
¼ cup lemon juice
2 Tbs onion, grated
Tabasco

Boil vinegar, water and sugar. Mix everything together.

CHEESE RECIPES

The following are miscellaneous recipes of my mother's that were also specialties of hers. She was a wonderful cook, and you might find that some ingredients have been added or deleted when you compared her recipes to others. She was her own person, and therefore, her own cook!

Cheese Grits

How can I write a book on being Southern and not include a Grits recipe? I never liked grits that well until I tried my mother's cheese grits. Oh, my stars, what a comforting food they were, and she obtained the recipe from Betty S. Talmadge, the ex-wife of a former U.S. Senator. Betty was also the niece of my daddy's law partner, and after her divorce became a very successful business woman, during an era when women weren't know for their successful business ventures.

Betty's Cheese Grits

4 cups water, with salt
1 stick butter
2 tsp salt
½ tsp worcestershire
1 cup grits
4 eggs, separated
2 cups extra sharp cheese, grated
milk, only if necessary

Bring salted water to a boil and add grits gradually. Reduce heat and cook for about 25 minutes, until thick and stirring frequently.

Add cheese, butter, and worcestershire while hot, and set aside. Beat egg yolks and add to mixture. If grits are too stiff, add a little milk. Grease 1 1/2 quart casserole. Next, beat egg whites until stiff and fold into grits. Pour grits into casserole and top with remaining cheese. Bake 350 for 35 minutes. Serves 6-8.

CHEESE SOUFFLÉ_(MEMA'S SPECIALITY AND A TREAT)

4 tsp butter
4 tsp flour
½ lb. grated cheese
1 ½ cups hot milk
6 eggs, separated
1 tsp salt
1 dash cayenne

Melt butter, add flour and blend. Add milk. Cook until thickened, stirring constantly. Add seasoning and cheese. Heat until cheese is melted. Add beaten egg yolks. Cool. Pour in stiffly beaten egg whites and mix well. Bake in 2 quart pyrex dish at 300 for 75 minutes. Note: Soufflé is successful if you beat your egg whites until they form a stiff peak. Remember you only have a few minutes to get it to the table once you remove it from the oven or it will fall.

CHEESE STRAWS

1 stick of butter, soft
6 Oz extra sharp cheese, grated
½ tsp salt
½ tsp cayenne pepper
1 ½ cups flour

Preheat oven to 350. Mix everything except flour. Add flour and knead until smooth ball. Put mixture into a cookie press and press out onto un-greased cookie sheet. Remove from pan and let cool. Bake until golden.

MISCELLANEOUS

These last recipes are miscellaneous goodies that mother always made. I mentioned earlier how my daddy did not like "store bought" mayonnaise. I believe he was spoiled because mother always made it for him. After our Sunday lunch, there were always numerous veggies left over. Mother would take them and freeze them to be used later in soup or stew. Living in the South, where corn is bountiful during the summer months, everyone seems to make some type of relish. Our favorite was Corn Relish. Putting up summer vegetables and making corn relish or pepper jelly was just a normal part of my growing up Southern.

Corn Relish

18 ears of corn
4 onions
2 red bell peppers
1 cabbage, large
½ box mustard
2 lbs sugar
½ cup salt
2 Qt. vinegar
celery seed, Dash
turmeric, just for color

Scrape corn off the cob and add all ingredients to a large pot. Cook first four ingredients until done. Add other ingredients and bring to a boil. Then add vegetables and bring to a s second boil. Pack and seal.

Pepper Jelly

2 bottles cento
3 peppers, large
12 hot peppers
5 lbs + 1 cup sugar
¼ cup water
3 cups vinegar

Cut up peppers. Boil sugar, water and vinegar. Add peppers and cook until it boils good. Remove from heat and strain. Add cento and green coloring.

Mayonnaise

1 egg
1 ½ cups vegetable oil
1 Tbs lemon juice
1 ½ Tbs cider vinegar
½ tsp salt
1 tsp pepper, white

Put egg in mixer and slowly add the oil. When the desired consistency is there, add other ingredients. Refrigerate for at least an hour.

Chapter 4

My Siblings

On October 13, 1932, my parents welcomed home their first born child, Harvey Lamar Jay, Jr., a handsome blonde, blue-eyed baby boy. As a mother of a firstborn, mother always said that she thought he was the most handsome baby in the world. She loved being a mother, bonding with her baby, and staying at home while my daddy was at work.

Mother, Daddy, and Harvey were a threesome for six years before they ever thought that there would be additional children in the family. Harvey told me that he had grown up being scared because mother was often scared. When I looked dumbfounded, he replied that daddy would go back to the office at night to prepare for a case the next day, leaving Mother and him at home alone. I am not sure why but mother never told me that she was scared when she was a young bride.

By the time I came along, eleven years later, daddy never went anywhere at night. By then, he was well established in his practice, and did not have to go back to work. I think the humorous part was that mother often told me that she didn't know why but that Harvey had always been a scary child. I never could imagine Harvey being scared, but now I think I know why!

There were two other favorite stories about Harvey that mother told me about through the years. The first one was that when Harvey was only four years old, he looked out the window one day and saw frost on the ground. Not knowing what frost was, he ran into the kitchen calling "Minnie, Mother, come quick. Somebody has spilled grits all over the backyard."

The second story mother liked to tell was that when she left for the hospital to have me that Harvey was concerned about her losing another baby and he sobbed violently. Once daddy returned, and told him that he had a new healthy baby sister, he became so excited that he jumped up and down. Actually, he bit his tongue almost off. Little did daddy know that he would hardly get home from the hospital before he would have to take Harvey to the doctor. The doctor tried to repair his tongue, but it was somewhat difficult, especially in those days.

When Harvey was growing up, our neighborhood was filled with nothing but boys. There was Johnny Spell, Johnny Williams, Zeke Williams, Billy White, Johnny Patterson, Billy Hargrove, and the legendary Lauren Hargrove. Since we had the largest front yard, the boys turned it into a football field with a goal post at either end. I cannot believe mother allowed that to occur, but she agreed so that they would stay in her yard. Yes, our yard was larger than some yards, but it was most definitely not large enough for a football field!

Whenever there were lots of neighborhood boys around that meant there were often neighborhood disagreements. Mother said that she looked out the front window one day, and saw all of the boys fighting. She said that she honestly thought they were going to kill one another. She went outside, broke it up, and said if there were any more fights in her front yard, she would have the goal posts taken down. Now, according to Harvey, all his friends loved his petite, blonde mother and thought she was the prettiest woman they had ever seen. So when mother told them that, they looked sheepish, and obeyed. The next time there was a disagreement in our front yard, the boys did not fight there, but instead took it to the park median, directly in front of our house.

Daddy often said that mother would call him at the office, crying about the boys fighting, even though they were in the park. She would beg him to come home before blood was spilled. Of course, they never went to that extreme, but from the stories, they were a group to behold. They were just a bunch of high energy boys that went on to belong to the only State Championship Football Team in the history of Fitzgerald High School.

No matter how many children you have, each one is different, and each has his own personality. Harvey had a temper when he was younger and tried mother often. Most of the time, he was the brother who always took up for me and thought I could do no wrong. I am sure having a younger little sister wasn't always the neatest thing.

One time, Harvey decided that he wanted to leave home, and if he was leaving, he would take me with him. In a fit of anger, he grabbed my hand and put me in the car with him. Thankfully, we weren't gone for very long. Harvey was also the brother who taught me that the best-boiled peanuts were the "squeegee" ones rather than those that were large and filled out. Duh, right?

Mother said that Harvey's friends, remember those boys that liked to fight, were still a "mess" even when they were older. She relayed that sometimes Harvey would come in late, and she would cry, and say: "Harvey, you've had a beer." His response would almost send mother over the edge as he replied: "No, mother, I've had two." Then, she would start crying then he would feel bad about his actions and try to console her. I am not sure it always worked, but he was known to be a pretty cool operator!

Harvey belonged to the class at Fitzgerald High School that had the right to graduate at the end of their eleventh-grade year or stay on and go twelve years to high school. He had a late fall birthday, so he along with most of his friends, spent another year in high school. After graduation, he first went to North Georgia College and later graduated from Mercer University before entering the US Army.

I only remember going once with my parents to a Family Day at Mercer University while he was a student there. I will never forget that we were visiting at the Sigma Alpha Epsilon frat house. One of the brothers showed me a trophy that Harvey had captured. I looked at the inscription which read "Best Bull Shooter." I was dumbfounded because I knew that my younger brother, Charles loved to hunt, but I never knew that Harvey did! Now, please remember that I was only 8 years old and was still a platinum blonde.

After a two year stint in the Army as a Second Lieutenant, Harvey returned to Mercer University to attend law school. While at Mercer, he met his wife, Barbara Hodges, of Macon, Georgia. When I asked her how they met, she answered that she became curious about a boy in her class named Harvey Jay. It appeared that every day, someone different from the SAE fraternity answered to the name, Harvey Jay! Barbara's curiosity got the best of her, and finally on one exam day, the intriguing young man appeared, and she finally got to meet the one and only student named Harvey Jay.

After a year of dating, they married in Macon and moved to Atlanta. Barbara taught at Morris Brandon Elementary School, and Harvey worked for an insurance company. Harvey graduated from law school, but he honestly never wanted to be an attorney. He detested the thought of being cooped up in an office or a courtroom. Harvey would have been the fourth generation of lawyers in our family. It is easy to understand why he felt the pressure to attend law school. There is no doubt that he made the right decision not to become an attorney.

Harvey and Barbara moved to Jacksonville, Florida in the 1960s. They had two children, Harvey III, and Marjorie. Both of his children graduated from The Bolles School in Jacksonville, Florida. Harvey III graduated from Stetson University in Deland, and the University of Florida in Gainesville. He did carry on the tradition of becoming a lawyer, and today he is a Court of Appeals Judge. Marjorie is a homemaker and lives in Tampa, Florida.

Harvey and Barbara have five grandchildren. Harvey has been engaged in real estate for the past fifty years which was a perfect career choice for him. He is very personable, likes being outdoors, and enjoys getting to know people. Barbara has spent her time rearing their children, volunteering, and being a homemaker.

The first ten years of my married life, we were blessed with Harvey visiting us about every two months on business. Harvey is a walking encyclopedia of sports facts, and he always enjoyed discussing them with my ex-husband, and our son, Rob. Rob adored his Uncle Harvey, loved for him to visit, and always insisted that he sleep in the downstairs bedroom with him. I firmly believe that Harvey kept him up, late into the night, teaching him every sports fact he knew because how else would Rob have known what he did at such a young age? The two definitely shared camaraderie with one another, and to this day, if you need an answer to a sports question, give either of them a call.

My youngest brother, Charles Allan Jay, was born on May 15, 1938, in Fitzgerald. Charles was the brother you didn't want to have because his mother thought that he was the perfect child. He was quiet, mild mannered, and always behaved as he was expected. Of course, Harvey and I often tried to make him look different in our mother's eyes, but we never succeeded. Not wanting to think badly of anyone, she only saw the good in Charles. Of course, I am really kidding, but how could this book resonate of truth if I didn't put in a little sibling rivalry?

I don't remember Charles and his friends from the neighborhood, playing football in our front yard. I do remember them setting up the bases and playing baseball there. Buzzy Garrison and the neighborhood boys often played baseball with their make shift home plate, on the south side of the lawn facing Palm Street.

I do not know exactly how many times they hit the baseball over Palm Street into one of my grandmother's windows, but it was quite often. When they hit the ball and broke one of my grandmother's small glass windowpanes, mother would make whoever did it go over and tell her that they were sorry. Being the gracious Southern lady that Two-Moms was, she always gave them a hug and told them not to worry about it, that it would be fixed before nightfall. Yes, you guessed right. It was always fixed immediately.

Breaking windows and baseball soon took a backseat when Charles decided he wanted to learn to play golf. The idea certainly suited my mother who wanted to plant some pine trees in the front yard. My daddy loved the game of golf and played every Wednesday, Saturday, and Sunday afternoons. Soon, he began to take Charles out and taught him to play golf.

Charles, a child who liked to stay home, got so involved with golf that he decided he wanted a putting green in our backyard. He had sand brought in, made a concrete roller, and made his own putting green. I always loved to sit on the little, sparkling white, front porch of my playhouse, and watch him putt around the yard for hours. My poor, poor mother. For twenty long years, she went from having goal posts and bases in her front yard to a putting green in her back yard. No wonder she was so ecstatic when a baby girl was finally born!

Charles was a friendly, outgoing, and a very popular student in high school where he played football, baseball, and ran track. He was Mr. Fitzgerald High School, president of the student body, among numerous other accolades. The best advice he ever gave me was something he always practiced. He told me to always be friendly, especially to those who weren't your closest friends, who maybe needed a friend the most. He was so right. He explained that those needy friends were the ones who would value your friendship most when your other friends might not always be supportive. That is a lesson that I have tried to teach to my grandchildren because there is a lot of credence in that philosophy. I firmly believe that if others practiced this belief, there would less bullying in society today.

Charles, unlike his brother Harvey, loved to hunt and fish. Whenever he was not involved in sports, that is how he spent the majority of his time. Mother encouraged the hunting hobby because she loved for him to bring home quail and dove for her to cook. Charles sometimes brought frogs and fish home as well but fishing, next to golf, was my daddy's hobby, so he always kept us supplied with an abundance of fish.

There was another hobby that Charles loved and that was playing with snakes. Yes, I said snakes! He would always come in from hunting, pulled the birds from one of his coat pockets, and then maybe pull a snake out of the other pocket. Once, Charles brought one home, and when he went to get it out of his pocket to show me, it wasn't there. I thought my brother Harvey was going to kill him as we all searched and turned the house upside down. None of us got much sleep for the rest of the night, because we never did find the snake. I spoke of how Harvey taught Rob to love sports facts; I am afraid that Charles taught Rob his fascination with snakes!

Charles was not a child or teenager who roamed around on the weekends nor ever got into any kind of trouble. He loved to spend his time with Eli Vickers, at Lake Beatrice, most often referred to as Lake B. On every Friday and Saturday night, you could find Charles out there dancing with everybody. Charles always had lots of girls waiting in line to "jitterbug" with him, since he was an excellent dancer. To this day, when I see girls close to his age, they always ask about him and then comment about what a great dancer he was.

After Charles graduated from Fitzgerald High School and Mercer University, he enlisted in the US Army for two years. After returning from the military, he moved to Perry, Georgia where he began his career in the savings and loans financial institution. While in Perry, he met his bride, Kerry Finlayson, who lived in that county, and was a student at Tift College. They married in the late 1960s and moved to Macon, Georgia.

In Macon, Kerry taught school for two years, and Charles became President of Home Federal Savings. They built a beautiful home there and shortly thereafter, they were blessed with two daughters Kristy and Kelly. Kristy graduated from Agnes Scott, and Mercer University, while Kelly graduated from Auburn University. Kristy still lives in Macon, but Kelly has recently left Macon and moved to Atlanta. Charles and Kerry have nine grandchildren and enjoy every minute with them. In fact, for approximately fifteen years, they hosted dinner for all thirteen of them every Sunday night after church.

Charles, like the Jay men before him, has always aspired to be a servant to others. I rarely meet anyone from Macon that does not tell me that is exactly how he spends his time. Every Saturday morning, you will find him visiting the local hospitals and homes of his church members and friends. I might add that he does set aside every Saturday to do so, unless Georgia Tech is playing football in Atlanta. If the yellow jackets are there, rest assured that he will be at the game with his grandson, and namesake, Charles. I am certain that my daddy is smiling down from heaven since some of us have been traitors and switched to being a Georgia bulldog.

Visiting the sick is not all that Charles does, but he has also taught other male friends in Macon how to wear pink. He did this long before real men were wearing pink and eating quiche. If you are wondering why, it is because Charles has served several terms as chairman of Macon's Cherry Blossom Festival, and their color is pink.

According to the acclaimed *Macon Telegraph* writer, and well-known Georgia author, Ed Grisamore, Charles was one of the city's leaders who taught men to wear pink during the Cherry Blossom festival. As the festival began in the early 1980s, Charles convinced William Fickling, Sr., Bill Simmons, and Lee Crayton to order pink sports coats, like he had. Yes, they have been the brunt of sneers and comments, all dressed in pink, but the best story was when they were in Washington, D.C., at a Cherry Blossom Festival reception. According to Ed Grisamore, the four pink pioneers were on the elevator when on came some muscle men. Needless to say, they looked at these four men in pink somewhat askance. Charles' quick response, being a diehard Georgia Tech fan, was that they were members of the University of Georgia Wrestling Team. Wouldn't you loved to have seen the look on those men faces? Today, Charles' pink jacket is enshrined at the "Cherry Blossom Hall of Fame," in downtown Macon.

If there is an award out there, Charles has probably received it. He has been a trustee at Tift College and Mercer University, Georgia's

Outstanding Jaycee, Man of the Year in several communities, Macon's Sertoma Club Service to Mankind Award, as well as many others. Charles was also the President of Idle Hour Country Club and one of a few people who was not a Macon native, to hold that esteemed position.

But of all his honors, the greatest to me is that he is a child of God. Upon arising from bed each day, he prays "Thank you, God, for another day. Don't let me die until I am dead." I must say that is the best description of my brother and to me that says a lot about who he is. Charles feels that he has seen too many people walking around who are already dead and doing nothing to make life better. He does not want to be one of those people; for he wants to live life to the fullest, taking out everything he can, but putting back a little more than he takes out. This valuable lesson taught by our precious daddy.

Relationships with siblings can sometimes be trying, but how special is that relationship between your siblings and you? We understand one another better than anyone else. We share the ups and downs of our own family that others might not know. Indeed, I am proud of my brothers and am thankful that God selected me to be a part of their family. They weren't always at home when I was growing up. I do know one thing though; without the love and adulation of both of them, I am not sure where I would be today.

MY SIBLING'S FAVORITE RECIPES

The main foods my two brothers wanted growing up and when they returned home for family events, were fried chicken, ham and vegetables. Until our mother's death, they never came home that she did not have everything they liked on her table when they arrived. My daddy used to ask mother "Don't they have fresh tomatoes, peas and corn in Macon and Jacksonville?" He asked that because not only did she prepare many homegrown vegetables for them, but also she bought enough for them to take home to their family.

WHITE ACRE PEAS

2 pieces ham hock
2 lbs peas
1 onion, small and chopped
1 cup water
salt and pepper to taste

Put the cut up ham hock into a large pot and cook for 2 minutes over medium heat. Add the peas, onion, water, salt and pepper. Bring to a boil, turn down the heat and cover. Simmer for anywhere from 30 minutes to an hour or until they taste good. The longer you cook them the creamier they become. (This recipe can be used with any kind of peas or butter beans.)

FRIED OKRA

1 lb small okra
¾ cup cornmeal
1 tsp salt
½ tsp pepper
1 egg
1 cup vegetable oil

Rinse the okra and cut off the stem. Be sure to use only the small pods because the larger pods tend to be tougher. Mix the dry ingredients together and put the beaten egg in another bowl. Put the okra into the egg mixture and then coat with the dry ingredients. Drop into the oil in the black cast iron skillet and fry for about 3 minutes. Last, drain on a paper towel.

Corn Casserole

1 ½ cup sugar
1 ½ pints sweet corn
1 cup milk
½ stick butter, melted
1 tsp salt
3 eggs
1 Tbs flour

Bake at 350 for 35 minutes

Scalloped Potatoes

6 potatoes, small
½ stick butter
white sauce, any recipe

Peel and cook potatoes for five minutes. Slice potatoes as thin as possible. Place in a buttered casserole and add white sauce. Add butter to the top of casserole. Bake at 350 for one hour.

Squash Casserole

2 cups squash, cooked and mashed
2 eggs
¾ cup milk
¼ tsp salt
¼ tsp pepper
1 Tbs onion
1 cup cheese, sharp
½ stick butter
2 pieces bread

Scald milk and add butter. Soak bread in milk and add to seasoned squash. Beat and fold in eggs and other ingredients. Bake for 35 minutes at 375.

Scalloped Oysters

1 qt oysters
2 cups cracker crumbs
1 egg
½ cup milk
½ cup buttered crumbs
3 Tbs butter

Combine crumbs, butter, salt, pepper and sprinkle them into a greased baking dish. Arrange the oysters over them. Top with the rest of the crumb mixture. Bake at 350 for 40 minutes.

Southern Fried Chicken

6 chicken breasts, cut into two pieces
1 cup flour
½ cup milk
salt and pepper to taste
1 quart of vegetable oil

Season chicken pieces with salt and pepper and dip in milk. Get a brown paper bag and fill it with flour. Put chicken in bag and shake until every inch is coated. Put chicken in hot oil, cover and let fry until golden brown. Turn the pieces once and cook for about 15-20 minutes. Take out of skillet and place on a paper towel to drain off all the grease. Note: My brother Charles has been known to eat eight pieces of this fried chicken in one sitting!

Extra Special Pork Chops

8 pork chops
8 onion slices
8 lemon slices
2 cans of tomato soup, diluted
1 cup water
salt and pepper, a sprinkle

In black skillet, brown pork chops on both sides. Pour off drippings. Sprinkle chops with salt and pepper. Top each one with a slice of onion and lemon. Stir in cans of soup diluted with 1 cup water. Cover and cook for 45 minutes.

Shrimp and Artichoke Casserole

6 ½ Tbs butter
4 ½ Tbs flour
¼ cup sherry
¾ cup milk
1 Tbs worcestershire
¾ cup Half and Half
salt and pepper
1 13 oz can artichoke, drained
1 lb shrimp, cooked
1 cup parmesan cheese
1 6 oz can mushrooms

Preheat oven to 375. Melt butter, stir in flour. Gradually add liquid, stirring constantly. When thick, add salt and pepper, sherry and worcestershire sauce. Arrange artichokes on bottom and top with shrimp. Add cheese, mushrooms and top with sauce. Add additional cheese and paprika if you like. Bake 25 minutes.

Jeanne Hunter's Fruit Salad

6 oranges
2 grapefruit
1 can white cherries
1 fruit you like
1 can pineapple, small
4 envelopes of gelatin
½ cup cold water
1 pinch of salt

Combine everything and refrigerate overnight. Makes 18 molds.

Frozen Eggnog

1 egg yolk
¼ cup sugar
3 Tbs whiskey
½ pint whipped cream
1 bottle cherries
1 cup nuts

Crush vanilla wafers on bottom of pan. Stir all ingredients together and put on top of wafers. Freeze.

Two-Moms's Rock Cream

1 qt milk
½ box Knox gelatin
4 eggs
¾ cup sugar
vanilla flavoring, a dash

Put gelatin in milk to soak and bring to a boil. Beat egg yolks light. Add sugar and hot milk. Cook until thickened in a double boiler. Cool. Beat egg whites until stiff with 4 Tbs of sugar and vanilla. Add to the custard.

Chapter 5

My Childhood

The greatest generation was definitely those individuals who were born in the early 1900s and served our great country. These heroes were in at least one of the two major world wars that actually defined who they were. I was not born until November 1943, but how blessed I was to live in a time when I could leave home in the morning to go play and not return until afternoon. I could even drink water from the garden hose when I got hot and thirsty. I never thought about locking the door when I left home because the only fear I had was fear of my parents.

It was a time when we were somewhat unsupervised. We had been taught valuable lessons by both of our parents and were expected to make wise choices. I often wonder what can I do today to help young people become more trustworthy and more responsible, as my parents did for me. Even though my generation is not known as the greatest generation, I firmly believed it was the best generation for children. We were able to grow up in an environment where we always felt safe from harm.

"It was the best of times, it was the worst of times," according to the first chapter of *A Tale of Two Cities.* Somehow the best times seem to describe the small town world I grew up in, while the worst times appear to be the world in which we live today. In so many ways, our world is better with all the inventions of the 20th century. In other ways, we are more handicapped and divisive. Our world revolves around what the media informs us in regard to what is happening at that minute around the world. We seem to live where opinions and reasons come a "dime a dozen." During my childhood that was not necessarily so. I often find myself questioning what is normal, what is steadfast, and what is enduring today?

Most mothers, with whom I came into contact, were home during the day and spent their time baking cookies, soothing souls, bandaging and kissing "boo-boos," and making sure there were three meals on the table each day. There were no fast food restaurants, so cooking was of great importance. Maybe that is why everything we do down south is still centered around food.

Food is used to honor people, presented as a gift, and used to "soothe one's feathers" following a disagreement. Even though we always had a cook in the house, my mother took great pride in planning, and managing her meals for us. We didn't eat our meals in shifts, but instead we all sat down together and enjoyed our meal, whether we wanted to or not. And, if for some reason we decided we needed to leave the table before everyone was finished, we had to ask permission. Can you imagine that in today's world?

I remember my parents talking about their parents and grandparents living during the times of tribal American Indians and the Civil War. They told stories of how they lived to see the banks close and the WWII German POWs being relocated to Fitzgerald. These POWs were only three blocks from my home at the Blue and Gray Park.

My parents also reminisced about seeing the U.S. military on horseback looking for German submarines on the beaches at Ponte Verde, Florida. Mother told me that my daddy did not go to war because of his age and the fact that he was the Mayor of Fitzgerald during those days. Can you imagine living through what our ancestors lived through and endured during those troubled times? I loved hearing these stories over and over and am so glad that I did; otherwise, I would not be able to share them with future generations.

I was a baby during those days of POWs, so I was unaware of what had occurred at that time in Fitzgerald. Of all the war stories I heard my parents tell, my favorite story about WWII was when they heard about the sighting of German submarines. While my parents were vacationing off the northern coast of Florida, they were told to turn off their cottage lights at night. A military horseman would ride up and down the beach blaring out instructions via a megaphone because a German submarine had been spotted offshore. I can only imagine in my wildest dreams! Could it be that those stories actually began my fascination and love of the ocean and beaches, or did they began my fascination with history?

The statement "It takes a village to raise a child" was undeniably just as true when we were children as it is today. Everybody in the neighborhood helped to mold us into the people we are today. They felt a responsibility to take care of all the children in the neighborhood.

It never entered the minds of our neighbors that it was not their legal right to discipline us if they saw us doing something wrong. If they thought we were hungry, they would invite us in to eat, or if we were to hot, they would give us a drink of water. It didn't take us long to realize that we were in trouble though when they called us by our formal name such as Lydia Elizabeth Jay! The neighbors truly felt it was their bona fide responsibility to make us do what was right in their own eyes because they saw each of us as a reflection of their community.

In a small town, people know what you did even before you can get home to tell someone. Many years ago, I heard the following on a television interview with Sam Nunn, a former US Senator from Georgia. Senator Nunn spoke of how he spent his early summers finding the fly balls at the Little League field in Perry, Georgia and returning them for $.25 a ball.

One summer, Senator Nunn found a brand new shiny baseball. Rather than turning it in to the officials at the park, the small boy hid it under the bleachers to retrieve it at a later date. When he arrived home that afternoon, the first thing his parents asked him was where was the shiny new ball he caught. He was dumbfounded and could not believe that they knew about the incident. He had hardly walked in the door, when he discovered that someone had called them about what he had done.

The experience of Senator Nunn was typical of growing up Southern where an entire community helped to rear you. They wanted to keep you safe, and they kept you honest because they saw everyone's children as their responsibility. One was always under the watchful eye of a friend's mother who felt that it was her civic duty to mold you into a respectful human being. Honestly, about the most horrific incident to occur in a child's life was to be reprimanded by someone else's mother. There was an unspoken rule or understanding that it would be even worse for you once they got home.

Today, we are bombarded with tips on how to keep children safe in our community because we are so busy that often we do not even know our own neighbors. Yes, back then, we were taught not to talk to strangers, even though the consequences were not the same as today.

As a child, I remember walking home from a friend's house that was only two blocks away. It had just begun to rain, and this elderly gentleman pulled up beside me in his car, and offered me a ride home. I said, "No" immediately and scurried home as fast as I could. When I got home, the gentleman, Mr. Arrington, was in the driveway talking to my daddy. I started to cry when I saw him because I was so scared. This kind gentleman knew I was frightened, so he had driven straight to my house to let my daddy know that he was the poor soul who had offered me a ride home. He did acknowledge and praise how I had evidently listened well to my parents about not accepting rides from strangers.

Those were the days when people did not lock their doors, they kept the windows open so a cool breeze would invite any and everyone into their homes. Still, our parents instructed us not to talk to strangers. Today the world is vastly different. I just hope that we are not spending so much time worrying about strangers that we forget our gentleness and kindness to others in need.

I wish every child could have had the experiences I had growing up in a small community. I spent many gilded days of summer going on picnics with my parents to the pond or to the Boils. The Boils were a spring that majestically bubbled up out of House Creek and were located about ten miles north of town. It was owned by a family friend, Paul Stone, so our Sunday afternoons were often spent there. There were several families such as the Dorminys, Stones, Parrotts, Garlands, and others, who joined us and brought covered dishes of food for an early supper. Notice, I said supper, and not dinner because in the South, we have dinner at noon, and supper at night.

Everyone loved it when my mother brought her homemade ice cream to our Sunday afternoon get togethers. She would boil the eggs and milk at home and put the container in an enormous cooler. We would then stop by the Fitzgerald Ice Company to pick up a bag of ice.

By the way, did you ever go inside a large ice company in the 1950s? It was unbelievable! It was just one massive room with a floor of ice blocks that the attendant would pick up with gigantic tongs. He then would break them up with a sledge hammer, and put the small pieces of ice in your cooler.

Once we arrived at the Boils, the children would fight over who got to lick the freezing cold cast iron dasher when mother removed it from the churn. She covered the top of the wooden freezer with a plug and a towel, until it was time for dessert. One must remember that there were no electric ice cream churns in the 1950s, so we all had to take turns "hand churning" the ice cream. In between the churning mother would add rock salt and more ice. What work that was, but we honestly did not see it as such because we knew how enjoyable the end reward would be.

Individuals who didn't have a neat place like the "Boils" to swim often went to Bowen's Mill which was just "down the road a piece" which means that it was one mile or it could even be ten miles. Bowen's Mill had two swimming pools, a huge wooden structure that housed a bowling alley, and a dance floor. I will always remember the ditty we sang as we approached the entertainment center. It went like this, "Around the curve, and over the hill, here we are at Bowen's Mill." There was an old wooden Grist Mill on the property, but I never saw it in operation.

Later, came Lake Beatrice, which was built on the same principle as Bowen's Mill. It housed several swimming pools, bowling alleys, and a dance floor. It was run by an immensely caring proprietor Eli Vickers, who became a surrogate parent to so many restless teenagers during that era. Mr. Eli was there to make sure that you behaved and were safe. While he monitored the establishment, he basically became a counselor, father-figure, and friend to everyone who entered.

Another swimming hole was Crystal Lake, a natural lake that provided entertainment to families for generations. It was located about 15 miles away, in the next county. For some unknown reason, it always had difficulty staying open. It was consistently in the midst of opening, closing, and then reopening.

All of these three public places, were nothing but cheap, cinder block buildings. They often were in need of a little paint and fixing up. Oh, if those walls could only talk and reminisce about the memories that were made at those three hangouts. In the late fifties, the city of Fitzgerald built a public swimming pool, and playground at the American Legion complex. Today, none of the above establishments are in operation.

My love of the families that we enjoyed at the Boils continued into adulthood. Those same families hosted significant celebrations in my family's life. I can still see the round tables that Elene Dorminy had made for my wedding rehearsal dinner, and the exquisite pink flowered table cloths. There were fresh roses that Gladys Stone and Elene had cut for days from their rose gardens and refrigerated.

The day before the dinner, Gladys Stone, whose garden was the dinner spot, fell and broke her arm. "No, problem," said Elene, who was helping to host the event. "I'll just move the dinner to the Play House," a building she owned next door to her house, and that she did. They hosted approximately 50 guests that particular night which was not unusual in that era.

Friendships, like those with the Dorminys and Stones, cannot be bought. Those of us who are still around cherish these memories and treasure our friendships as well. My mother hosted bridesmaid's luncheons, teas, anniversaries, and other auspicious occasions for these families throughout the years. It appears to me, as I reflect, that most events held in those days were what we would call today "intergenerational" parties. If you don't understand the term, it is a party where the guest list spans several generations. The mixing of different age groups certainly makes it much more interesting.

My earliest remembrance of having a best friend was a little girl named Mary Smith. Mary lived around the corner from me on South Lee Street. She was the daughter of a prominent local physician, Dr. John Edward Smith, and his wife, Dorothy Kiker Smith. Dorothy was my mother's cousin, and the two had grown up together in Cordele, Georgia. When Dorothy married John Edward, mother and she were thrilled to be neighbors once again.

Our families were extremely close, and I referred to him as "Uncle John." We were no blood kin, but his children called my daddy "Uncle Harvey." This was another custom that was a symbol of love, endearment, and respect towards your parents' best friends.

I remember well how Uncle John would put Mary and me in the back seat of his car when he had to make house calls after hours. I still remember his black, two door car, and Uncle John folding up the front seat for us to climb into the back. We always loved to go with him on calls. We would take our baby dolls so that we could entertain ourselves while he visited and cared for his patients.

Early on the morning of December 6, 1946, Mary Smith's mother, Dorothy Kiker Smith, and her other two children by a former marriage, came by my house. It was the time for our annual Christmas trip to Atlanta so Dorothy blew the horn for mother and me. My mother went out to the car and told Dorothy that I had a fever during the night. She had debated but decided that we would not go with them this time. They drove out of our driveway with my precious mother not knowing that she would never see Dorothy and her three children again.

During the predawn hours the next morning, this family was among 119 people who died in America's deadliest hotel fire at that time. It occurred at The Winecoff Hotel, located in the heart of downtown Atlanta on Peachtree Street. The hotel had been built in 1912 as a fireproof hotel but did not have a fire escape or fire plan. There were very few people who escaped this blazing inferno but I can add that one of Dorothy's nephews did survive. Our dear Uncle John, called my daddy to give him the devastating news of the deadly fire and his loss. My daddy lamented throughout his life that being a pallbearer for four caskets was something that he hoped he never would repeat nor would he ever forget.

On that cold December morning, God had other plans for my mother and me, and I will always be thankful that mother and I did not join our dear friends. Some forty years later, John Ed's last wife, Margaret Smith, brought me Mary Smith's sterling baby cup. Mary and I had been best buddies for almost three years. The baby cup today has a special place in my home and is one of the few items that I have taken with me each time I have moved!

Another special development was when Uncle John's daughter, Margie Smith Maris, by his second wife, shared with me the discovery of a movie from when I was a child. Margie's dad had taken a movie of Mary and me riding our tricycles on their South Lee Street sidewalk. I cannot express the emotions it evoked as I remembered the times that we had spent together growing up. Margie's dad and my daddy entertained one another at ball games, suppers, and on numerous fishing trips. These memories exemplify the meaning of "It doesn't matter what you have in your life but rather who you have in your life."

Several years later, Uncle John, my daddy, and two other friends bought some land on the Bethlehem Church Road. There they built a pond and stocked it with bream, bass, and catfish. My daddy had taught my brothers and me how to fish, so we were ecstatic about the pond. We envisioned a place where we could now store our fishing paraphernalia and make memories together. We named this haven, "The Pond."

I can still visualize the first time I saw a turtle and its babies sunning on a log. The turtle experience was much better than my seeing an ugly snake as it swan across the water. My mother did not care that much for fishing, or the outdoors, but my brothers and I certainly did. My daddy liked to play golf on Wednesday, Saturday, and Sunday afternoons, but when he finished about 4:00 p.m., he always came home. Then, it was our time to go out to the pond to fish. Sometimes, because mother did not want to be left behind, she would pack a picnic for us. We would fish for a while and then have a picnic. Often, there was little left after our nibbling on the way to the pond.

I adored and admired "Uncle John" as a loving physician, but most of all, I loved him for his attitude. He lost his first family in the Winecoff Hotel fire and then married a lovely lady named Anne Shelton from Atlanta. Together, Anne and he had one boy and two girls. When Anne was in her 40s, and their youngest child was only four years old, she died of breast cancer.

Later, Uncle John married another fine woman, Margaret Tolbert. "Aunt Margaret" was widowed, childless, and as fine as anyone that I have ever known. When they first married, she commented to mother that the greatest thrill of her life was having the back door open and hearing children calling "Mama" to her. Aunt Margaret had cancer several times before Uncle John died of Parkinson. Prior to his early death, I remember that he was asked how he had survived so many tragedies. His response was "If I put everything good that has happened to me in one hand and everything bad that has happened to me in the other, the good would far outweigh the bad." Now, to me, that defines a true Christian soul.

I love to read, but I was certainly surprised when I came across an article recently from the 1943 edition of a Fitzgerald newspaper. My mother was not good about saving articles but my sweet grandmother was. The article discussed the 25th celebration of the Carnegie Library's Book Week. Children were to light a candle, and place it on the Christmas tree. The children were also asked to put 50 cents in the basket. With those donations, the Library would use the money to buy new children books. The article from the newspaper also mentioned that the youngest child who had a candle lit in her honor was as follows:

> *Little 'Baby Jay,' daughter of Mr. and Mrs. Harvey Jay, just two hours old, even before she found a name she likes, has asked her little cousin, Dotsie Jay Adams, to go down and light a candle on the Silver Anniversary cake at the library for her. She states she wants a pink one with a pretty ribbon. She also says she will have a name in time to register in the Silver Book before Book Week is over.*

Several hours later, that little baby was named Lydia Elizabeth Jay, which was me! Other names I recognized that appeared in the article for lighting candles were Ceciley Abrams, Dotsie Adams (Milne), Gary Cohen, Max Elders, Linda Hopper, Dotsie Humphries (Taylor), Billy Mann, Johnny Nall, David Payne, and Nancy Stone (Hough). Even before I was a day old or even had a name, my love for books had begun.

I don't have any idea how old I was when my mother first took me into the Carnegie Library for my very first library card, but I do remember getting it. The librarian who helped me that day was Miss Louise Smith, who was also my Sunday School teacher. She wore little wire glasses on the bridge of her nose and smiled the biggest smile as she said to me,"You are now the owner of your very own library card." Wow, what an exciting day that was for me. Miss Louise gave me instructions on how to behave in the library and what part of the library I would find my books. She further informed me that after making a selection, I was to go to the checkout desk and have the book stamped before leaving the library.

I will never forget experiencing that enormous room filled with so many books. My very first thought was how will I ever be able to read all these books in my lifetime? Of course, that was not reality nor did it ever materialize, but I have certainly done my best by trying to read as many books as possible. While some children played school, my favorite game was to pretend that I was a librarian. I requested a hand stamp one Christmas so that I could used it to check books out to my imaginary friends.

The only bad day that I remember at the library was when I was invited to a library dedication. I was asked to stand by Dr. Haile, the financier of the new children's addition to the main Carnegie library, to have my picture made for the local newspaper. I am not sure why I was selected for this prestigious honor. In my child's mind, it was that the librarian and her helpers knew how much I loved my library books.

After the picture taking sessions were completed, I was walking back to the car with my parents. I had on a black and white taffeta dress and new black patent shoes. As I was getting into the car, I realized that I had stepped into a package left on the ground by a canine. I was devastated. My beautiful black patent shoes never looked as shiny after that debacle. And I never wanted to buy another pair of black, patent leather shoes again. Only, after becoming an adult, and I could purge that thought from my mind, did I buy another pair.

Growing up, a perfect day was when my mother allowed me to walk the four blocks from home all by myself, down the back alley, to the Carnegie Library. Upon arriving there one day, I remember watching the library staff load up this huge, black but conspicuous bookmobile. The bookmobile was designed to deliver books to children who lived outside of the city limits. I always wanted to ride in that big, dark bookmobile surrounded by nothing but books. I was never so lucky. Still, I often thanked God that He came up with this idea. It was wonderful to think that those who couldn't walk to the library like I could were able to get a library book from the bookmobile.

I could only imagine the long, dusty backroads where these books went, and the white-haired ladies who would stop along their route to deliver books to the residents. In my mind, that was pretty close to a near perfect job. I often wondered if the recipients of the books could also belong to the Summer Reading Club as I did. It was somewhat of a status symbol to belong to that summer club and meeting your reading goal. Whenever you completed your goal, you were rewarded with a coupon for ice cream.

Miss Louise Smith, the wonderful librarian, along with her helpers Miss Pauline Ennis, another of my Sunday School teachers, and Miss Petrie were my adult mentors, who led me on my journey around the world each summer. I have often pondered whether it was the three of them or my daddy who inspired my desire to read as well as to travel. I understand that today we mostly read from our electronic books, but I still love to feel and turn the pages of a printed book. How many times have you walked through a room, seen a book you read years earlier, heard it calling out your name, and then picking it up and rereading it? Can you say that about an electronic book? I certainly don't think you can.

Another favorite place for me to walk was to downtown Fitzgerald, which was only three blocks from my house. I loved walking on the blue and gray hexagon pavers depicting our heritage, to the McClelland's Five and Dime Store, the Dixie Store or Dixieland's. All of these stores were referred to as "dime stores." I enjoyed these local stores where I could purchase multi-colored magic cubes, coloring books and crayons, or delicate little goldfish. In small towns like Fitzgerald, these stores were much different from those in cities like Macon and Atlanta. Our local dime stores did not have lunch counters where you could sit on a bar stool and enjoy a coke. I do remember however, that Haile's Drug Store and the Central Pharmacy did have those neat red stools. Many a day did I spin around on one and enjoy a coke or 7-Up Float. Do you remember when we bought a coke, we first hand to look on the bottom of the glass bottle to see where the bottling plant was and to check if anyone had one stamped "Fitzgerald" on it?

On my trips to Macon, I remember that enormous "dime store" called Woolworth's. It was located on Cherry Street in downtown Macon. It was on my left, separated from Davison-Paxon's department store, with only a paved alley. My family went often to Macon to our dentist, Dr. Valentine. If I didn't cry at the dentist, my parents would take me to Woolworth's. After my small purchase, we would head to their shopping venture, Davison-Paxon, which later became known as Macy's. I loved going out of town with my parents, but most of all, I enjoyed walking to my little dime stores in downtown Fitzgerald. They were the best to me!

On Saturdays, my friends and I would walk to The Grand Theatre, better known as "the Picture Show." At the show, we pretty much spent the entire afternoon. Saturdays were extraordinary days growing up not only because we did not go to school but also because it was the day that everybody came to town. The farmers and farm hands came to town to purchase supplies for the next week. They would always bring their families with them. For those living in town, we went to town so we could see everybody too. It appeared that the theaters were a good place for the children to congregate while their parents did their weekly shopping.

We had the Grand Theatre located on Main Street and the Pine Theatre which was located on East Pine Street. My friends and I normally went to the Grand. I loved all the cowboy double features and serials on the weekends, as well as Edward R. Murrow and the news.

Cowboy movies were the main feature of Saturday matinees with such heroes as Roy Rogers, Gene Autry, Lash LaRue, and Zorro. Actually Lash LaRue and Zorro came to Fitzgerald and signed autographs. How could I ever forget Lash LaRue walking the streets of downtown Fitzgerald popping his whip and visiting with everyone?

My parents would give me a quarter since the movie cost fifteen cents to get in. I then had enough money for a nickel coke and a nickel bag of popcorn. If I was really fortunate, I could scrounge up another nickel for a candy bar or a pack of peanuts. What fun it was to pour my peanuts into my coke bottle, and shake it up well. Once in a while, we would splurge and buy an ice cream cup, just to see what movie star's picture was on the inside lid of the cup. Certainly, it is difficult for anyone to fathom today that you could attend a movie for only fifteen cents. I think it is ridiculous what movies cost today and how many families are unable to see movies due to the cost.

At the time, I knew no difference, but now I am saddened to think that I grew up in a segregated south. At the Grand Theatre, there was a white and colored section. In other buildings throughout our town, there were also white and colored entrances and white and colored water fountains. Even though sometimes the colored children would call me a "soda cracker" when they walked past my house, I virtually knew no difference. I am thankful for that belief. Having been brought up to be a true Southern lady, I never used the "n" word nor associated with people who did. I was a grown woman before I even heard that word.

On Sunday afternoon, if I was not with my grandparents, I would be with Pat and Shep Dunn, who lived across the street from me, and go out to their farm off of Highway 129 South. Their daddy, Big Pat, would drive us out there in the back of his Willis jeep. Oh, what an adventure that was for me. The only other farm I had been to was my Two Dad's farm, off the Evergreen Highway. When I went with my grandparents, I never got to stay very long but not so at the Dunn farm.

I can visualize Pat, Shep, and me running through the open fields, the wind flying through my long blond hair, laughing, and playing so hard. After a few minutes, we would literally fall in the tall green grass, and roll over and over, until we almost threw up. Once, the boys even gave me a puff of their rabbit tobacco they had picked at the farm and rolled up in a newspaper. To this day, I have wondered how they knew it was smokeable, and who taught them to do such a thing. What blissful days of childhood those were to me!

"Little Pat" was the oldest of the two Dunn boys and was just a year older than I. His brother Shep and I were born two months apart with him being the younger. As I would look out my window, I could see other children and Little Pat walking to their kindergartens. Some of the neighborhood children went to Ms. Warren's kindergarten while others went to Ms. Lee's.

I remember one day Pat rang my doorbell, and I ran to the door. He told me that I could walk with him to Ms. Lee's kindergarten only three blocks away. I went to tell my mother who came to the door and tried to explain to Pat that neither his brother nor I were old enough to go to school. I spent half the morning crying over not being able to go with my friend Pat to his school.

After about two hours of crying, my mother finally took me down to Ms. Lee's kindergarten. We went inside where I watched the other children sing songs, listened to a story being read, and played on the little playground behind her big red house. This big red house is now painted white and is owned by Dr. Dylan Reach. It is the house that recently was used by the movie crew that came to Fitzgerald to make a movie in December 2018. It is so vivid in my mind that even today, I can see the big red house as clear as crystal.

Childhood friends have to be the best friends ever, and what fun it is when you are able to enjoy them when you become adults as well. I remember the very first person to pay me a visit when I got engaged the second time was my dear friend Pat Dunn. And, his brother Shep, to this day, is referred to as my "boyfriend" by my husband, even though our relationship has always been nothing but platonic. His wife and my husband laugh about the relationship that we still share. Shep's beautiful wife, Susan, once told him that I am the only one that he could marry if anything ever happened to my husband or to her. I guess that is what you call being really good friends.

There is not a doubt in my mind that if I ever needed Shep Dunn, he would be there for me, regardless of the day or time. Now, that is what you call love and true friendship in the South. I cared deeply for those two boys even if they did make me eat "mud pies" on many rainy afternoons in the old white barn behind their house. How blessed I feel that God allowed me to revisit my childhood through the Dunn boys who have been my dear friends for seventy-four years, until the sudden death of Pat just this past year.

My best girlfriend growing up was Martha Anne Dorminy who reminded me at her brother's funeral last year that I had been her very best friend in the whole wide world. She was two years older than me but only a grade ahead of me in school. Our parents were best friends so that made for lots of lasting memories together. I remember walking down the "dirt road," which was in reality an alley, but I saw it as a dirt road, leading me the two blocks to Martha Anne's house to visit her. I always thought it would be neat to live out in the country so in my little old mind, it was my own "country road." We used that alley like it was a superhighway between her house and mine. Essie Mae, their nurse, was enthralled with my long, platiumn curls, and always wanted to brush my hair and sometimes she would even try to braid it for me. Martha Anne had long light brown hair that was easy to braid but my white curly hair was definitely an adventure for Essie Mae, and she reminded me of that until her death.

Essie Mae and Minnie, our nurse, would often take Martha Anne and me to the Park which was almost at Martha Anne's back door. We loved for the two of them to swing us "as high as the sky" in those huge silver iron swings. They would sit there and visit with the other nurses as they watched us enjoy being outdoors. Once, I remember asking Minnie if she had children and she told me the only children she had were Harvey, Charles and me. After that time, I asked her more often because it always brought a smile to my face and an opportunity for me to give her a hug and a big ole' kiss.

My mother had instructed Minnie to spank us if we did not behave or obey her but I don't ever remember her spanking us or telling on us when mother inquired. Minnie left us when I was in the third grade and it broke my heart. The story I was told was she had a large family in the North and wanted to be with them. Later, in my life, I discovered that the real reason she left us was because she was pregnant, not married, and completely embarrassed by her situation. Another sign of how times have certainly changed.

When I was at Martha Anne's house, my favorite thing to play with for hours was a huge, wooden doll house. It had tiny furniture, tiny curtains and even tiny people. I never forgot that doll house and later in life, I built one for my own daughter, Jaye, complete with many of the accessories similar to those that Martha Anne had in her doll house.

I am sure it appears strange that we survived without having a swimming pool in our yard or in our neighbor's yard but somehow, we all did. Our swimming pool afternoons actually consisted of someone's mother setting up an oscillating sprinkler in the backyard where we played. It was much like going to the pool because we had on our bathing suits as we sprinted in and out of the fast turning sprinkler.

Now, my best friend Martha Anne did not enjoy getting wet as much as I did so when we no longer played with dolls, we would normally play "dress up" and would prance around our front and back yards acting like movie stars. We would always find the highest heels we could find in our mother's closets, a few of their strapless dresses and a pair of their shiny, dangling earrings. For many years, when I saw a picture of us dressed as such, I thought Martha Anne was the most sophisticated looking person I knew, while I looked just like a child playing dress up, but oh, how I treasure that picture and memory today.

Through the years, the two of us spent many days at her house or my house, even through our college days. In college, Martha Anne decided she wanted to be called Marcie, but she was the same person whether we were ensconced in our bedrooms, at either house, or just discussing life and boys. Her life basically centered around dance and piano, and today she is a well-known concert pianist who has played from New York to Austria. Before her brothers and she left for school every morning, they were required to practice the piano. Martha Anne and I took music from the same stern, gray-haired lady on West Magnolia Street, named Mrs. Belvin. I took for eight years until one day, Mrs. Belvin told my mother that unless I practiced more, she was just wasting her money on my lessons. Not true for Martha Anne, who practiced every day and whose talents have taken her around the world, while mine have—well, on second thought, I have not yet discovered my talents.

Martha Anne had two brothers, John, who was nine months younger than me and Jim, who was three years younger than me. Both of them have spent their adulthood living close by, so we have been able to continue our close friendship through the years. Jim's brother, John, was my Ob-Gyn for thirty plus years, so our paths crossed more frequently than mine did with Jim, who later in life moved to a nearby town. Not long ago, Jim told me that he thought of me often when he went into his Fitzgerald office. I looked very inquisitively at him when he reminded me that on the brick wall, above his office desk, I wrote my name with a rock or a coin when I was a child. His local office is located in the house in which he grew up but I sure don't remember ever doing such a thing as writing on someone's wall. Probably Martha Anne wrote her name and suggested that I write mine as well. You "reckon?"

Two years ago, I got a call at the lake early one morning, that my dear childhood friend, John Dorminy, had died of heart complications. I immediately returned to Fitzgerald and as I entered his house, I was able to have one last visit with him before he left this earth forever. Several weeks prior, I had gone out to see Katarina and John, and he reminded me about our trip to the Smokey Mountains together as children. He said that his family could not figure out why my mother kept throwing Kleenex out of the car window, which I might add was before we were taught not to litter. When we finally arrived at Fontana Dam, in North Carolina, they discovered that I had gotten deathly carsick going around the mountains and that my mother was constantly have to clean up after me. We also spent time discussing that I was writing a book and hopefully soon I would be able to share it with him but that did not come to fruition.

Three days after John's death, we celebrate his life with a luncheon at First Baptist Church after his funeral, for 85 out of town friends and family members. On each table, were spring flowers placed in colorful hats and framed in gold was the following sentiment which I had written in his memory:

> *Spring is symbolic of new life and new beginnings. Just like spring, our precious John brought new lives and new beginnings to thousands of families and for this, we are all blessed. This celebration of life is for you, John. You will be grievously missed, but 'Thank You' for the love and compassion you shared with your patients, friends, and family.*

Martha Anne, John and Jim's parents were extremely close to my family and not only did we go on vacations to the mountains and beach together, we also enjoyed having dinner together on a regular basis for years. Many a night, our parents would put the four of us in bed, and when it was time to go home, my parents would come in and wake me up so we could go home. Until their mother, Elene's death, my mother and she rarely went a day without conversing with one another either in person or on the phone. One of mother's favorite stories about Elene was how she would come blazing into our house, change all the furniture around to suit herself, but once she left, mother would move everything back the way it was. They were just that kind of friends.

When Elene died of cancer, my mother was at the beach, and my "death companion," Aunt Rosie and I drove to Fernandina to give mother the news and bring her back home. My daddy did not want mother to be told over the telephone, so he sent us down and he agreed to "pick up" my children from school that sad day.

To this day, my daughter still remembers how my daddy cried when my mother arrived home that afternoon, and he saw her pained expression over the loss of her dear friend. Friends such as that are difficult to come by and how heavy my heart is today that I have lost another of my special childhood friends, John Dorminy. It also weighs heavy on my heart because I felt as my best friend Martha Anne and I said goodbye after John's luncheon, that I just might not see her again since she lives so far away, and has such a busy lifestyle, and rarely comes back home. I know it is difficult for my children and grandchildren to understand that during my childhood we seldom took pictures. Therefore, I have to live with the pictures in mind to carry me through my senior years of remembrances.

There were other friends that grew up in my neighborhood, but they have since moved away, died or I have little or no knowledge of their whereabouts. There was Johnnie Lewis, Jane Cannon, Howell Sweat, and Mary Jane and Kay Henderson, just to name a few. Of course, there were many of my childhood classmates at Third Ward School that I am blessed to still have as friends, such as Pat Puckett Willcox, Rachel Strickland Bishop, Freddie Melton Nation, Stan Sumner, Frankie Griffin, and Buzzy Mitchell. All of these childhood friends had a significant impact on my life in one way or another. Later, in high school, I met people from all the schools and grew to love many of them, especially Glenda Stone McKenzie, Janet McGlamry Barrs, Kay Clark Stewart, Thomas Tomlin and Bill Luke.

Do you remember going on vacation in the "humpback cars" and later the "big fin cars" or the "muscle cars" that screamed "speed?" When some people went on vacations, to pass the time, parents would often teach their children to count cows or telephone poles. This was not true in my family because my daddy had better ideas. He would give each of us words to define and often I believe he enjoyed our bewilderment in not being able to figure out the meaning of a particular word. He would say, "Well, if you don't know the word, just write it down and we will look it up in the dictionary when we get back home." Dictionary, that's an almost obsolete word today, since we are now living in the age of technology. I honestly believe that family ritual helped me become infatuated with words. To this day, I enjoy learning new words, and if I don't know their meanings, I look them up on my I-pad or phone.

Growing up, I was blessed because for as long as I can remember, I have spent time at the beach, just like my mother and daddy before me. Growing up, my mother spent the winter months in St. Petersburg with her mother and at Indian Springs, Georgia during the summer months, all prior to her school days. However, the only time my grandparents took my daddy to the beach was during the summer months. My daddy, as well as his daddy, loved swimming at the beach and instilled in me a love for the beach and the smell of the ocean. How many times did I hear my daddy acclaim the beauty of the ocean and lament how anyone could look at the majestic sea and not believe there was a God. "How else could one explain its beauty?" Daddy would always say to us.

I remember that the only time my family could go to the beach was during August because my daddy, who was a District Attorney and a practicing attorney, something that is not allowed today, always had court in June and July but not in August. Sometimes, my grandparents went with us but usually my parents' friends, such as the John Dorminys or the John Ed Smiths, accompanied us to Florida. My mother was in charge of the rentals and always found us a perfect house on Jacksonville Beach until we decided to move further south to Ponte Vedra Beach.

I remember how we took Minnie, our nurse who today would be referred to as a Nanny, with us to the beach and our friends took their nurses with them as well. When night time came, our parents would take the nurses to another house to spend the night, a house that had been secured by the rental agency. At that time, I could not understand why they did not stay with us even though there was not an extra room and also why our parents had to rent them a room in someone else's home.

Later in life, I learned it was because of segregation and "Colored people," a polite and not derogatory expression during my childhood, were not allowed to stay in certain neighborhoods, something that had never crossed my mind. In my childlike mind, they were a part of our family, and during those days, no one used the term "race" except in reference to a competition of some kind. Today, I am thankful my generation understands that in diversity there is beauty and strength.

I am not sure who enjoyed the beach or being away from home the most, Minnie or us. She loved our beach trips and we would hardly get home from one before she was asking when were we going back. I realize now what a distinct change it must have been for her to travel with us even though when we stopped for gas, the stations had bathroom restrictions based on color, which I did not realize at that time. It was much later in life before I understood why my mother always packed a picnic lunch. At that time, there were color restrictions on restaurants and we would never have been able to all eat together inside. Also, let me add, that there were few fast food establishments back in those days.

After reaching our destinations at the beach, every night after the dinner meal, we would all go to the Boardwalk. My parents didn't like the carnival atmosphere but since we were children, it is what we loved the most and why we were not happy when they decided to move down to Ponte Vedra. What mayhem we experienced at the colorful boardwalk. I can still see the waxed head of a woman in a glass box who told your fortune for only a nickel, the ferris wheel, the bumper cars, picking up ducks, trying to ring a basket, etc. Today, I wonder how we survived these trips, in a car, not an SUV or van, without air conditioning but rolled down windows, in the oppressively humid South Georgia and North Florida summers.

Summers were sweltering hot in South Georgia and one must remember there was no air conditioning in homes or automobiles in the 1940s and 1950s. You either rode with open windows or lived with an attic fan or a large oscillating fan. My brothers and I would stand in front of the giant oscillating fan and talk which made our voices sound strange and distorted. As we did so, we would laugh and dance around in hysteria, while the cool breeze ran through our bodies and we could hardly catch our breath. No matter how hot it was, we always played outside and rarely wanted to be indoors; something very different from children today.

Reminiscing about childhood brings the imagery of my days at my elementary school, Third Ward School. I started in the First Grade when I was only five years old while the beginning age was six years old. They, I am not sure who they are today, decided that another girl and I, who both had late birthdays, should start First Grade in the Fall of 1948. We were told that they would decide at Christmas whether to leave us there or take us out so that we could start school the next year with our own definitive age group. I was able to stay in school that year and loved to read books about Dick and Jane and their dog Spot but that always made me the youngest person in my grade.

I remember the names of most of my childhood teachers at Third Ward, and even to this day, I can visualize the classroom with the scarred wooden floors, the silver radiator heaters, and the huge tan window shades that operated on a pulley type mechanism. My first grade teacher was Miss Abby McCall who I dearly loved. Like my daddy, I was left handed and my teacher's sister, Miss Julia McCall, came in the room one day and had a "conniption" that I was writing with my left hand. She walked over to me, popped my hand with the ruler and informed her sister to do so every time I did anything with my left hand. Why? According to Miss Julia, it was not feminine for girls to be left-handed, so she informed my teacher that she needed to change me. Henceforth, I learned to use my right hand but am triumphantly joyful that I still can do some things left-handed as to say, "Nana Nana boo boo," to Miss Julia for making me change my dominant hand. I have always attributed my confused mind to the fact I was changed from being left brained to being right handed in a left brain body. No wonder I am often confused!

My oldest brother Harvey was in the eleventh grade at Fitzgerald High School when I was in the first grade at Third Ward School. The one memory I have of him coming to my school was when he would come over, during recess, to work with our elementary football team. I truly thought that I was "big time" because Harvey would always stop by the store across from my school and bring me a treat.

The little neighborhood store where Harvey went was owned by Pete Roberts, a kind man who adored all children, and they adored him as well. I can still remember sticking my hand down into his old, faded red drink box and touching that frigid water, as I pulled out my nickel bottled coke. Oh, I believe that was the coldest water that I have ever felt! On some days, when I got to go to his store before or after school, and if my best friend that day did not have money to buy a drink, I would share my Co-Cola with her and I didn't even get sick.

Being the first born in a family is not always easy because so much is expected. Harvey was probably the smartest of the three siblings in that he had somewhat of a photographic memory, so school was extremely easy for him. To him school was palatable, but his real love was playing sports and having a good time. Being younger than

Harvey, I can only vaguely remember his playing football at the old Blue and Grey Football field and at the annual football jamboree on Thanksgiving Day between Fitzgerald and Tifton. Even though I don't remember much about the old football field on East Palm Street, I do remember having to hurry through Thanksgiving dinner to get to the stadium early since there were often 4,000 plus spectators during this annual event.

Harvey was a junior the year that the Fitzgerald Purple Hurricane football team won the state championship, something that has not occurred in our community since 1948. That was an exciting year for this group of boys and several articles, as well as books, have been published about this team's win in Columbus, Georgia at the Peanut Bowl. The star of the show was Lauren Hargrove, the "fabulous phantom of Fitzgerald" who scored two touchdowns and kicked the winning extra point against Decatur High School that year. According to most people in our community and throughout the state, Lauren was the most sought after football player in the nation that year. He went on to the University of Georgia, played for Coach Wally Butts, and was drafted by the Green Bay Packers, shortly before he was drafted into the Army. In my lifetime, Lauren has often been referred to as the "Herschel Walker of his day" by sports enthusiasts.

I cannot talk about the Fitzgerald High School Purple Hurricane football team without mentioning my daddy. Maybe it explains why I grew up loving sports even though I was not very athletic. I had always heard, from others, that my daddy was a great football player, but I honestly did not realize how good he was until I read some of the newspaper write ups and comments in the book, *Purple and Gold Boys,* by our homegrown author and attorney, Charlie Roy Adams.

In Mr. Adams' book, he relates that as a sophomore at Fitzgerald High School, my daddy, Harvey Jay, was the best end that the school had ever had. During my daddy's senior year, which was 1922, he was elected Captain by his teammates and scored the first touchdown of the year against Cordele as well as scoring three more touchdowns in that one game. After high school graduation at 16, Daddy planned to play college football that fall but encountered a back injury the very first month of practice at Georgia Tech.

My brother Charles, who was only five years older than I, was a safety patrol guard at Third Ward School when I was in the first and second grades. He was allowed to spend a week in training at the

School Safety Patrol Camp at Lake Blackshear, near Cordele, Georgia so that he could earn a badge and the distinction of being a school safety patrolman. Charles also got to wear a uniform to school on the days that he was a patrolman. In his brown vest and his cute little brown cap, his responsibility was to guard the crossing at Highway 129 South or better known as Grant Street. Charles would see my friends and me walking home and would stand in the middle of that busy highway to hold traffic for us to cross the street. I was most impressed and always enjoyed letting others know that Charles Jay was my brother!

Another thing that Charles did for me in elementary school was to pull me on the back or the front of his big blue bicycle up that HUGE hill, only in my mind, to Grant Street where he assumed his patrolman post. You must understand that his bicycle was no ordinary bike for he had put baseball cards between the bicycle spokes, and everybody didn't do that. Charles also had to roll up his pants legs so his pants would not get hung in the spokes. He would assume his post and then I would have to walk the next block home, huffing and puffing.

Now, Grant Street was the busy street where my dear friend, Buzzy Mitchell, got hit by a semi truck and had to be homeschooled for a long time afterward. When I think of that horrific day of Buzzy's accident, it makes me realize how precious life is and how Buzzy should have never lived through such a collision. I am certain the impact must have had an effect on his friends, Stan Summer and Frankie Griffin, who witnessed it all. It immediately brought to my mind from then on "timing is everything."

When I was in the fourth grade, the hardest grade ever and had Mrs. Gurganus for my teacher, I remember being so excited to tell her that we had just purchased a television, and how elated she was for me. She told me to share with the class what all I could see on a television. Doesn't that sound archaic? Our TV was a Sylvania model with a halo light surrounding the screen, it was black and white, and had a set of rabbit ears on top. Outside of our house, we had a tall antenna that was necessary for us to be able to receive more than one television station and even then, the station might have a "snowy" image. The television stations would come on at 6:00 AM and go off the air at 12:00 AM, with the playing of the national anthem. I can remember being the only one in my class with a TV that year and how proud I was of that television.

There were very few television shows on during the first few years that we had the set except for musical variety shows. I remember watching The Bob Hope Show, CBS News, and later westerns such as Gunsmoke, featuring Miss Kitty, my heroine. One of my parent's favorite music shows was the Lawrence Welk Show which became known as the "champagne music" hour. Mr. Welk was a bandleader and often played the accordion as he traveled across the United States.

I did not like the boring television show that Lawrence Welk hosted but rather I enjoyed the Ed Sullivan Show which introduced me to such artists as Elvis Presley, rock and roll, and later the celebratory Beatles. I will never forget the first time that Elvis appeared on the Sullivan show. My parents were so embarrassed that they turned off the television. They saw him as vulgar, as he rolled his hips and thrust his pelvis, and they were not sure I would be able to watch him again. However, that did not last long because he introduced the country to "rock and roll," a new kind of music that was based on blues, gospel and soul music that had been around for years. I can still remember the long lines at our Grand Theatre, when Elvis' first movie, "Love Me Tender" played, and the first one hundred patrons, received a free picture of him.

The emergence of "rock and roll" was an exhilarating time for preteens and teenagers. It was just the beginning of our own era of music which most girls loved as well as some boys. However, most of the boys were still hung up on and loved old cars with loud mufflers, gear shifts, and saw the speed limit as only a mere suggestion.

I am sure that you are wondering what we did before television, but that was simple, we had mammoth console radios. There were certain programs that came on our local stations, WBHB or WSIZ, that we learned to operate our lives around. Rarely were we, as children, allowed to pick and choose what we wanted to listen to on the radio. My daddy loved to listen to Amos and Andy, The Jack Benny Show, and the Zebedee Parsons' Gospel Hour, hosted by a local personality. My brothers, waited with gusto, for the Roy Rogers and Skye King adventures. On Sunday afternoons, we all gathered around the radio and listened to a spooky show called "The Shadow." These types of story programs were soon replaced by music programs and then came television.

The radio performed other services to the community such as when the fire siren would go off, we could know the location of the fire. All we had to do at home was excitedly rush to the radio to hear "The Justice Company" report on the fire. Later, when I became a teenager, how privileged I thought I was to find the Big Ape, WAPE, in Jacksonville, Florida or WOWO in Fort Wayne, Indiana on my car radio. Yes, you read right, not stereo but car radio. By then, I certainly thought I had arrived even though I was still not allowed to select a station at home.

When I was in the seventh grade at Third Ward School, Mrs. Emily Hattaway was my teacher and my principal. Her daughter had been a close friend of my aunt and later, her granddaughter, Emily Tyler, from Ocilla, became my close friend. In small towns, it is amazing how many friendships are formed due to generational friendships. Mrs. Hattaway was a persistent teacher but oh, how I loved that lady and that year in school. It was similar to being a senior in high school since you were the oldest ones at that particular school. Mrs. Hattaway selected me to be her "runner" so that whenever she had a message to deliver to the other teachers or students, I was the chosen one.

Also, during my seventh year, my brother Charles came over to the school to work with our little football team, just like my older brother Harvey had previously done. Even though Charles was not as fortunate to claim his fame from being on a state championship team, he was still an outstanding athlete. Charles was much smaller in statute than Harvey, but he lettered in football, track, and baseball during all four years of high school. His determination and athletic prowess followed him into the military and into his adult years. In the military, when he was asked by his sergeant to do 25 pushups, he would do 35 pushups because he wasn't tired at 25 even though that did not make his sergeant very happy. In his adult life, he has continued to run ten miles several times a week, play golf, play tennis, and exercise daily.

I loved Third Ward School and can easily remember the aroma of the chalk, the dusty erasers, the dark, dingy cloakroom closets, but I remember as well watching movies on rainy days when we were unable to have recess. I always enjoyed recess even if I was always one of the last girls picked for the baseball games. These memories take place at my red brick, one story elementary school, which I attended from first through seventh grade.

I was talking with my granddaughter one day and mentioned that I was always the last one picked for the baseball game during recess. Her response was "Mama and you had something in common. Mama said it didn't hurt her feelings not be picked, but I bet it hurt yours, MeMa." My response was "No, not really. Everybody can't do everything, and sports were just not my forte." Anyway, my personal feeling is that life is filled with ups and downs and not being selected to be on a team was a learning experience that certainly didn't dampen my spirits.

My brothers always had chores around the house to earn extra money, but I never got to earn any money. I remember Charles and Harvey having to go out to the garage or to the coal shed, located at the back of our garage and bring in coal and wood during the winter months. We had six fireplaces in my house growing up, so there was always a need for "more coal and more wood" for the fire. When I was still in my single digits, age wise, my parents added on a great room to our house. I wanted another fire place in the new room but as expected, no one but me wanted another fireplace.

My family was blessed in that we did not have to utilize the fireplaces totally for heat. We had a coal furnace in the downstairs hallway and later a gas furnace that heated our house before central heating and air conditioning. As a young child, I can remember my mother bringing my clothes downstairs and helping me to dress for school by the warm furnace. Girls were not allowed to wear pants to school at that time, but if it was extremely cold, we could wear warm corduroy or flannel pants under our dresses. The only other chore I remember that my brothers had was to take the trash out to the alley for my mother. Later, when they were in high school, both of my brothers worked as bag boys at Jitney Jungle and at Harmon's, both independently owned grocery stores, to earn additional spending money.

How well I remember an incident with my oldest brother while I was in childhood that scarred me. It is something that I have never been able to get over and it led me to being claustrophobic. Harvey was in college, the military or the workforce most of my life but I remember on a few occasions, he was forced to babysit for Charles and me. Once, Harvey was on the phone talking with his girlfriend, and I kept interrupting him. He literally picked me up, took me to the bathroom and locked me inside. To this day, I cannot stand to be closed up in a small area and yes, I will ride in elevators, but not by choice. I guess, growing up with two older brothers, I have done pretty well if that is the only scar I carry from childhood.

Believe it or not, there were no cafeterias at any of my schools, so everyone had to either go home or bring their lunch in a brown bag or a small, tin lunch box. In the South, the main meal was called "dinner" and was served in the middle of the day. The night meal was much "lighter" in fare and was referred to as "supper." We always had two vegetables, meat, a salad and dessert for our noon meal. After we left the table from having dessert, my dad always ended his meal with a piece of Russell Stover or Whitman's chocolate candy. It was kept in a drawer by his recliner. He would offer everyone present a piece of candy, but he never ate but one piece after his meals. Now, if I had a box of chocolates by my chair, I would have eaten them until they were all gone but not my daddy. You can see the type of life he lived and preached; he truly lived his life with everything in moderation.

As I reminisce about not having a school cafeteria in elementary school and how we always ate meals at home, I tried to remember the first restaurants we had that were similar to fast food restaurants today. There was Johnnies and the Spotted Pig, where you drove up and waiters came out to take your order with a pencil and pad. Then came the Purple Duck Restaurant downtown. Soon after that came the Dairy Queen and the Tastee Freeze, where you walked up to the window and placed your order.

I imagine that there are not many alive today who remember that the first Dairy Queen was built on North Grant Street where Ward Chevrolet was later built and today that spot houses the Nazarene Church's Youth Center. Next door to that Dairy Queen, the owner Neil Peavy, a local druggist, also built our first Putt-Putt course. Presently, we have numerous fast food establishments, and I might note our third Dairy Queen has just been built in Fitzgerald. Things come, things go and some things come around again. It is difficult to remember much about life without fast food restaurants, but I do remember a time when they were few and far between.

Can you believe that approximately150 trains still rumble through Fitzgerald every day and that many people set their clocks by the trains? For so many years, we had a railroad shop here, and our town was viewed as a railroad community. If one was not a professional, the next best job in our community was the railroad, according to the community and pay status. At retirement, railroad men received a solid gold pocket watch, and that was a big deal back then.

I love trains: The headlights beaming, the noisy railroad tracks, and the smiling engineer waving as the train went through town. The tracks pass right through the middle of our town and preachers at the Methodist church often had to stop while preaching or conducting a wedding or funeral since it is right next to the train tracks. When I have visitors from out of town, they often have difficulty sleeping because of the train whistles blowing all night, but to me, its sounds vibrate peacefully through my body.

As a child, my mother would pack a lunch and the two of us would take the 11:00 AM train to Atlanta, arrive in Atlanta that afternoon and shop until dark. We would spend that night at the hotel and then take the train back home around 5:00 p.m. the next afternoon. We would arrive back in Fitzgerald around 1:00 AM and Mr. Simpson, who was a cab driver, would be there waiting to take us the five blocks to our home. My daddy couldn't go with us when I was a child because, according to him, he had to work, so that we could go and have a good time.

I remember numerous trips to Atlanta but the highlight was when Rich's Department Store, put in the much-publicized "Pink Pig." I can still visualize the first time I saw that monorail, high above downtown Atlanta in the 1950s, and had an opportunity to ride in the "little" pink pig. It wound through the toy department, where younger children squealed as they spotted items that they desired for Christmas. I felt somewhat silly since I was really too old to ride it. However, my mother would have died if I had not had the opportunity to ride the famous Pink Pig, which has now been enjoyed by my own children and grandchildren.

What wonderful memories I have of riding the passenger train to so many destinations since my daddy was the legal counsel for the Atlantic Coast Line and we were able to ride free. My parents and I rode up and down the East coast from New York City to Miami, and we always rented a sleeper or Pullman car on the train and what fun that was.

The bulging, green Pullman cars were exquisitely adorned with heavy brass fixtures, green drapes, leather seats and unique carpeting. There was a beautiful dining car and at particular stops along the route food was brought onto the train and could be purchased by passengers. There were white cloths on the dining tables and beautiful silver and china for the place settings, and there was even a smoking car where men gathered to smoke. Once on a trip to Miami, as I walked with my daddy to explore the dining car, we passed through the observation car, better defined as a place for men to gather for a drink or a smoke. In so doing, we encountered Mickey Rooney, the once famous actor, who was somewhat inebriated. Even so, it was a treat for me to see a real live movie star.

I always told my cousin, who lived in Honolulu, that it was a shame that the train didn't go across the Pacific Ocean because if it did, I could visit her often. Now, I understand that was particularly juvenile on my part but that was how my brain worked at that age. Trains are exhilarating but probably the most fascinating account of a train trip was told by my parents who had a friend who rented an entire Pullman car to attend the Kentucky Derby every year.

For approximately ten years, this contractor, H. G. Smith, took his doctor, banker and attorney and their wives to the Kentucky Derby via train where the pullman cars were parked right up to the Churchill Downs track. What luxurious tales my parents shared with me after experiencing the Kentucky Derby from a four bedroom pullman car. The Georgia Railroad used their cars for trips to The Kentucky Derby and The Masters Tournament until their retirement in 1982. What a life that must have been during the golden age of trains, for today the majority of trains we see are used only to transport cargo.

Religion and church have always played a special role in the lives of Southerners. Church is a place of refuge and relief, a gathering place for fuel for the soul, as well as a social place for interaction with others. I grew up just two blocks from the First Baptist Church of Fitzgerald, my beloved church. Every Sunday, rain or shine, my daddy and I walked to Sunday School and church together. I honestly cannot remember how my brothers got there unless they walked together, but I can remember holding my daddy's hand and his heart as we strolled by our neighbor's "front porches" on the way to church.

During the summer months at First Baptist Church, I remember the funeral home fans that were kept in the pews for us to use to "fan ourselves" so that we could stir the air around when the windows were raised as high as they would go. However, it was still hot inside the church, not from the firey sermons but rather from the South Georgia heat. I loved that church where at the age of 8, I joined on an Easter Sunday, was baptized, and later I was married there.

Speaking of the summer months, it appeared to me that school would never end. I never did understand why the first week we got out of school was when all of the local churches decided to have Vacation Bible School. Oh, don't get me wrong, I loved VBS, but it meant no reprieve from getting up early every morning, just like I was still in school! Each morning of VBS, we would line up outside the church, in the summer sweltering heat, and march inside to the tune of "Onward Christian Soldiers" with the "chosen one" carrying in the American Flag.

Once we were inside the sanctuary, we stood and pledged to the American Flag, the Christian Flag and the Bible. After a few songs and instructions, we were dismissed and sent to our individual classrooms or on field trips, according to age. There, we colored pictures, cut out pictures, glued them to paper and then each day took something we had made or something from a field trip home to share with our families.

On the last day of VBS, we created something extra special to take home to our mothers and fathers. For after all, those were the glory days when most children had mothers and fathers living together at home. I believe that I will always remember the brightly colored Kool-Aid, the vanilla crème cookies, and volunteer church members handing us a napkin rather than a plate to place the cookie.

I have mentioned Vacation Bible School, but I would be remiss if I didn't mention that Sunbeams, GA's (Girls Auxiliary), BTU (Baptist Training Union), Wednesday Night Prayer Meeting and Sunday School were all an integral part of my growing up. These religious activities defined me as a Baptist child, who spent many hours in the House of the Lord on Sunday mornings, Sunday nights, and Wednesday nights as well. We were instructed to be good ambassadors for Christ, and my memories are filled with inspiring individuals such as Mrs. Mary Mitchell, who made me want to be a missionary, and Ms. Louise Smith.

There were inspirational preachers at First Baptist Church such as Dr. Cary T. Vinzant, Dr. Carroll Carter and Dr. John Burch, who later led us as well at the new church on South Merrimac Drive. Later in my life, this church was bought and demolished by David Sims and my uncle, Clayton Jay, Jr. I acquired two of the beautiful stained glass windows that were in the choir loft. Today, one of these windows is located over the garage entrance at The Jay House, where I grew up, and the other I returned just a few years ago to my uncle for his pond house.

I love being a Baptist but probably not as much as my mother. In her last years of life, she told my dear friend, Butch Frye, who was a Methodist, that she liked everything about him but one thing and that was that he wasn't a Baptist. She belonged to the older generation that believed there was only one religion and that was hers; however, she was really tolerant of other religions because she always would end discussion of other faiths with "Well, we are all working for the same thing and that is to get to heaven."

I think of how fortunate I was to grow up in a community that valued religion as well as religious differences among its residents. Of all my heritage, I probably appreciate the acceptance of religious differences in my community as the pinnacle because I grew up not knowing that there was much difference between Gentiles and Jews. The majority of the first businesses in the 20th century in Fitzgerald were owned by Jewish men whose families had migrated from Romania or Russia.

Recently I discovered, in an old December 1934 issue of *The Leader-Enterprise*, where the Christmas spirit was stressed at the Woman's Club's December meeting by Mrs. Sam Abram, mother of the honorable Morris Abram, one time President of Brandeis University. Mrs. Abram shared with the club, her appreciation of the old toys that were donated to help make 125 children happy at Christmas. Another of the leading Jewish men in our community during my lifetime, was Martin Gottlieb, often referred to as our Jewish Santa, who left his estate for Christmas gifts to be purchased for the underprivileged children in our county. He selected an attorney to administer the distribution not through his own synagogue but rather through my daddy at the First Baptist Church.

Even though we were a small rural community, we were blessed to have a Jewish synagogue and a full time rabbi, Rabbi Kohen, for over 25 years. Our synagogue was indeed a regional congregation where Jews from numerous other communities migrated on their Sabbath and other holidays to Fitzgerald. Jewish mercantile or manufacturing families such as the Abrams, Eastmans, Embers, Gottiebs, Halperins, Harrises, Hellers, Krugers, Kaminskys, Litts, and Tatels, all played a significant role is the economic and political development of our small town. Today, there are very few Jewish families in our communities and what a loss that is for all of us, especially for the children now growing up here.

I never realized that our Jewish neighbors were any different from my Methodist neighbors until I was working in Atlanta in the late 1960s. Two new attorneys were hired at the Attorney's General office where I worked, Robert Sherrell, who was dark skinned and curly haired and Gerald Cohen, a light-skinned blue-eyed blonde. With an office filled with single women looking for men, someone said to me that one of the new attorneys was Jewish, to which I responded: "So what, I'm Baptist." Thank God I grew up in a community where we sometimes went to the Synagogue, they sometimes came to our church, and we integrated our lives and values together and continue to do so today.

Growing up for me was a time when most businesses in small communities were locally owned mom and pop stores and not large conglomerates like Walmart or Target. It was a time when people trusted one another and your word was as good as your bond. We went to the drug store, grocery store, or clothing store and said to the employee, "Just charge it," and they did and we paid at the end of each month.

At night, mother always left an empty milk bottle at the back door for the milkman, who came by early in the morning and replaced it with a bottle of fresh milk. Weekly, we rode over to "Big Eulalie" Massee's house where we were met at the back door by Belle who sold us her homemade butter and eggs. The dry cleaners came by your home, picked up the items to be washed or cleaned and returned them in a few days unless otherwise instructed. Oh, how I wish I could smell and feel the freshly ironed sheets that arrived from the White Swan Laundry again. Yes, I do iron my pillowcases, not sheets, when I have guests coming for the weekend to allow them the pleasure of freshly pressed pillowcases but I certainly don't iron my sheets.

Summer nights were filled with lightning bugs or fireflies, as they are called in the North, mosquitos, and gnats if the truck with the toxic spray hadn't been through the neighborhood yet, but we barely acknowledged any of them during our childhood or youth. Summer days were filled with some of us going to the Ocmulgee River, where we learned to water ski with the Luke brothers, as we sped by large old trees that sometimes had a snake dangling from its limbs.

I had other friends who built fires on the river's sandbars and stayed out there until "dark thirty," something I was not allowed to do. Going to the river certainly spelled "independence" to us as we rode down the dirt or loosely gravel road to its banks, away from the eyes, in our minds, of the condemning adults. An interesting circumstance is that only a few of my friends smoked, but none of them drank, and just being together, whether at the river or the lake, was a pure unadulterated joy that we all shared with one another.

I am sure my grandchildren cannot imagine how I spent my weekends but they were filled with entertaining times. We went to Lake Beatrice dancing, to the walk-in and drive-in movies, cruised up and down Grant Street, and sat around in the parking area of The Spotted Pig, our local hang out. During the school year, our weekend nights revolved around football, basketball and baseball fields and wondering whose letterman's jacket or class ring we would wear next or who was dating whom. Remember how we would use either paraffin wax or tape to make the boy's class ring fit over our dainty fingers?

The only job I ever had, prior to college graduation, was at the City of Fitzgerald's swimming pool. This pool was built in the 1950s before the arrival of home pools It was a great place to meet friends, during the long, hot summers we experienced in south Georgia. I applied for the position of lifeguard and got it after passing several tests. You must remember that there were few options for teenage work, especially girls unless you lived on a farm during that era. Did I save any lives that summer? No because my primary job was to sit on the tower and keep a lookout, while I worked on a rich golden tan! Did I ever sweat with this South Georgia heat? Of course not because Southern girls are taught not to sweat or perspire, but rather we are taught how to just "glow."

During those years, I am reminded of the drive-in theaters of which we had two in Fitzgerald. We would sneak as many people as we could in the back of the trunk into the movie so that they would not have to pay. Once, we were inside, everyone would unfold, and get out of the car. Not me, however, because I was too claustrophobic to even think about getting inside a trunk. As teenagers, we always had so much fun at the drive-in theaters, but most of our parents set rules that we were not allowed to go there on dates unless we were "double dating" or sixteen years old. I firmly believe that sneaking someone into the drive-in theater was possibly the "worst" thing we did in high school.

I will admit that the worst night of my life was when I was dating an older boy and we went to the drive in. I knew well that I wasn't supposed to be there unless I was double dating but I wanted to be "cool" as the other teenagers, so I went. I thought I was pretty cool until I heard my mother's voice calling me as she went up and down the rows at the drive-in because she had heard I was going there. I certainly tried to follow my parents' rules even more closely after that incident, and I will admit that was the first time that I actually broke any of their rules.

I didn't always wear a watch but thanks to the outdoor clock at my dear friend, Pat Puckett's father's chiropractor office, I was never late coming in from a date or being with my friends. My parents were strict disciplinarians and I had enough fear and respect for my parents that I always tried my best to obey the rules set for me and it certainly made life a lot easier. It might sound boring to you today, but my life was seldom dull.

I often reminded my mother that she was young when my brother Harvey was a teenager, but old for me. It appeared to me all of my friends had much younger and less strict mothers than me. I was a tenth grader before I was allowed to date, and I thought that was terrible. My mother was full of dating wisdom such as "If you let a boy kiss you by the third date, he will think you are easy," "Don't date anyone you wouldn't want to marry," "What's done in the dark will always come to light", and probably her favorite was "When your date walks you to the door, do not linger" and if I did, she switched the porch light on and off several times. Embarrassing? What do you think? I guess my fear and respect of my parents kept me out of a lot of trouble that otherwise would have been tempting.

The fun-filled days of high school are something I will always treasure: from reading summer novels, to being a lifeguard-not because I wanted to be a heroine, but because I needed a glowing suntan, to visiting the sick or making cookies for shut-ins, or water skiing in the Ocmulgee River. My nights were filled with the drive-in theatre or the downtown theater, hanging out at the Pig, or cruising Grant Street. Those summers were just as great as the school year to me.

Later, I understood that everyone did not feel the way I did about high school. Those people who were not contented or happy appear to still "tote" feelings of resentments and jealousies. I definitely do not fall into that category. Reflecting, it might be because high school was all I could have ever wanted it to be. I was fortunate to receive such honors as Miss FHS, Homecoming Queen-escorted by Fitzgerald's own Harold Brown, Most Popular, Valentine Sweetheart, class officer, and other accolades. It is easy to understand why I feel no resentments. As far as jealousy goes, I have a myriad of faults, but none of them include jealousy. I have always been happy when others acquired things I didn't have and could never comprehend why it made others feel despondent.

In the South, hair is often referred to as a crown of glory, but while big hair is still big down here, you must understand that wild hair is not. You might not comprehend this Southern theory, but what I have always heard is that the bigger or higher the hair, the closer to God you were. Do you think that is why some religions do not allow women to cut their hair?

When I was a child, ladies used to have a standing appointment at their beauty salons every week to have their hair fixed. Now understand that I said fixed and not styled. A Saturday night ritual at my house consisted of my mother twisting my hair around her finger into little curls and then using a bobby pin to hold the curls in place. I had to sleep with the bobby pins in my hair. Then when she woke me up for Sunday School, all she had to do was unpin my hair and comb it out.

When I became a teenager, I did my own hair and went to the Beauty Bob Shop just for hair cuts. I had some friends that would use empty Co-Cola cans rather than hair rollers to get a bigger bouffant look. I did not use hair spray, but rather in the South in the 1960s, we called it spray net. We also would sleep on satin pillowcases a trend that has reemerged today. Some teens would hang their heads off the bed so that their hair would not get messed up during the night. When I reminisce about this, I guess we really did believe that our hair was one of our greatest virtues.

As older teenage girls, some of us began to wash "Summer Blond" into our hair while others dyed their hair "Light Golden Blond," both products of a well advertised company. The majority of us sported the bubble or pageboy hairstyle. It was not just girls but teenage boys peroxided their hair during the summer months to show off their fabulous tans as well. When it came time for school to open back up, they wore a buzz cut to get rid of most of the blond. It is interesting what those of my mother's generation did. They would wash their hair with octagon soap or lemon juice. Then, they sat out in the sun to bleach out their new bob hairstyle.

High school days were not just about learning to fix our hair but also about experimenting with makeup. I loved wearing Revlon's "Cherries in Snow" or "Fire and Ice" polish on my lips and on my toes. I had an older friend who was living in the North during this time. She told me that as soon as her flight arrived at the Atlanta airport, the first thing she did was pull out her bright red lipstick. Then she applied it to her lips before heading further south to Fitzgerald. Inquiringly, I asked her why? According to her, northern girls wear very little lipstick while us Southern girls love us some color on our lips. If you don't believe that to be true, just check the female newscasters on television.

I loved the school year, but oh, how I loved summer time! How we would slather our bodies with suntan oil, which was actually nothing but iodine and baby oil, to get that golden tan. Then one day, that guy in Daytona came up with suntan lotion called Hawaiian Tropic that we all adored. Our number one goal for summer was to have a glow that looked as if we had just been kissed by the shining sun. Everyone did not achieve a glowing tan because some would get blistered during the day. When dusk fell, they would take oatmeal or vinegar baths to cool their bodies down.

Thinking about suntans makes me remember our delightful trips to the beach, remember the laughter when we went out at night and saw the old men in their tropical shirts, Bermuda shorts, black socks, black plastic sandals, and knobby knees. Can't you still hear the laughter and shrieking that transpired over these ugly sights that were not typically seen in rural South Georgia?

An unsuccessful trip to the beach meant that you did not meet a lifeguard that got your phone number, called you, or stopped by for a visit before you left the beach. This adventure did not end with my generation. I remember well when my daughter and niece, Kelly Jay Cross, were with me at Fernandina Beach one week. Breathless, they came in squealing one day and screamed that the count was at 19. My response was "What?" Jaye answered, "Oh mom, you know! We have already met 19 boys on the beach today." It unquestionably reminded me of the days when lifeguards were everywhere on the beach, and our perfect day was to see just how many lifeguards we could meet.

I know it is difficult to comprehend, but I was in high school before my family owned more than one car. Living just three blocks from my daddy's office, he enjoyed his daily walk to and from work as he visited with friends along the way. If daddy went out of town on business, he took the family car. Then, if my mother needed to go anywhere, she just made other arrangements with her friends. I understand that it appears as if we were deprived, but I knew of no one who owned more than one car in the 1950s, except for a few farmers who had to have a truck.

When all of us children were allowed to have cars while in college, daddy gave us one, but he felt that mother and he still only needed one car. He felt that way until my brother Charles left his car at home when he went into the military. During those few months of basic training, my daddy decided it was really quite nice to have a second car. He bought himself a car, but he continued to buy my mother the nicer sedan.

Daddy was also a firm believer that you never bought a car until you could pay cash for it. He also believed that no one should drive a car if it had more than 50,000 miles on it. Once it reached that magical number, daddy felt it was time to trade the car. What a different world it is today with cars being built to last much longer. Fifty years ago, it was the era of cheap gas and thoughtful service station attendants who helped you take care of your car.

In so many ways, life was simpler then. Remember how we drove up to the gas station or the filling station, as we called it then, and told the attendant how many gallons of gas we wanted. The caring service attendants, like Lloyd Bedford, Johnny Beck, and Clyde Bailey, not only filled up our gas tank, but they also washed our windows, checked our oil, and swept our floorboards out as well.

Today, a trip to buy gas means you drive up, get out, and pump the gas yourself, unless you are like a friend of mine. My dear friend drives up to the pump, looks around pitifully, and asks someone else to pump the gas for her. To this day, this true Southern Belle, Quita Carswell, has never pumped her own gas! I do believe that she must be smarter than most of us.

There is little doubt that I grew up with a close to perfect childhood. My grandmother used to tell me that I had the world by the tail because I enjoyed life to the fullest. I lived across the street from my daddy's parents. My sweet grandmother would say that I walked across the street, between our two houses, like I owned it. I am certain that is true because I loved life and everything in it.

My memories of childhood are filled with many more friends than foes. There is little doubt, at that stage in life, that I firmly believed everyone loved me. Why would I think such a thought? I assume it is because I loved everybody so why would they not love me? Actually, I was an adult before that realization entered my life. Was I ever surprised, but blessed since that usually occurs earlier in life. Indeed, that was an epiphany to me.

Oh, how I still love my friends today, especially my girlfriends. Young people need to understand that to have great friends, you must first learn to be a friend. Yes, it does take a great deal of time and energy. True girlfriends are those friends that even though you are separated by years, emotionally you are not separated from one another. When you reunite with them, the bond and conversation is still there, something that most men will never comprehend. Just let a death occur in your family and friends from all stages of your life will appear. Without even asking, they seem to know just what to do, what to say, and what your needs are.

Lifelong friends are indeed the most precious. They have been there with you through thick and thin and that history makes it even more special. Friends truly validate from whence you've come, where you are today, and where you are going in the future. Haven't you seen a group of women on the beach or at a restaurant and their laughter draws attention from everyone within earshot? They just resonate the belief that there is nothing like "good ole girlfriends." During a lifetime, there will be marriage, babies, divorce, death and other major life issues when you need someone there for you. I was taught at an early age that boys may come and go, but genuine girlfriends were always here to stay. I definitely believe that is a bona fide statement.

I read that a sign of a really good friend is one who can fill in the blanks when writing an obituary or help you to plan visitation after the death of your loved one. A good friend is also one who knows how proud you are of that new grandchild and asks about him, before you ever mention his or her name. A friend can also tell by your voice, even over the phone, how you are feeling that day. I sometimes wonder if maybe they don't know you better than you actually know yourself.

Even though I have commented on the value of girlfriends, women who have boyfriends are dually blessed. It is not that boyfriends are less valuable or less treasured, but men do not always understand or recognize the needs of women. I am reminded of when my daddy died and I was a single mother. I had two of my dear male friends, Jim Dorminy and Shep Dunn, who appeared early the next morning to see if I needed help with anything. In fact, I did! These two friends hauled off my trash and were there to assist with other small matters, so that I could focus on the significant issues at hand. We all have heard that, "A friend in need is a friend indeed," and these two men personified it in every way.

I once heard that women give you their ear, but men give you advice. Yes, that is probably true, but we must remember that a well-balanced life needs both. When you have such valuable friendships, life becomes much easier for you as you walk through good and bad times.

Just a few months ago, I received a plaque from my dear friend, Ethelyn Underwood, that reads "Friendship isn't about whom you've known the longest… It's about who came and never left your side." There are times you feel like "killing" your friend for what she said or did, but if you genuinely care, you just move on. You are able to move on because you know in your heart of hearts she really didn't mean what she said or did. I firmly believe that investing in friendships is probably the best investment one can make and always gets a 100% return.

How many times did I play hopscotch or monopoly or ride the merry-go-round at the old park on Lee Street, a block north of the synagogue? How many times did my mother stand at the front door and call out my name to come home? The times are too numerous, but I do know that my childhood consisted mostly of outside play. I spent hours making mud pies with the neighborhood boys, running and playing in the sprinkler, or playing dolls in a friend's playhouse. I feel blessed that I grew up in an era where I was able to do such things.

I could ride my bike or walk to a friend's house, where we played for several hours, before returning home at dusk, without my mother fretting about me. Some of my male friends would leave their houses in the morning and stay gone all day. They would spend their day visiting or playing ball with their friends where the only major decisions were made with a simple eeny-meeny-miney-mo? My hometown was a place where others treated you like they want to be treated. Life, as a child, growing up in a small town, where you were nourished and loved, has to be the very best that life has to offer!

My Favorite Recipes

Cream Puffs

Puffs:
½ cup butter
1 cup boiling water
4 eggs
1 cup flour

Place butter and water in pan. When it boils, add flour all at once. Stir hard and remove from heat. Add unbeaten eggs, one at a time. Beat hard and drop by spoonfuls on buttered sheet, 1 1/2 inches apart. Bake 10 minutes at 400 degrees. Makes 8 puffs.

Filling:
¾ cup sugar
2 eggs
⅓ cup flour
2 cups milk, scalded
1 tsp vanilla
salt, pinch

Mix dry ingredients, add eggs, slightly beaten, and pour over the scalded milk. Stir until mixture is thick and then cool.

Fudge Cake

Melt the following together and let cool.
2 squares dark chocolate
2 sticks butter

Beat the following:
4 eggs
2 cups sugar
1 ½ cups flour
1 ½ tsp baking powder
2 Cups pecans

Bake at 350 for 30-40 minutes. Cut off the ends and give to your children or honey. While cake is hot, split marshmallows and place on top of cake.

Icing: Bring to a boil the following:
½ stick butter
3 Tbs sweet Milk
4 cups powdered sugar, 10x
½ cup cocoa

Cover the cake with the icing.

FROZEN FRUIT SALAD

2 cream cheese pkgs., small
½ pint whipping cream
4 Tbs mayo
½ tsp salt
1 tsp lemon juice
½ lb. marshmallows
1 small can pineapple, crushed
1 can white cherries
¾ cup red cherries
½ cup nuts

Add fruit to cheese mixture. Beat cream and fold into fruit mixture. Let stand in "ice box" for 3 hours.

CALLIE SUE'S ROLLS

3 cups flour (level)
½ cup Crisco
¼ cup sugar
1 pkg Yeast
1 Egg
1 tsp salt

Cream flour, sugar, salt and crisco together until smooth. Dissolve 1 pkg of yeast in 1 cup of tap water. Add egg to creamed mixture. Last, add yeast. Leave in bowl for 1 1/2 hours to rise. Bake at 350 for 15 minutes.

AUNT MARGARET'S BAKED FRUIT

1 can pineapple
1 can peaches
1 can apricots
1 jar apple rings
1 stick butter
½ cup sugar
2 Tbs flour
1 cup cooking sherry

Arrange fruit in dish and melt butter, add 1/2 cup Sugar, 2 Tbs flour, and mix thoroughly. Add 1cup sherry and stir. Cook until smooth and thick. Pour over fruit and cool. Bake at 325 until bubbly.

Chapter 6

Life After Fitzgerald

In my family, there was never a discussion about whether I would attend college after high school but instead where I would attend college. It was in the stars or maybe in my parent's horoscope that I attend a girl's school. I selected Stephens College in Columbia, Missouri because it sounded exciting to go far away from home.

After high school graduation, my best buddy, Buzzy Mitchell, was going to Auburn University in Alabama. He came over one night and helped me talk my parents into letting me go with him for summer quarter. There was only one catch and that was that I had to go to Stephens after those six weeks at Auburn.

Dreaming of faraway places, it never entered my realm of thought that I might get homesick. After six weeks at Auburn, away from home, friends and family, I realized that I was homesick. After my summer jaunt at Auburn, I decided that Missouri was just too far away and needed to devise another plan of action. My parents and I discussed my options which were limited, since it was only six weeks before Fall semester began.

A good friend, Dekle Rountree, who had lived in Fitzgerald, but had moved to Gainesville, Ga, came to my rescue. Dekle happened to live next door to the Dean of Women at Brenau College, a girl's school located in Gainesville. In fact, it was not just a girl's school, but the girl's school that my namesake, my great Aunt Lydia, had attended. My friend spoke with the Dean and the Dean said for me to submit my application which I did. The Dean rushed it through, and soon I was on my way to a place unknown to me.

September 1961 arrived, and I became a freshman at Brenau College, a college I had never seen before, but where I spent the next four years. Initially, I had planned to attend Brenau for two years and then transfer to Auburn University. However, when I realized how many hours I would lose by transferring, I decided against it.

It wasn't all bad being at a girl's school especially when you had the University of Georgia and Georgia Tech only 45 minutes away. The weekends were filled with frat parties and football games. We sported gold mums for homecoming games at Tech while at Georgia, we sported white mums with black and red ribbons. Later, came concerts, dances, new friendships, and the typical college item, fake IDs.

My freshman year, I had a roommate who was from Hershey, Pennsylvania, who was certainly unaware of our Southern colloquialism. The very first night, our suite mate walked into our room and exclaimed, "We are 'fixinto' go walk downtown to get some supper. Would y'all like to join us?" My roommate, Sue, looked at me and said, "What did she say?" Later that night, she asked me to help her call home because it appeared the telephone operator could not understand her brogue. The next morning, our dorm room was stuffy so I asked her if she would "crack a window." I think that statement just about did her in. She looked at me unabashedly and said, "Will I ever understand how Southerners talk."

Many young women of my generation attended college only to earn their M.R.S. degree which stood for finding a husband and getting married. My college days, however were filled with other things besides sorority and fraternity parties. There were circle pins, strand of pearls (a must in any Southern girl's jewelry box), scarab bracelets, and Youth Dew perfume of which I knew little. There were Pappagallo and Bass Weejun shoes, McMullen and Villager blouses, and sweater sets with matching skirts. We all wore raincoats over our shorts since pants were not allowed at Brenau. There were sign in and sign out sheets in the dorms for when we left campus and a permission form from our family to leave campus for the weekend. It is difficult to imagine that I loved it all. I am sure to a teenage girl today, it resembles her definition of a convent!

My freshman year in college, I pledged Alpha Delta Pi, a sorority founded at Wesleyan College, in Macon, Georgia. Sororities are a vital part of a young woman's life in the South and one can understand why when they discover how many of them originated in the South. I have several friends from the North, and they claim that sororities are not as important in the North, but that is not so down south.

Nothing can ease your feelings of loneliness or the confusion of your freshman year than to achieve the camaraderie that you do in a sorority. After all, haven't we been taught that when trials appear, the best way to get through them is by talking through the issues? Can you think of a better way to do that than with your congruous network of sorority sisters or friends? My sorority sisters also introduced a new term to me which was "sursy." In case you do not know, it is a small, unexpected gift or a surprise. It was exciting to return to the dorm and find a sursy on my bed from one of my new sorority sisters.

At a small girl's school, sorority life is the center of your daily life. These new friends usually become lifelong friends, as you bond through community service, rush week, socials with fraternities, teas, and becoming new sisters. Sorority life also provides you with a connection to other sisters when you visit other college campuses.

I loved serving as Rush Chairman my junior year, but the achievement I was most proud of was being President of the Panhellenic Council during my senior year. Can you imagine the average college girl traveling to Mississippi today to a Panhellenic Conference, with the dean of women from their college and feeling comfortable with her? Well, I did so with Dean Scholtz. Interestingly, in my thirties, the two of us were still corresponding with one another and actually scheduled lunch together. I feel that our relationship and the essentials that I learned while being a sorority girl at Brenau College helped to bridge the age differences.

As much as I enjoyed my freshman year of college, I had an incident occur which has affected me through my adult years. I rode the Greyhound bus every Friday morning after class, excluding winter and summer holidays, to Atlanta to Dr. Herbert Alden, a prominent dermatologist. Dr. Alden gave me the latest treatment for acne, which I had begun to experience while in college. This particular treatment was called radiation. I can still remember after my procedure, riding the bus back to Gainesville with my face feeling like it was on fire. As I reflected on it, years later, I realized that this treatment occurred about 50 times that year.

Twenty years later, I began my bout with melanoma and basal cell skin cancers. A local doctor, Charles Durden, told me that the medical profession only did these radiation treatments for approximately two years. During that time, they realized the repercussions and damage that it could cause later in life and stopped radiation treatments for acne. There has only been one other person I have know who had such treatments and that is one of my dearest friends, Patricia Waters. She, like I, has had multiple skin cancers through the years.

In June 1962, mother and I packed up my clothes from college and were heading home to Fitzgerald. Mother could never pass through Atlanta without encountering a stop over, so once again we spent the night there. We arrived late that Saturday afternoon, checked into a motel, and enjoyed a nice meal.

The next morning, as we were having breakfast, we saw the headlines of the Atlanta Constitution. A group from the Atlanta Art Association had crashed at Orly Field, in Paris, with no survivors. The plane had just taken off from Paris when the Air France Flight 007 tragedy occurred. What made it significant to Atlanta was that Air France had just opened its office there and this was their inaugural flight.

Among those 130 individuals killed were some of Atlanta's most well-known citizens. There was one couple who were special friends of my parents, Carol and Sykes Young. What a devastating revelation that was for my mother and me on that hot, summer Sunday morning. The Young's best friends, who were along on the trip, had a brother who flew over to Paris that day and relayed a meaningful commentary of what had occurred. Captain Hunnicutt was most kind to send a copy to the friends and families of these four individuals. The letter always held a special place in my mother's heart and significantly helped the healing process.

Another interesting as well as unique event occurred two years later, when I was a junior and I was allowed to have a car at college. One Friday in October, I met my mother in Atlanta where we were going to spend the weekend together. Our plan included meeting that day at Lenox Square, doing some shopping, going to dinner, and then to our hotel.

We were late having dinner that night so when we came out of the mall, my mother drove me over to where my brand new car was located.

As I was getting into my car, I noticed wires hanging down where my radio had been. As I looked further, I saw that the tachometer on my dash was gone, and that my car was a mess. I motioned for my mother to stop and wait as I realized that my car had been burglarized.

About that time, the mall patrol came riding by, and I flagged them down. Interestingly enough, immediately they knew what the problem was. The policeman asked me to raise the hood of my sporty new car, and perplexed, I did so. It was then that I realized that my engine was gone! It appeared that these car thieves would back up to a car with a wrecker, raise the hood, and lift out the engine. They had perfected it so that within the time that the mall patrol could make one lap around the mall, they had robbed an engine. Needless to say, of all my exploits in college, that was the most astonishing that happened to me.

During my college years, there was a Baptist minister, Martin Luther King, from Atlanta, Georgia who headed up the Civil Rights Movement in the South. Dr. King was best known for his nonviolence movement. I knew little of him since I was living in a cloistered girl's school in the mountains of North Georgia. I guess the first and other time I heard about Dr. King was in 1962 when he lead a march in Albany, Georgia, sixty miles from my hometown.

Being in college, loving life and thinking only about me, I didn't pay a whole lot of attention to the civil rights movement that was emerging. Like college students at that time, thinking it did not affect them personally, I did not recognize the significance of this movement. In 1963, the spring before Kennedy was assassinated, King organized a March on Washington and delivered his memorable "I have a Dream" speech. It was only then that I realized the importance and implication of this movement. I can attribute some of my innocence to the fact that I was not involved in a community except my own little world of academia.

The South was finally beginning to integrate when Dr. King was assassinated in 1968 in Memphis, Tennessee. Even though I had heard of the NAACP and the Ku Klux Klan while growing up, I knew very little about either group. Believe it or not, I never knew anyone who belonged to either group. Truly, that is difficult to believe in this day and time, but without the inundation of the media, most people lived in their own little world. Certainly, that is not the case today with news broadcasts twenty-four hours a day.

Where were you when John F. Kennedy was shot in Dallas in 1963? I remember well that November day when I was a junior at Brenau College and was sitting in a Sociology class. Someone came into the classroom and told the professor. My professor looked shocked as he told us that John F. Kennedy, the President of the United States had been shot. Needless to say, he dismissed class. I can remember running back to the sorority house in a trance and wondering what the world would be like tomorrow. When I arrived at the house, all my sorority sisters were gathered around our one TV. They were intently listening to the news, and I don't mean CNN or Fox, because we had neither at that time in life.

Life is interesting because until those times in my life, I had never thought about where I was when a significant event, like the death of John F. Kennedy or Martin Luther King, occurred. How well I remembered my parents talking about where they were when World War II began, Pearl Harbor and when they dropped the bombs on Hiroshima and Nagasaki. Often, they would talk about the ending of the war and how many of the local men survived and arrived home.

A little note of relevance to wartime is that as a child, I was informed that our local radio station, WBHB, stood for "Welcome Back Home, Boys." Now, I don't know if that is true or not but it was established about that time in history. During that time in my life, all those things seemed foreign to me. As an adult, I understand and find myself reminiscing about where I was when significant events occurred in my lifetime.

During my junior year at Brenau College, several of us decided to go to Europe for a few months before our senior year. The tour group, headed by Mrs. Franklin, a former Brenau woman, met in New York and spent a few days before leaving for Europe. My college roommate was Caye Miller Gregory, from Sylvania, Georgia. Caye was also my roommate throughout Europe and what a time we shared. It was a glorious experience as we sailed on the Cunard line for seven days before arriving at Southampton, England. After our time in Europe, we returned on an extended eight-day trip, through a harrowing storm, from Le Havre, France to New York.

It is difficult to believe, but while we were in Belgium, I discovered a young man from Fitzgerald. We were on the hotel elevator and when this man heard my voice, he asked if I was from the South. It turns out, he was a friend of my brother and his name was Ben Bryant. He was also the brother of a good friend, Jack Bryant, and was serving with the international press corp.

A few days later in Holland, I met a couple who were friends of my parents, from Camilla, Georgia. As we were watching cheese being made, they were buying Gouda cheese at the factory and realized we were from Georgia. On that trip, I also met a new friend whose father was the legendary baseball Hall of Fame player "Pee Wee" Reese. One never knows who and where they will run into someone who knows a friend or has a relative from the South.

Throughout Europe, the sights were magnificent, and I must admit that my favorite country had to be Italy. I am not sure if it was because I was a history major or if it was because of the beautiful and diverse countryside. I am most thankful that we were instructed to read *The Agony and The Ecstasy*, prior to our trip, for that definitely had an impact on the knowledge I acquired in Italy.

Being only twenty years old, the scenery in Europe was not only comprised of academia but also of meeting new friends. There were the local boys in every port, crew on the ships, as well as the SAEs from Florida State University. These new beaus made our itinerary even more intriguing. What stories we had to tell. Even after this adventure, several of us continued our friendships with these newfound friends. I am sure that this might sound immature to you, but you must remember, I was still a young woman and the male species was high on my agenda, Darling!

I was most blessed to have a daddy who felt that one of the best educations was travel. Rarely did I not thank him for exposing me to an entirely different world. It was a grandiose experience from England, onto the continent of Europe, and all the way down to Pompeii and back up to Austria. We ate well, learned well, and certainly spent our daddy's money well.

Probably, one of the most intriguing stories to relate was when we were in Brussels, Belgium. As you might know, there is no finer lace than handmade Brussels lace. We went into a shop and being young girls, dreaming of our prince charming, we tried on some of the delicate, handmade lace wedding veils. They were exquisite. This scenario was toward the end of our stay in Europe, so our funds were beginning to diminish. It was delightful trying on veils with friends, even if you knew you were too low on cash to purchase one.

After finding the perfect veil, minus the perfect husband, I informed the owner of the shop that I did not have enough money to buy a wedding veil. Much to my chagrin, his response was "Oh, little one, do not worry. Take it home with you, and just mail me back a check." Can you believe that I took the wedding veil with me and mailed him a check when I got home?

Now, I am sure you are wondering why I did not put the veil on a credit card, but I had only Travelers Checks and no credit card. About the only credit cards available in the 1960s were gas credit cards and department store credit cards. There were no Visa, Master Card, or American Express cards! I realize that must be difficult for the younger generation to comprehend, but that is how it was in the old days!

Lastly, I need to add a little note about the postcards that were sent to my parents during those European days. The postman and dear friend Richard Mathis, was a well-read individual who enjoyed traveling, but he traveled mostly through the postcards that he delivered. When my mother would see Richard coming, she would run to the front door to see if she had a postcard from me. Before she even got to touch the post card, Richard was telling her about where I had been, and what I had done that week. One could say that is a prime example of what we call "sharing our experiences" with others in the South.

Speaking of the postman makes me think of how often I looked for mail from my mother, daddy or boyfriends while in college. Mother always kept me informed about what was going on in Fitzgerald. Daddy always loved to write me humorous and uplifting letters. It really didn't matter what the letters said or who they were from, it was just great to go to the campus post office and have mail in your box.

I'm not sure what was better getting letters or getting phone calls from home. In those days, no one had their own phones in their dorm or sorority house. When the telephone rang, whoever answered it, called out your name, and you went running down the hall to answer the phone. You talked out in the hall with all ears listening. With the onset of mobile phones, I know this situation is difficult for younger generations to comprehend.

I graduated from Brenau College in June 1965 and began to realize that my carefree life would be no longer. I realized that the time had come when I needed to make decisions that would personally influence my life. I began to reflect upon the many lessons that each of my parents taught me. I guess we have to mature before we truly understand that who we are is based upon who our parents were and where we have been.

My daddy strongly felt that children should be given opportunities but not advantages. He believed, similar to Warren Buffet, that parents should give their children enough to do anything they desired, but not enough so that they would do nothing. Having a head start is fine, but a ticket for a free ride is not, according to him. I must add, I entirely agree with him. My daddy taught me that no one owed me anything, that respect must be earned, and that I was to always take responsibility for who I was. Wherever I went in life was my own doing and it should always be without blame of anyone else.

As I reflect upon my daddy, it is difficult to express the most significant legacy he left to his family. He gave us a good name, a love of nature, strong morals and ethics, an example of how a Christian should live by putting others before yourself, and lastly, God and family should always come first. For the last twenty-five years of his life, he gave each member of his family a monetary gift based on his age. This was how he lived and exemplified his belief in "putting others before yourself." We would often kid him that we hoped he would lived to be the oldest man in history since he gave to us based on his age!

My mother was filled with words of wisdom for me. Mother was the disciplinarian in our family and would send us out to pick our own switch. There was a tree next to the garage where we had to go and pick our switches. If we did not select a "good" one, mother would go out and select the best she could find. She did not just "tap" us but rather she whipped us.

Today, if teachers saw such marks on a student, it would definitely be reported and DFACS would come. I guess one could say that she taught me irony because when she spanked me, she always said: "This hurts me much worse than it does you." Was she kidding? How could that be? However, once I had children, I understood. Other words of wisdom my mother bestowed upon me was to be sure I had on clean underwear in case of an accident, and I guess that is called foresight. Another lesson she taught me was "When you get to be my age, you will understand," and guess what, she was right!

Of all my mother's words of wisdom though, the most valuable lesson was to always find something nice to say to everyone with whom you come in contact. For example, when you are going through a drive-through, always find one virtue about the person waiting on you, and compliment them on that virtue. It might be a "little untruth" sometimes, but a little white lie is nothing more than a kind gesture made to someone less blessed. Who knows, that random act of kindness might be the only positive thing that they hear all day!

It was only after I became an adult that I realized that everyone did not live their lives as I did, nor did everyone have good, congenial Christian parents like I had. Now, I understand that people only learn what they are exposed to, whether it is good or bad. Few days go by though that I don't thank my almighty God for selecting the parents he did for me. Also, I am most thankful that he enriched my life by teaching me that everyone is different and that is fine.

I had a dear friend, Marianne McLendon Busbee, whose parents bickered constantly with one another, and yet apart, each was as good as gold. Her mother, Alma, worked outside the home, and her daddy Richard, worked on the railroad. The railroad was a coveted job in our community, especially if you were not a professional or owned your own business. Marianne's daddy was so good to all her friends.

When Richard was "off the run," he would take us wherever we wanted to go. Sometimes, he even took us to a little wooden building that was actually a bar called "Flournoy's." The owner had built a pool, from a round metal tanker. It was located behind the building where his patrons could leave their children to swim while they socialized inside. As children, we were only allowed inside to buy a root beer, coca cola and penny candy. I was enamored by this "den of iniquity" because it was definitely a place my parents would have never taken me.

It was always fun times with Richard because he did just what we wanted him to do. One day, Richard heard the famous "Goat Man" who lived near Macon was heading into Fitzgerald. He came home and put Marianne and me in his car and we headed to Sultana Drive to encounter this legend. This old man, with the nasty grey beard, lived up to our expectations and his notoriety. The Goat Man had at least a dozen goats pulling his ramshackle, clanging wagon, which was loaded down with his pots and pans. It was difficult to believe this man was a preacher because he was not like any preacher I had ever encountered. Boy, did he ever smell!

Richard decided to take Marianne and me out to the golf course to try to teach us to play golf. After an exasperating experience, he took us back home. Later, when he saw my daddy, he told him that it was impossible for us to learn to play golf. Why, you might wonder? Because, Richard claimed that our hands were softer than a "baby's behind." Now, if you knew Richard, you would know that I changed the language a little bit. He was a good man but one who never believed that thoughts should be only thoughts and not always expressed.

I relate the stories about my friend's daddy to demonstrate that everyone is different and that is a big part of the South. I was so blessed to have the wonderful parents that God gave me. I must also remember that I was blessed to know individuals who were very "colorful" individuals who enriched my life in many ways.

Please understand that it doesn't mean that my parents were better or worse than anyone else's parents. I am just implying that my life was filled with unique individuals who made me who I am today! It reminds me as well that whenever my dear mother saw someone who was less blessed than us, she would always say, "Except for the Grace of God, there go I." Now you see how profound her lifelong lessons were and what she taught about living life!

Let me say, however, that I thank God every day for giving me the parents he gave me. Most of all, I thank him for the incredible influence that both of them had on my two children, Rob and Jaye. To this day, they often remind me of something positive in their lives that stems back, not to their father or me, but instead to my own mother and daddy. How gratifying that is to me!

Sorority Recipes

Instant Hot Tea

½ cup instant tea
2 pkg instant lemonade
2 cups Tang
3 cups sugar
1 tsp cinnamon
½ tsp cloves

Mix all together and store in a tightly closed container. Put in a mug and add boiling water.

Instant Hot Chocolate

8 quart box non-fat dry milk
2 lb boxes Nestle's Quick
1 jar Cremora, 6 oz
½ cup powdered sugar

Mix together and store in tightly closed container.

Party Punch

2 bottles ginger ale, large
1 can pineapple juice, large
2 bottles cranberry juice, large

Mix all together in container. You can freeze 1/2 in pan and use as your ice when serving.

Cocktail Smokies

2 pkgs cocktail smokies
1 bottle BBQ sauce, 18 oz
1 jar grape jelly, small

Mix sauce and jelly together on high until jelly melts. Add smokies and simmer on low until done.

Cheese Ball

1 pkg cream cheese, 16 oz
2 Tbs minced onion
¼ cup bell pepper, chopped
1 pkg, chipped beef, 8 oz

Drain pineapple. Mix ingredients and form into a ball. Roll in crushed pecans. Serve with crackers.

Cocktail Dip

4 pkg chipped beef
1 lb cheddar cheese
1 jar Cheese Whiz, medium
1 jar mushrooms
Dash or Worcestershire

Mix well and cook over medium heat. Serve with melba toast.

Cheese Biscuits

2 cups cheese
2 cups Rice Krispies
1 stick butter
2 cups flour

Mix together and drop on uncreased cookie sheet. Bake at 400 for 15 minutes.

Extra Special Dip

1 8 oz can artichokes, drained
1 cup mayonnaise
1 cup parmesan cheese
¼ tsp garlic salt
½ cup onion, chopped
1 ½ tsp lemon juice

Mix all together and bake at 375 for 18 minutes or until bubbly and browned. Serve with crackers.

Chapter 7

Life After College

A few weeks before my senior year of college, a significant world event occurred. It was the beginning of the Vietnam conflict due to the Gulf of Tonkin. This particular incident escalated into a serious issue for my generation when the North Vietnamese PT boaters fired on the USS Maddox. The USS Maddox was a destroyer located in the Tonkin Gulf, off the coast of North Vietnam.

By the time I graduated from college in 1965, the US government had deployed regular combat units into Vietnam. There were too many friends of mine who were joining the fight while others just stayed home and protested against the war. It was not until the end of the twentieth century that most Americans realized that it was a war that should have never been. The Vietnam war led to the significant loss of lives and the beginning of many other conflicts.

It appears that war and military conflicts are often a precursor of things to come. The 1960s was no exception. For some of my friends, who were a few years younger and not home having babies, there was another significant event that occurred in the late 1960s. Betty Friedan wrote a book entitled *The Feminine Mystique* which sparked a wave of feminism in America and led to the women's liberation movement.

I can only imagine how strange it must have seemed for the older generation of women, who in their life time, had just been given the right to vote. With this feminist movement, the group presented newfound opportunities and careers for women that had only been in a male oriented marketplace.

Truly, it was the first time in history that women, even women of my own generation, had more than three significant career paths in college. Most women could become a secretary, a nurse, a teacher, and that was pretty much it. This is the movement which also led to the introduction of maternity leave, abortion, and the birth control pill. These new movements and ideas were being accepted but were also being challenged by other groups.

I must admit that during this time, I was preparing for a career but I had no idea what I really wanted to do. College graduation came and, being undecided, I went to work at the State Attorneys General office in Atlanta, Georgia. Desiring to be a female attorney, something rare in the 1960s, I decided that working in the field of law would be exciting. There were few law schools that would accept women in the 1960s and most were in the North. I also felt if I could do anything in the law field, it would make my daddy proud since he was in that field.

Realistically, probably the main reason I went to work at the Attorneys General office was that my daddy's college roommate at Mercer University was Eugene Cook. Mr. Cook was the Attorney General of Georgia, and he offered me my first job. I obviously loved my job and the dear friends that I met there. My new friends were Jack Cooney, George Hearn III, Marion Gordon, and Susan Lowe. Only a few months after I was hired, Mr. Cook resigned, and Arthur K. Bolton became our new Attorneys General.

After the first six months, at the Attorneys General office, I met my future husband, Robert Sherrell, from Atlanta. Now, if there were ever two people from more diverse backgrounds or personalities than Robert and me, I don't know them. I suppose we proved the theory that opposites attract and once we began dating, neither of us dated anyone else.

I must admit that I was enamored someone like Robert, with so little financial means and opportunities available to him, could achieve the goals that he set and obtained for himself. Robert was born in Atlanta, Georgia to Oakland and Geneva Sherrell on September 9, 1936. He was a Seventh-Day Adventist and attended Adventist schools in Atlanta and Collegedale, Tennessee. There were no competitive athletics at these schools, except for tumbling and Robert became a participant. At Collegedale, he was given the nickname of "TT" which stood for Tennessee Tumbler, a name that followed him for many years.

After high school graduation from the Collegedale Academy, Robert went back to Atlanta and worked at a bank for a year to earn enough money to attend college. It was also during that time that he bought his first car. It was a 1941 Ford and he paid a little over a hundred dollars for it.

Having several friends who played college football on scholarships, Robert accompanied one of them, Billy Benton, to Presbyterian College in Clinton, South Carolina. There, Robert persuaded the football coach to let him become a "walk on." Later, he received a full ride. Robert played in the Fiesta Bowl, in Orlando, Florida, his senior year. After graduation from Presbyterian College, he enrolled at the University of Georgia law school. Robert entered school with very limited resources, but when he graduated in 1965, he actually had a relatively stable saving account. I hope this relates to you how frugal he had learned to be in order to accomplish what he desired.

Robert and I met at the Attorney General's office in January 1966 and began dating the next month while working after hours. There was a policy at the Attorney General's office that there would be no dating among employees; therefore, we had to devise a plan. There was no discussion about our not dating, so the discussion was built around who would leave the office.

Six months later, I resigned from the Attorney General's office. I took a job as a social studies teacher at O'Keefe High School which was on the campus of Georgia Tech. O'Keefe High School was an intercity school but was an interesting and innovative school in which to work. At Christmas that first year, Robert gave me an engagement ring. Six months later, we married with a beautiful wedding in my hometown.

On June 24, 1967, at the First Baptist Church in Fitzgerald, Robert and I married. Dr. Carey T. Vinzant, President of Tift College and a lifelong friend, conducted the ceremony. The reception was held for over 500 people at the Fitzgerald Country Club. Robert and I thought everything was perfect at the time. However, little did we know that several of our friends from Atlanta had been in a terrible automobile accident a few minutes before the wedding. They were only ten miles outside of Fitzgerald when the tragedy occurred.

After the reception, Robert and I went back to my parent's home to change clothes for the honeymoon. My daddy and Uncle John came upstairs and told us that there had been an accident. Robert's friends, Albert Pickett, David "Cooler" Inglish and his fiancee, were outside of Fitzgerald, near Irwinville, when they were hit head-on, by a drunk driver. We were informed that my Uncle Clayton was helping Albert, who was uninjured, to get back to Atlanta. David and his fiancee of only one day were headed to the Tifton hospital for observation. Uncle John and Daddy advised us to leave for our honeymoon as planned. They said there was nothing we could do for them at that time and we could see them when we returned.

When Robert and I returned from a week in the Bahamas, we were confronted with the disastrous news. We were told that David's fiancee had a severe brain injury, was rushed from Tifton to Columbus, and had died the next day. Truly, we could not believe that such a catastrophic event had occurred during such a joyous time in our lives.

The week after our honeymoon, I was in my former college roommate, Patricia Coffee's wedding, in Eastman, Georgia. It was a beautiful wedding with a reception at her parents' home, with live doves and lovebirds in exquisite white cages, strategically placed throughout the backyard. It was an exciting time as well for us because this was our first social event as a married couple.

An interesting and an amusing article about the Coffee wedding appeared in the Jacksonville, Florida newspaper. It stated that Patricia Coffee had married Miles Brewer, had become Patricia Coffee Brewer, and they were now residing in Cocoa, Florida. What an anomaly! Today, my dear friend lives in Macon, has two grown children, and beautiful grandchildren. The only sad part is that neither of us visit one another as often as we should.

Robert and I spent our first six months living in my apartment in Atlanta as we looked for a house. We were lucky to find and buy a small but darling house at 329 Eureka Drive in Peachtree Hills. It had a full basement that we rented the entire time we lived there. There is probably nothing as "cute" to a young couple than their very first home. I must add that we paid under $20,000 for the house in 1968. The following year, we sold it, and made several thousand dollars on it. Interestingly enough, several years ago, that same house in Peachtree Hills, was appraised at over $400,00. Now, that is what real estate agents call location, location, location!

What an enjoyable time that was being newlyweds in Atlanta. We attended UGA football games and even went to Georgia Tech games, with our dear friends, Stan and Sissy Gann. If you are from the 1960s era, you will recognize Stan Gann as "Stan the Man," a notorious football player at Georgia Tech. These were great times with some of our other close friends such as the Billy Bentons, the Jack Cooneys, the Jimmy Rakestraws and the Larry Rakestraws. You might also recognize this last name, Larry Rakestraw, because he played football at Georgia, and also played with the Chicago Bears.

Six months into our marriage, I became pregnant. We were both thrilled especially Robert. He wanted to have children early in our marriage because he was seven years older than I and he did not want to be too old when they were born. I was able to complete my second year teaching at O'Keefe High School which was good. It was a long, hot summer after school dismissed, especially since our little house did not have any air conditioning. It was also the last few months of my pregnancy.

I revisited my summers growing up in Fitzgerald by spending most of those hot afternoons in the confines of the Atlanta Public Library, which was air conditioned. Of course, that was until my brother Charles and his new wife Kerry came to visit us for the weekend. All they had to do was mention to my mother how unbearable our little cottage was since there was no air conditioning. Shortly thereafter, Mother arrived with two air conditioning units from Rich's Department Store.

I had finally achieved my lifelong dream of being a wife and mother with the birth of Robert Ashley Sherrell, at Piedmont Hospital, in Atlanta, Georgia. All I wanted was to stay home, and how blessed I felt to be able to stay with Rob. When Rob was only six months old, my daddy was searching for a young attorney to join his law firm. He discussed the options of attorneys with Robert. He asked him to think about who he knew in Atlanta that might like to live in a small South Georgia community.

After much discussion with his boss, Arthur Bolton, as well as consideration on Robert's part, he found an attorney for my daddy. Robert decided to join my family's 73-year- old law practice, Jay, Garden and Jay, unbeknown to me. With no discussion whatsoever, Robert announced at my parent's breakfast table in May that he was joining the firm. Honestly, I had no idea, but two months later, we moved back to my hometown. On a sweltering July 1 day, in 1969, we moved to Fitzgerald with a precious nine month old little boy.

When we moved to Fitzgerald, my new friends informed me that things were different there since I had left. They informed me that the only thing to do back home was to either play bridge or have babies. Having the motherly instinct, I decided on the latter. A year later, I had our second child which was a little girl. Prior to this, friends were most kind to invite me to join an afternoon bridge club, the Gateway Garden Club, the DAR, and the Book Review Club. I became an active member of all of the above and enjoyed them for many years.

The year after we moved to Fitzgerald, I did have a beautiful baby girl, Sally Jaye Sherrell, who was named after my maternal grandmother Sally, and for my maiden name Jay. Fitzgerald is when I learned about that awful tasting paregoric drug. Mothers were giving this to their little ones when they were sick or had restless nights. Today, that drug has been outlawed, but I must add that it allowed many mothers of my generation to enjoy some restful nights.

Several of us stay at home moms would go at least annually to Atlanta on a girl's shopping trip to see the latest styles in fashion. We always tried to schedule a trip around the highly acclaimed Fashionata at Rich's Department Store. Our special friend, Martha Jo Felson Katz, from Ocilla, Georgia was one of the top models to walk the runway at the fashion extravaganza. We were elated by her success and elegant beauty but little did we realize Martha Jo would become a mega star in Atlanta's charities one day. Her success in Atlanta charities makes me even more proud of her. I am blessed we became good friends through my best Ocilla friend, Emily Tyler McBride.

Fashionata was held in the 1970s at Rich's Magnolia Room and what a treat it was for us small town girls. It was not just a fashion show but also a musical directed by the legendary fashion icon Sol Kent. I remember him assisting my mother, along with Mrs. George, in the Regeny Shop, and what a treat that was for me. He was the man behind the fashion success of Rich's during that era. Remembering Mr. Kent made me think of the lunches, especially the frozen fruit salad, mother and I always ordered in the Magnolia Room after shopping. My friend, Beth McIntyre, reminded me how shopping had been such a significant part of my life growing up, and I had not even realized it. With my mother, I guess it was just second nature.

I loved having two babies, 24 months apart and had hoped to have several more, but Robert felt that since we had one of each, that was sufficient. I soon learned that in order to stay home that I needed to do something so I could have spending money to provide the extras for our children. Robert nor I wanted me to work outside the home, so I had to devise other ways to earn additional money.

I spent my first few years after the birth of our children, hosting Doncaster and Young Traditions clothing shows, making bejewel sweatshirts, selling bagged pecans in an Atlanta drugstore, and teaching reading at Modern Fibers. These little enterprises helped me to subsidize my shopping vice. It also allowed me to be somewhat self-sufficient rather than having to ask my husband for money.

An older but dear friend, Eugenia Garland, and I decided in 1972 to open a gift shop together and we called it *The Little Shop.* It was located in a historical house on Grant Street. The shop was housed in a five room residence that was built in the early 1900s. It featured a wrap around porch with gingerbread ornament along the roof lines. The gift shop specialized in Hallmark cards and featured unusual gifts for babies, children, teenagers, men, and women. Living in a small community, we never purchased more than two of any one items so that no one would have the same items in their home.

Starting the new business was a fun adventure and both of us worked only two days a week. This allowed me to spend five days with our two small children. At the end of the second year, I decided it was time to sell out so I could stay home and devote my time to family and others. Being a business owner was an enjoyable undertaking and one I do not regret. It was an incredible learning experience in the world of business for me. Forty odd years later, I resurrected The Little Shop in a downtown Fitzgerald French Market called "Bella Rue." I loved working with young friends and enjoyed it for a few years before I began to have health issues.

Reflecting upon my return to Fitzgerald, I am often reminded by friends of an extraordinary party Robert and I had in our new home. Our law firm was trying to entice an attorney from Warner Robins to join the firm. I worked for weeks trying to get our home ready for these special guests.

In the meantime, Robert instructed our friends to be on their best behavior at the party. Now, that was something for him to request, since his dress was often the topic of conversation! Robert was known to appear at a formal party in a most casual outfit. Once, he even arrived at a neighbor's party in his swimsuit. I know that sounds rather eccentric, appearing in his swimsuit, but he had just decided to swim across the lake to the party. You can virtually see why our friends were shocked when Robert asked them to dress appropriately and behave.

Little did we know, what our friends had planned for entertainment. When the party time arrived, the front doorbell rang. Robert and I went to the door, all bedecked in our cocktail apparel. We opened the door, with our honorees with us, and there stood our friends, decked out like the "Beverly Hillbillies." They had not arrived in a limo but rather they arrived in a caravan of pickup trucks. Some of the trucks even had lawn chairs in the back of them with decked out passengers. I will never forget the look on the face of our guests, as well as our faces. Aimlessly, I wandered throughout the house blowing out the candles in my sterling silver candelabra. Needless to say, our guests did not decide to relocate to Fitzgerald nor to join Jay, Garden and Sherrell.

My Favorite Recipes

Frozen Fruit Salad

8 oz cream cheese
¾ cup sugar
10 oz strawberries, frozen
½ cup nuts
1 pineapple tidbits, 16 oz
2 bananas, sliced

Cream cream cheese and sugar together. Add other ingredients, place in 9x12 dish and freeze. Take out the salad about 15 minutes before serving.

Extra Special Chicken

3 oz ham or dried beef
3 chicken breast, boned
6 bacon slices
1 can mushroom soup
1 cup sour cream

Arrange ham or beef on bottom of casserole dish (12x8x2). Place breast on top and then bacon on top of breast. Bake uncovered at 350 for 45 minutes. Drain off some of the grease. Combine soup and sour cream and pour over dish. Cover and place back in oven for 30 minutes longer.

Orange and Date Cake

4 cups flour
1 cup butter
2 cups sugar
1 ½ cups buttermilk
4 eggs
1 cup nuts, chopped
1 cup dates, chopped
1 tsp baking soda
2 Tbs orange rind, grated

Cream butter and sugar, adding one egg at a time. Dissolve soda in buttermilk and add alternately with flour. Fold in dates and nuts. Add rind. Bake at 325 for 1 1/2 hours. Put 2 cups sugar, 1 cup orange juice and grated rind in small pan and stir until dissolved. Spoon over cake.

Pineapple Cheese Ball

1 cream cheese, 8 oz
1 cream cheese, 3 oz
1 crushed pineapple, small
1 cup nuts, chopped
¼ cup bell pepper, chopped
1 onion, small-grated
1 Tbs seasoning salt

Combine all ingredients together and shape into a ball.

Rosalind's Slaw

3 lbs cabbage, chopped
1 ½ cups sugar
1 bell pepper
1 cup veg oil
1 cup vinegar
2 Tbs celery seed
1 Tbs salt

Mix first three ingredients and set aside. Boil the last four ingredients and pour over cabbage. It will last for three weeks if put in a glass container.

Chocolate Sheet Cake

2 cups flour
2 cups sugar
½ tsp salt
1 stick butter
3 Tbs cocoa
½ cup oil
1 cup water

Sift flour, sugar and salt together. Melt butter and cocoa. Add oil and water and then dry ingredients. Add eggs, buttermilk, soda and vanilla. Bake at 350 for 18 minutes.

Icing:
1 stick butter
1 box powdered sugar
4 Tbs cocoa
1 tsp vanilla
¼ cup milk

Melt oleo, add cocoa and sift sugar with milk. Add vanilla and nuts are optional. Spread on warm cake.

Sour Cream Cornbread

1 cup corn meal, self-rising
1 sour cream, 8 oz
⅓ cup oil
2 eggs, beaten

Combine everything and put in well greased pan. Bake at 375 for 30 minutes.

Chapter 8

My Children

Robert Ashley Sherrell was our first born, very precocious, but oh, the pride that filled our souls was indescribable. He was born to a young mother and father who had fallen in love while working together at the Attorney General's office. Rob, as he was called, was born on September 9, 1968, at Piedmont Hospital, in Atlanta, Georgia.

I will never forget that early morning, as Robert and I drove through our neighborhood, with Robert blowing his horn to inform our neighbors that we were on the way to the hospital. As I walked into the hospital, they immediately told us that our baby would be born within the next few hours. Rob wanting to make a statement that he wasn't ready to arrive on time, something he seldom does, became traverse. The doctors had to slow down my contractions, so that they could go in with forceps and turn him, if he did not turn himself.

Thankfully by that afternoon, Rob flipped himself and was born. I have often thought that maybe that was an omen for his unique personality. What excitement arose as we saw that we had a beautiful baby boy. During this era of birthing, no one knew the gender of their baby until it was born. Robert immediately went down and bought cigars with blue bands to hand out to his friends. The first thing my mother said when she saw Rob was "Look at how his little ears lay flat against his head." You might not comprehend that statement unless you knew his daddy and then it would be obvious.

From Rob's earliest days, he has been hyper and full of life. When he was nine months old, we moved back to Fitzgerald for Robert to join my grandfather, daddy and uncle in their law practice. How well I can remember the moving van pulling into our new house on Walker Avenue that sweltering, summer day in July, 1969.

Rob was a large child and at one year old, he weighed 31 pounds! I can see that chubby little fella right now at his first birthday party. We celebrated it with neighborhood friends like Duboise White, Lee and Len Hogan, along with other friends like Clay, Hank and Todd Cook, Lee and Tom Mann, and David, Joey, Terry, and Jamie Mann. The only little girls at the party were the Dunn girls, Dana and Emily.

How precious Rob looked in his blue and white linen sailor suit with his white and blue oxfords that were stuffed with newspaper in the toes. Why you might ask did he have newspaper in his shoes? The day before I sent his daddy and him to get shoes from Reuben's, our best shoe store in town. When his daddy came back home, he had bought our little boy a pair of shoes from another store to save money. When I noticed how big they were for Rob, his daddy informed me that he had bought them too big so that Rob could grow into them. Enough said! I guess I just wasn't smart enough to pick up on how my life would be henceforth.

When Rob's baby sister, Jaye was five months old, Rob set our house on fire. Yes, it is truly unbelievable that a 29-month-old could do such a thing, but not so if you knew Rob. He had walked into Jaye's nursery to tell me that he wanted some French fries. I instructed him to wait until I finished bathing Jaye and then I would get him some fries.

Rob left me, went into the kitchen, and pulled open the freezer compartment. You must understand that our freezer compartment was located on the bottom of our refrigerator. Rob then proceeded to get out a bag of frozen fries. He pushed a chair up to the cabinet and got out the Wesson Oil. As Rob tried to pour the oil into the pot of fries he had placed on the stove, he got it all over the stovetop. Then, he turned the stove on.

Rob left the kitchen and came back to Jaye's bedroom where I was. He quietly, that should have been a clue, sat down to watch me finish bathing his baby sister. I had no idea what had transpired until

I began to smell smoke. When I walked out of the nursery, smoke had engulfed the hallway. I wrapped a towel around Jaye, grabbed Rob, and went to the kitchen to call the fire department. The closest phone to the outside was in the kitchen and you must remember there was no such thing as a cell phone. After calling, the three of us ran outside to flag down the fire truck.

Before the firemen even arrived on the scene, my childhood friend and local building contractor, Shep Dunn, heard it on the scanner and drove up to help me. By the time I told him what had happened, he grabbed Rob, and took off looking for Rob's daddy. It just so happened that Robert was in court that day in Irwin County, an adjoining county.

My daddy was returning from his golf game and heard on the radio that there was a fire on Walker Avenue. Laughingly he thought, "I wonder what Rob has gotten into now?" Of course, he did not think it was truly our house. Thankfully, he came on out and was there with me. Our kitchen and den were severely burned and there was smoke damage throughout the house. It did not take us long to realize that we would not be able to live there for a while as they were remodeling it. Robert found another house and we immediately moved into it. It was located on Sims lake and was the house that our children lived in until they moved away after college.

Rob seems to have excellent taste in male role models and John Cook was no exception. We enjoyed trips to the beach and to the country club with the Cook boys and their parents. Recently, I was reminded of the first time we went to the beach with them. Rob was almost two years old and still taking a bottle at nighttime. Robert and I had tried to break him of the habit before our new baby arrived, but it was to no avail. When we got to the beach, Robert suggested throwing Rob's bottle out in the ocean for the fish to enjoy. That idea seemed to appease him, so Robert did so.

Everything was going fine until the next day when we left the beach. En route home, we decided to meet the Cooks in Albany for supper. While enjoying our supper, Clay, the oldest of the Cook boys, looked at Rob and said, "Rob, I bet those ole fishes are sucking on your ba-ba." Needless to say, we had to leave the restaurant because of the screaming that Rob engaged in after that statement.

Rob was two when "Lee-Tom," which is what he called Lee Mann and Tom Mann, gave him their little football uniform, shoulder pads, pants, shirt, and helmet. Rob loved his new gift so much that when that night came, he begged and cried to wear it to bed. He even wanted to wear the helmet and shoulder pads as well. I let him do so, but the next morning when he awoke, he was not in the best of spirits. Sometimes, children have to learn the hard way. On an interesting note, not long ago, Rob sent me a picture of his own little boy sleeping with his basketball. My first thought was that the apple doesn't fall far from the tree!

Being a mother of a hyper son, our pediatrician suggested Ritalin for Rob when he was only three years old. Being somewhat educated, I did not want to start him that early on it so I did not. Yes, it was not always an easy job, but people do it every day, just like I did.

An entertaining story was when Robert, Rob and I were sitting in the balcony at First Baptist Church one Sunday morning. We were listening to John Burch, our beloved preacher, preach his sermon. Dr. Burch lowered his voice to a quiet tone for emphasis, but when he did so, Rob yelled out, "I can't hear you, preacher." Oh my, I said it was an entertaining story, but I must admit it was not so cute at the time. As soon as my parents, who were sitting downstairs in their "assigned seat" heard that voice, they knew it was Rob Sherrell. I will also add that even the preacher got a chuckle out of this incident.

Rob loved playing outside and hanging around his adult male neighbors. He has always gravitated to males. I feel that part of it was that his father, being a trial attorney, was not home as much as he would have liked. There were two neighbors, Penn and Foster, who were railroad men, and adored having Rob around on their days off. He went to the store with them, helped them plant their gardens, mowed grass with them, did repairs with them, and all the other things little boys like to do with males.

One day, Penn and Foster were playing with Rob out in our yard. A friend of theirs, Winfred Tucker, drove up with a little black puppy. Seeing Rob, and knowing who he was, he asked him if he wanted a puppy. Of course, you know the answer to that! Rob came running into the house and told me there was a man in a truck outside with a black dog. He then lamented, "And, guess what Mama? That dog's name is Sherrell, just like my name." Of course, dear Winfred knew Rob's last name and told him that was the dog's name, just a ploy to make him want the dog even more. I told Rob that we would check with his daddy and let his newfound friend in the black truck know later that day. Believe it or not, we did not get that dog!

Speaking of dogs, we certainly had our share of them. We probably had seven or eight dogs through the years. The neighborhood joke became if you wanted to get rid of a dog, just give him or her to the Sherrell family. We loved our animals, but much to our sorrow, we did have great difficulty in being able to keep them alive. I do believe that living on a corner did not help in their longevity.

I am reminded of several other adult male friends that Rob adored, such as Shep Dunn and Alan "Snake" Dixon. When he was about four years old, he was unhappy because he wanted to go off with his daddy. His daddy said no because he was going to a friend's house to watch a football game.

After his daddy left, Rob came downstairs with his little suitcase in hand. I asked him where he was going and he said: "I don't know, Mama, I'm just running away." We talked a few minutes about what he had packed and how long he thought he would be gone. Then, Rob walked out the door, as I was telling him to be very careful and not walk in the road.

When I looked out my window, I saw Rob "lollygagging around" in the yard because he really didn't want to leave home. I called his daddy to come home and talk with him. Robert and his friend, Shep, drove over. As Shep drove up to Rob, he asked him what was he doing. Rob looked at him pitifully and said that he was running away. Shep asked him if he wanted to go get an ice cream cone before he ran away. Of course, Rob said yes. Shep reached down and threw Rob's suitcase in the back of the pickup. He then lifted him up into the truck and the three amigos rode off into the sunset. Rob loved Shep more than any adult I know. In fact, he loved him so much that once he even named his new dog after Shep. Now that says something, right?

On our last trip to Ponte Vedra, Florida with Mary Jean and John Cook, I remember another fun story about Rob. He was four years old and Mary Jean was fixing the four boys a peanut butter and jelly sandwich for their supper. When she asked Rob if he wanted one, he replied: "Yes, but I don't want Jelly on mine. Oh, and I don't want bread on it, either." In other words, Rob just wanted a jar of peanut butter. It was also on that trip that Rob was constantly commenting on John and how lucky the Cook boys were to have John as their daddy. I was certainly touched by the fact that at such a young age, he was able to identify good role models to emulate later in life.

Robert and I had spent a lot of time at Ponte Vedra and decided that we would love to own a beach house or a condo. We knew that the market there was too expensive for us so we moved up the coast to Fernandina Beach, Florida. Robert had heard that Charles Frazier, who had successfully developed Hilton Head, South Carolina, had plans for a similar development at Fernandina.

It was July, 1972, and we were on our first family trip to Fernandina Beach. There was only one motel, The Surf, that was located near the beach, so we bunked there while Robert went looking at the new development. When he arrived at Amelia Island Plantation, he was greeted by a realtor who was located in a trailer. You need to understand that there was nothing there except a trailer and a set of blueprints showing the new development.

While Robert was at the Plantation, Rob, Jaye and I were in the pool at the motel. Jaye's beach ball got away from her while she was sitting on the steps. As she reached for it, she fell in. The next thing I knew, Rob was dragging her out of the pool. She was fine, but scared. It isn't often that an almost four year old can save an almost two year old from drowning. To this day, Rob has never let Jaye forget that he saved her life and she owes him something. We left Fernandina with lots of information on plans for new developments there but realized that the Plantation was too expensive for our blood.

Robert, Shep Dunn and Steve McIntyre had invested in cattle, a decision that turned out to be a disaster. The cattle were constantly escaping, and often there were phone calls at night to come and rescue them. After that debacle, Robert shared with them about the new developments at Fernandina Beach.The three of them decided to give up the cattle business and invest in a condo at Fernandina Beach.

A few years later, Shep and Steve decided to sell their interest in the condo, Amelia South, to Robert. He owned the condo for the next eighteen plus years. Robert rarely went down, but the one time he went for a few days, a nor'easter came in, and we were condo bound for days. It wasn't the best of times, but there were several other families like the Braddys, Stricklands, and Halls there so that helped to pass the time away.

The first summer at our own condo, Shep Dunn's brother in law, Allen "Snake" Dixon and his wife, Belinda, were staying on the same floor near us. In fact, they were just two doors down from us. Early the next morning, after their arrival, I heard our door open and close. Immediately, I went to see where Rob had gone. When I looked outside, there sat little Rob with a toy in hand, by Snake and Bee's door. I walked out and asked him what he was doing. His answer was, "I'm waiting on my friend, Snake, to come out and play with me." Sometimes, it is only through the eyes of a child that one can view the true meaning of love and friendship.

As you can surmise, there was never a dull moment with our first born, Rob. By the time he was five years old, he had numerous close encounters. The first incident that I remember was when he set the house on fire, something that I related to you earlier. The next incident was when he got a fish hook in his hand and we had to go to the doctor to have it removed. Another serious adventure was when he was riding with my mom and was leaning on his car door. As she turned the corner onto Walker Avenue, his door opened, and he flew out onto the Irwinville Highway, into the traffic lane. A mom of a friend of mine, hit her brakes, and ran off the road to keep from hitting Rob.

The last episode happened at our house on West Roanoke Drive. Our sitter, Eloise Shelton, was in the house with Jaye. I was going to town, and as I started to get into my car, I realized I had left my purse in the house. I went running into the house, leaving my car door opened, and the phone rang. I answered it and talked only a few minutes. I then went outside where I saw my car rolling across the street, straddling two huge pine trees, and finally coming to a stop. This was an occasion that I cannot truthfully say who was the most scared, Rob or me. If you remember, in my very first sentence about Rob, I described him as precocious, but I am not sure that was the correct term to use!

Rob had a September birthday, and at that time, the decision about when a child would start school was left up to his parents. He appeared to be academically ready so we sent him early to five year old preschool. Dana Dunn, Emily Dunn, and Rob were carpooled by Susan Dunn and me to First Baptist Preschool. Those rides were filled with entertaining and interesting conversations. Through the years, I have told other young parents to savor those times because "carpooling" days were some of my favorite times with my children. Oh, the myriad of things you could learn from them!

After Christmas that year, we were told by his teacher, Rita Pryor, that Rob was ready for the First grade in the fall. Yes, he was ahead of the game, was already reading, but that was not to be. Robert wanted him held back so that he would be older when he became involved in sports. After research and conversations, I agreed that Rob would benefit from being one of oldest in his graduating class. I had always been the youngest in my grade and often wished I had stayed back a year. Robert and I agreed to hold him back the next year which was a decision that neither of us have ever regretted!

After attending the five year old program at First Baptist Church Preschool, Rob spent the next year at home with me. In February of that year, Jaye had a tonsillectomy. The first night home, she cried out for me from her bed about 4:00 in the morning. I awoke, went to check on her and laid with her a few minutes. Being half asleep, as I was walking back to my bedroom, I missed my bedroom door, and instead step out into the stairwell. I fell down thirteen steps, landing on my neck, and was unconscious for several days. I was blessed that I did not break anything, but have suffered repercussions during my senior years from the fall, just as the doctor told me I would.

A friend, Kay Paulk Hannah, offered to take Rob, along with her daughter, Lynn Paulk Brady, to the Presbyterian Preschool, while I recouped. It was most definitely a help because now I only had one child rather than two children at home. I will never forget her graciousness during that time, along with my other friends who stood ready to help, while I healed. It was difficult to be a shut in with small children. One day, to perk me up, two friends, Susan Dunn and Belinda Dixon, came over to visit. Right there and then, they decided to pierce my ears. I must admit that certainly added some excitement to my life while I was in bed convalescing. Was I ever a "pretty sight" with a neck brace on and straws in my ear lobes?

There were other good friends Rob enjoyed playing with while growing up in Fitzgerald. Rosalind and Billy Mann had five boys, David, Joey, Terry, Jamie, and Chris Mann. Rob considered them to be his special friends. In fact, much later in life, when Rob married, Jamie was in Rob's wedding. The Cooks, Dunns, Manns and Chris McIntyre were his childhood friends that he has kept up with through the years. What memorable experiences Rob was blessed with by living in a small community. A community where we all came together and were fortunate enough to be part of each other's families.

Rob was a precocious little boy and loved to captivate others while singing "The Devil Went Down to Georgia" and "Bad, Bad Leroy Brown." We had a dear friend, Betty Brown, and he loved to tease her because of her infectious laugh. Whenever she came over, Rob loved singing "Bad, Bad Betty Brown" to the same tune as Leroy Brown.

There is little doubt that he was definitely an entertainer. In later years, rather than appearing on the stage, he turned to entertaining others on the athletic fields. From little league through high school sports, he excelled in baseball, football, wrestling and cross county. What a delight it was for us to watch him as he participated and demonstrated his love of sports.

Our summers were spent at the baseball field and at the beach through the years. What marvelous memories Rob, Jaye and I accumulated together while their daddy felt the need to stay home and work. One of the most memorable experiences at the beach took place with Rob and his good friend from Waycross, Wayne McGee. Wayne's family had a condo in the same complex, Amelia South, and we thoroughly enjoyed our summers together.

Late one afternoon, several mothers were in Jane McGee's condo playing bridge when Wayne and Rob came running inside. It turned out that the two little boys had found some sparkles from our Fourth of July celebration. They had lit them and thrown them over into the sand dunes which caught the sea oats on fire. Someone on the top floor saw what was going on and immediately called the fire department. Praise the Lord that was before the environmentalist movement began, or we would have all been in deep trouble. Enough said about that incident!

One of the most challenging parts of Rob's growing up for me was when he first entered puberty. He asked me while we were at Lenox Square for a picture for his room. I agreed so he went into a store to buy one, but when I saw it, I almost died. It was a picture of the celebrated Farah Fawcett in a red bathing suit, somewhat subdued compared to life today, but still a shock to a boy's mother.

After the Lenox Square experience, I did not truly realize what was in store for me with a son. I will never forget, Rob, Jaye and I had gone out to a farm and picked tomatoes for me to make ketchup. I had a "bee in my bonnet" to make homemade ketchup because I had read that there was going to be a shortage that summer. The next afternoon I was busy making ketchup, when I looked out my window, at the kids down by the lake. There, I saw a young girl, two years older than Rob, next to him. She was standing there in a bikini, by the boat, flirting with my 12-year-old son. I almost died, ugh! I realized at that moment that the era of PAC-Man, Atari, toy soldiers, and collecting baseball cards had come to an end. His life and mine would never be the same and it wasn't.

Rob's teenage years were filled with his love of sports and his lettering in cross county, football, wrestling, and baseball as a ninth grader. There is little doubt in my mind that his being so involved in sports kept him out of a lot of trouble. Of all the sports that he participated in, I firmly believe that wrestling built the most character. As I reflect, maybe it was because of his celebrated coach, Mike Ellis, who built his character.

Coach Ellis is a legend in his own time. He was comparable to the early legend, Joe Compton, whom I loved and respected just as much! I will never forget during Rob's first year as a wrestler, seeing Coach Ellis holding him by his neck, against the brick wall of the gym. Rob had just beaten his opponent 16-2 so I could not understand why the coach was so upset with him. Afterwards, I asked him what had Coach Ellis chewed him out about, and he answered, "Mama, he did what he should have. He said, 'Rob, if you could beat him that badly, you should have pinned him.'And, he was right, Mama." That is exactly the respect and love that Mike Ellis' wrestlers had for him and why the gym at Fitzgerald High School was dedicated in his honor.

Wrestling is an interesting sport because it is only you and your opponent on the mat. Therefore, the wrestler cannot blame anyone but himself, when he wins or loses. I will always cherish seeing his peers wrestle or drop down a weight class so that others could wrestle in that spot. I will also remember the expressions on the faces of those wrestlers who had never been out of Ben Hill County or stayed in a classy hotel before going to the Atlanta matches. Those are some of the memories that I hold dear from Rob's four years of wrestling.

When wrestling, the only thing that Rob did ask of me, being a single parent and being protective, was that I not sit on the bottom row of bleachers. He often said that he could envision me sprinting onto the mat when his opponent had a wrong hold on him or when the referee made a bad call. As a mother, I could sit and listen to others lambaste my son, the quarterback, when he played football or question how the center fielder missed the fly ball; however, watching him wrestle was a whole different game. If you don't believe me, you just ask any mother of a wrestler.

The summer before Rob's eleventh grade year, his daddy told Jaye and him, on Father's Day, that he was unhappy and that we were going to divorce. Rob jumped up from the table, left the house in his car, and we did not see him for several hours. I understand why he was confused and upset because his daddy and I rarely had a cross word. Looking back, I realize now that was probably a part of the problem which led to our divorce.

A week later, when Rob realized that it was his daddy and my anniversary, he came into my bedroom. He pulled out his wallet and handed me his little paycheck from Wendell Patton. He told me to go out and buy me something special. Of course, being a mother, I did not want his money. Rob insisted so I bought a statue of a little boy patting the head of his dog, a gift I still treasure to this day.

I did not want Rob to assume the role of "man of the house," but he found himself doing so for the next few years. He tried to please me, as best he could but definitely did not when he brought home a special gift. Rob decided to take his paycheck and buy himself a snake. When he brought it home, and shared it with me, while I was in bed with the flu, I almost died. I allowed him to keep it, with the understanding, he was never to bring it to my bed again. Afterward, Rob kept the snake in an aquarium and only took it out twice a day. That made us all happy, especially Sue Jordan, who came to clean my house twice a month but refused to clean his room.

Rob's plans after high school graduation was to attend Georgia Tech to wrestle. At the very last minute, much like his mother, he decided he was tired of having to maintain his weight to wrestle and wanted to go elsewhere. I completely understood his feelings at that moment even though I was not sure where he would be able to go at this late date.

I was totally surprised when Rob said that he had decided to go to UGA. My response was that it was fine with me, but it was probably too late for him to apply to UGA. At that comment, he went upstairs to his room and showed me a letter from the admissions office. It stated that he was accepted to UGA because of his tenth grade PSAT scores and his being a Quest/UGA seminar finalist, when he attended earlier. I almost dropped my plate because I had never seen this letter before.

Rob and I went up to Athens to secure an apartment, since all the dorms were full. We had been there only a few hours when I saw my 80-year-old mother whiz by his new apartment in her car. My mother just couldn't stand not knowing where Rob was living and how he was set up. After we left, she decided that she would just join us in Athens, and that she did. I pray I have that kind of determination and love for my grandchildren when I get to that age.

Rob was born to be a Georgia Bulldog, I decided. He loved wearing red and black while gathering with 82,000 fans between the hedges on Saturdays. He felt it was a privilege to be a Georgia Bulldog. From the moment that he set foot on the Athens campus, he never had a doubt that he had made the right decision. He saw it as a honor to study under the tutorship of the great men who proceeded him such as Lewis Gizzard and Larry Munson.

While a freshman at UGA, Rob pledged Pi Kappa Alpha fraternity. My mother would ask him, whenever they talked, if he had gone to church yet in Athens. Rob always told mother no but that every single day he did go by the Baptist Student Union. What he did not tell his grandmother was that the BSU building was only two doors down from his frat house. In order for Rob to get to class daily, he had to walk by the BSU center. I wish I had a nickel for every time mother told me that story because she told it quite often. She desperately wanted to believe that he was going to a Christian center for religious purposes.

Probably the best story that exemplifies the time Rob spent at UGA was in 1989 when the Atlanta Braves were playing in Cincinnati, Ohio. I was watching the Braves late on a Monday night and listening to Skip Carey, the Braves announcer. I was well into the game when I heard Mr. Carey say, "We have some UGA students who have driven all night to be here this afternoon for this game. Let's give a big shoutout to Brownie and Rob Sherrell." As soon as I heard the name Brownie, I knew what was coming because they were always a pair looking for a good time.

Immediately, my phone started ringing. The first of several calls from was from Bill Hammond saying, "Are you watching TV?" to which I replied, "Yes, but I pray my daddy isn't since it is exam week at UGA." Of course, I don't know what my daddy could have said because he left Georgia Tech one night and rode the train to New York for the World series in1929! In a lot of ways, they were "cut from the same cloth."

Speaking of the Braves, I am reminded of 1992 when the Braves were playing for the National League West Championship. On a whim, I decided I wanted to go to the game. I called Jaye and Rob, both in college, and asked if they wanted to go with me to the game, if we could get tickets. Rob immediately said, "Don't worry, Mama, I've never been to a sporting event that I couldn't get tickets."

I picked Jaye up at Wesleyan College in Macon and we drove to Atlanta to meet Rob at the stadium. Rob was perusing the crowd, trying to find us tickets, when he commented that this venue was really tight. He said he had never seen so few tickets available, but for me not to worry, he would find us something. Thirty minutes later, Rob came over and handed Jaye and me our tickets. He then told us to follow him through this one particular gate and we did.

Once we got inside, he told Jaye and me that he was going to find a seat and that we needed to do the same thing. I looked down to see where our seats were on the tickets. At that very moment, I realized at that our tickets were to another game that had been played months earlier. When I panicked, Rob said, "Don't show your tickets, mom, but just walk around until you find an empty seat and sit down."

Dumbfounded, Jaye and I just stood there while Rob went and found him a seat right behind home plate! Needless to say, Jaye and I walked around, afraid that we were going to be ushered out at any moment. What he had done was pay my hard earned money to a guy at the gate, who pocketed that money, and gave us some old Braves tickets so we could get into the complex. Only in our life with Rob Sherrell would this have happened.

Rob absolutely adored his four years at UGA and graduated with a degree from the Terry School of Business in Risk Management. He, like so many, was unsure of what he wanted to do. Actually, I must add, it was four years and one quarter because no one wants to miss fall quarter with the "dawgs" playing football. When I inquired about why he couldn't take the one class during the summer that he needed to graduate, he informed me that it wasn't offered then. Now, I didn't fall off the turnip truck yesterday and my elevator does go to the top floor, but I decided that it was easier to just "go with the flow."

After his December graduation, Rob came home and worked in construction for his good friend and former employer, Louie Harper, of Harper Construction. Rob had worked for Louie during his high school and college summers and on holidays. He thoroughly enjoyed it and had built a special relationship with Louie and his late wife, Jackie.

Working for Harper Construction for a couple of months, Rob secured enough money to go to Colorado. Brownie and he worked as waiters and enjoyed the new scenery. Yes, I said Brownie because they were still a twosome looking for adventure. I agreed for Rob to go but with two stipulations. He had to pay his own way and he had to be back home for Mother's Day. Rob enjoyed every minute of his time in Colorado and wanted to stay longer; but he knew he needed to get back home as promised.

Rob spent that summer and early fall at home while he, once again, worked in construction for Louie Harper. He took the LSAT that August to get into Law School which allowed him special time with his grandfather and idol, Pa. Rob didn't really desire to go to Law School, but he took the exam anyway. He thought that being an attorney would make his Pa happy, and he always wanted to please his Pa.

As we know, it is not always our plan, but God's plan, and by Rob staying at home that fall, he was able to be there when his grandfather died. He adored his Pa and his Pa adored him just as much. After his grandfather's death in October, Rob went to work in Atlanta. Within two years, he had purchased a house and had his own insurance agency, Citywide Insurance Company. A few years later, still loving the Georgia Bulldogs, he bought a skybox at Sanford Stadium as well as a Gameday condominium, in his beloved Athens, for the weekend activities.

Rob has always enjoyed life and spent approximately 11 years being single in Atlanta. Before the next year was gone, he had meet a beautiful young lady, Amy Steele of Albermarle, North Carolina. Amy graduated from the University of North Carolina, with a management and finance degree from that fine institution. I will also add that I finally had another ADPi in the house!

When Amy and Rob decided to marry, Rob had his original house imploded, and they built a beautiful "Charleston-style" house on the same lot. It was a brilliant idea to rebuild there because of the magnificent view of Atlanta. It was also inside I-75, which was the perfect location for them, since the two enjoyed downtown activities that were within minutes of their home.

Rob and Amy married on mutual ground, in Athens, Georgia, halfway between their hometowns of Fitzgerald, Georgia and Albermarle, North Carolina in June 2005. The wedding was beautiful in the UGA chapel and was conducted by our dear friend, Dr. Gene Wilder. The reception was held at the Athens Country Club, among their family and friends and was a glorious affair. Afterward, the two went to the Eleuthera Islands for their honeymoon.

Sally Jaye Sherrell entered this world, fifteen minutes after I walked into the Ben Hill County Hospital, in Fitzgerald, Georgia, on September 28, 1970. When my sister in law, Barbara saw her, she stated that Jaye was the most beautiful baby she had ever seen, and she definitely was to us. Robert and I debated over what to name her and finally reached the decision to give her my maternal grandmother's name, Sally, and my maiden name Jay. We also decided to add an "e" on the end of Jay to give it a more feminine touch.

Jaye was only six months old when we bought a house on a 17 acre lake and it is the house that she lived in for the next twenty-four years. The house was built by the Druckers, from New York, who were being transferred to Fitzgerald. They only lived in the house for a year before deciding to move back north. Now that is a situation that is rarely heard of in the South and might indicate how different they were.

It was a large house with six bedrooms (one that was used strictly for storage) and four bathrooms. It was often the place to be for everybody since it had a lake to fish or ski, a concrete basketball court, and a playroom filled with toys. Our house became the perfect place, for my siblings and their families, to gather for Christmas. It was centrally located between Jacksonville, Florida and Macon, Georgia, and what wonderful times we shared in our house with one another.

As I mentioned earlier, the men in our neighborhood were railroad men, who were often home, and were always helping with two-year-old Rob and our newborn baby Jaye. They taught both of them to love the many trains which came through our city, day and night. They also loved to take Rob fishing and when Jaye became older, she wanted to learn to fish just like Rob. I, being available more so than being a serious fisherman, was the one who taught Jaye how to fish.

One of my most memorable moments in teaching Jaye to fish came when I was instructing her how to put a worm on her hook. As we began to run out of worms, I told Jaye that it might be a good idea for her to break the worms in half so they would last longer. Being an obedient child, like she always was, when I looked over at Jaye, she was not breaking them in half, but rather she was 'stretching' the worms in half. If only I could have had an iPhone in those days to snap that Kodak moment!

Jaye was such a shy, apprehensive, and cautious child growing up. Until she met her new neighborhood friend, Amy Smith who was far from that description. Oh, the stories I could tell on these two sisters from different mothers. We always made the comment that when Jaye opened the back door and saw Amy, her smile was just as wide as it was on Christmas morning. But why should it not have been because it was like opening the door and having a bag full of surprises.

I remember telling Jaye that she was finally old enough to ride her bike down to Amy's house, which was only four houses down our street. I reminded her she needed to, look both ways, ride on the side of the street, and watch for approaching cars. When I went to the window to watch Jaye, as she rode away, she was riding on the grass, in the ditch, and barely able to stay upright. Poor child, she just wanted to be sure she was obeying my rules. Now, if it had been Rob, where do you think he would have been riding? In the ditch or down the center line of the road?

Could I ever relate tales about Jaye and her best friend Amy without ever having to embellish the story? Amy was a vivacious little tow-headed girl, always full of good cheer, but filled with inconceivable mischief. From the time, the two went to the Fall Festival and presented my distinguished daddy with free kittens to frolicking through the leaves at June Young's house, as she was outside yelling at them, they had not a care in the world.

One of the most memorable episodes was when the two young spirits wrote on Robert's brand new Cadillac's white leather seats with red lipstick. I was getting ready to go to the grocery store one morning and could not find my "Cherries in the Snow" lipstick anywhere. I thought to my self, just where could I have put my lipstick, when I had an epiphany. Wherever Amy and Jaye were, there would probably be my lipstick. I walked outside, and I was right. Amy hurridly handed the bright red lipstick to Jaye, who had lipstick all over her face, and then said, "Ms. Sherrell, I told Jaye she shouldn't write on her daddy's new car." Helplessly, Jaye looked at me with teary, wide-eyes, and shakily said, "Mama, I didn't do this."

Amy and Jaye spent most of their awaking hours together until school began and then it was mostly on the weekends. Amy's wonderful parents and our dear friends, Jim and Danna, often took Jaye with them to Lake Blackshear. On one of the trips, Jaye encountered a white duck that chased her everywhere and was penned the name of "Lake

Blackshear Duck." Pretty original, huh? They were also responsible for teaching Jaye to water ski on the same inlet that Gene and I have a house today. Isn't life filled with so many anomalies?

Amy moved to Alabama in the eighth grade and Jaye was in the sixth grade. When Amy came down to tell Jaye, you would have thought there had been a death in our family. Not only did Jaye cry, but all of us cried as well because we loved Amy and her family. Amy and Jaye have continued their friendship today even though they live a state apart.

There was so much happiness and sorrow that Jaye and Amy have shared with one another. The first time Jaye went to a summer camp, she went with Amy. The first time she went on a date was in Andalusia, Alabama while visiting Amy. They were in one another's wedding and were there when each other's first born arrived. They have demonstrated that love can defy all odds if you make it a priority. A valuable lesson here is that during the good times and the bad times, true girlfriends will be there for you always. This is just another reason why it is so vital that you keep those dear friendships alive.

One of Jaye's most favorite things to do in life was to spend time with her MeMa and Pa. She adored both of them, but it took her until she began school to truly warm up to her Pa. Jaye was a child who preferred being around women. I remember a dear friend, Fred Hancock, would always offer Jaye a quarter to give him a hug but she never would. Fred was such a special friend that the didn't hold it against her. Even though he had moved to Albany, Georgia, he still came to her wedding. Now, anyone that knows Fred, knows that he rarely goes to a wedding so that was special for all of us.

Jaye was a "mother's child" and as I said earlier, she always preferred women to men when she was growing up. Maybe it was because she loved to go shopping, wherever it was, with her grandmother and me. As Jaye began a relationship with her Pa, she was filled with as much adulation for him as she had for her MeMa. Jaye has never forgotten how his face would light up when she entered the room and especially when she walked over to give him a hug. Words are inadequate to express the love and adoration that she showed her MeMa and Pa through the years but even more so during their last years of life.

Jaye's life was never as adventurous as Rob's especially after Amy moved away. The most significant circumstance that occurred in her life was when her daddy and I divorced. Jaye had always been a child that sat in the back of the classroom, timid and painfully shy, and often said very little to anyone. However, this catastrophic event which took place the summer before her ninth grade year changed her significantly. When she was told the news by her father, she ran upstairs to her room and closed the door. When I followed her, she looked me in the eyes, and said adamantly, "No one will ever do that to me after nineteen years of marriage." There was little doubt in my mind that day that she meant that statement with all her heart.

God is always good but we seem to notice it more when traumatic experiences occur in our life. Doesn't he always seems to send you an angel or angels just at the right time? I know that he did when he sent a certain family to help Jaye fill the void in her life after her daddy left home. Sue and Howard Jordan, parents of her new beau, Troy Jordan, were there by her at every turn along the way. Not only did they become a stalwart for Jaye, they became one for me as well. They provided the sunshine in our lives with trips to football games, shopping malls, the beach, and even a cruise to the Bahamas. Neither of us will ever forget the sparkle they provided us during that dismal time of our lives. There is little doubt, as I think about it, that it was probably Sue who was most responsible for Jaye becoming an assertive "little Sue."

By Jaye's junior year in high school, she no longer sat in the back of the classroom, but rather she sat on the front row and became an assertive young woman. I must admit that she also had several teachers, such as Jane Floyd, Beverly Lavender, Charles and Jodie Lewis, and Al Strom, who passed their love and enthusiasm for learning on to her. Jaye always reminded me of how she strived to reach their standards but that Nancy Kimball and Kay Batton helped to establish her foundation. Those teachers could not believe how outgoing Jaye had become during her final years of high school and neither could she. Often she would said to me,"I wonder how different my life would have been if I had demonstrated my assertiveness earlier?" Lord, forbid, is all I can say!

Jaye went to Wesleyan College, in Macon, a girl's school that her maternal grandmother had attended. I will never forget her driving up to the campus in her white Mustang convertible, her graduation gift from me, loaded down with all her possessions. She informed me when we left home that morning, in separate cars, that there would be no crying, so I honored her request. As I left Wesleyan, I am sure I was crying just 15 minutes down the road, she was crying as well.

Jaye spent her freshman year at Wesleyan, detesting every minute of it. Many of the students in her dorm were "women libbers" and she was not. Like her own mother and maternal grandmother, all Jaye had ever wanted in life was to be a mother and a wife. Thankfully, unlike me, she had a backup plan. Her first desire was to be a teacher and when children arrived, she wanted to stay home with her children. I am pleased to say that Jaye achieved both goals.

Jaye and I agreed that she would complete her first year at Wesleyan College. After that, if she was still unhappy, she could transfer to a different school. Rob thought that UGA or the College of Charleston would be the perfect place for her, but Jaye had no desire to attend a large school or one out of state. By May of that school year, she decided to transfer to Georgia College, located in Milledgeville, Georgia.

Jaye moved into an apartment with three other girls without knowing anyone at her new college. Shortly thereafter, she roomed with a local girl and sorority sister, Carla Burrell. Jaye ended up staying at Georgia College for the next three years and graduated from there.

A Southern girl with strong roots, Jaye pledged a sorority at her new school. Our dear friend, Ethelyn Underwood, attended her induction ceremony where she pinned Jaye with her own Phi Mu pin. Of course, I would have loved for her to have pledged Alpha Delta Pi, like I had done, but I told her early in life that she was to be her own person. Jaye has always done what she thought was best rather than what I thought, and I am proud that she has done so.

Jaye's senior year in college, she met her future husband, Jay Mason. Jay was through with college and was running a family business, twenty minutes away, in Wilkinson County. When Jay Mason saw my Jaye, he told a friend, Richard Pentecost, "There's the girl that I am going to marry one day." Richard looked at him, and said, "You don't even know her name." Jay agreed, but said that he would find out her name. Sure enough, he did and two years later, he married her!

After college graduation in June 1994, Jaye returned home to teach for a year and prepare for her upcoming wedding to Jay Mason. We had millions of things to do as we prepared for the wedding but high on the list was to find my mother a dress for the wedding.

Helen, Mother, Jaye and I headed to Atlanta not realizing that it would be mother's last shopping trip to Atlanta. We first went to Lillie Rubin's, at Phiips Plaza, to find mother a formal dress to wear at Jaye's wedding. After about thirty minutes of their bringing out, dress after dress, mother said: "Your clothes are pretty, but they look like something that an old woman would wear."

The saleswoman then brought out an aqua full length sequin dress, with a cut out in the back. My mother looked at it and said, "I'll take that one." Needless to say, it took me two months to find a mother of the bride dress. If you are wondering why, it was because I needed something at least presentable if I was going to be sitting next to my 87 year old mother in her sparkly new dress.

I want to add that while we were heading out of Atlanta, my mother suffered another stroke. I drove from Atlanta to Macon in less than hour to get her to the Macon hospital. After this stroke, she walked with a cane for a few weeks but was determined not to use it at Jaye's wedding. She practiced, went to therapy, and when the wedding arrived, she held her head up to her majestical height of 5'1, and sauntered down the aisle. The wedding was everything Jaye had dreamed of except her precious Pa was not present.

Jaye had always wanted to marry at home, but her bridegroom wished to marry in the church. They arrived at a compromise and were married by our dear friend, Dr. Gene Wilder, at First Baptist Church in Fitzgerald. After the wedding, they had a reception in our backyard.

It took Jaye, me, and our entourage months to get my house and backyard in pristine order. We worked diligently as we began to "freshen up" the house and design the backyard for an upcoming wedding reception. Jaye faithfully helped me. She even decided to dig her own goldfish pond which was the topic of conversation and a highlight of the reception. Jay lent his support by building a shed in the back yard to house the reception supplies. My very special friends, Susan and Ron Singleton, were the gophers for everything we needed.

The day before the wedding, Jaye and Jay drove around the neighborhood, and placed flyers in the mailboxes. The flyers informed our neighbors that the wedding reception would be featuring a live band in our backyard and we hoped it would not disturb them. The flyer was actually designed to let our neighbors know that they were invited to come on over or persevere the music from their own backyards.

One of the sweetest and most touching events that occurred on Jaye's wedding day was the result of Jay Mason. Neither Jaye or Jay had seen one another before their wedding. After the bridesmaids and Jaye had their picture session completed, my niece Kristy Jay Wilson walked out, and Jay asked her for her lipstick. Then, he went into the bridal suite at the church and wrote in lipstick, "Can't wait to see you." Actually, if more men were that thoughtful, I believe there would be fewer divorces, don't you agree?

Interestingly, in our small community, the common ritual was to only mail invitations to out of town guests. Then everyone else was invited to attend just by word of mouth. It truly makes it difficult on the caterer unless it just happens to be E.S. Wynn. He was a magician who miraculously fed over 400 people on the auspicious occasion. Let me also add that even though we did not send invitations locally, Jaye still received over 600 gifts. I believe that describes best the generosity of our little community along with the fact there were three generations of us still living here.

People rode by our house numerous times on Jaye's wedding day to watch the men erect the two imposing white tents and outdoor toilet facilities. One friend even flew over our house and captured pictures of our beautiful backyard for Jaye. Parking was provided across the street from our house, in an open field owned by David Sims, with parking attendants and police at hand. The guests were served appetizers as they stood in line awaiting Jaye and Jay's arrival at the reception.

The band struck up and played for almost an hour before a horrific lightning storm came through and people began to leave while they could. To this day, people remind me of the storm and lightening which occurred that night. Not Jaye though, who always responds when I mention the storm, that she hardly noticed it. To her, the night had been perfect, in every way, and that was how it should have been.

A family friend, Joyce Massee, told me later that she had never seen a more beautiful wedding. She was enthralled with the wedding tents and said that she had never seen any so beautiful in Fitzgerald, except for her own niece's wedding. The niece that Joyce was referring to was Eulalie Massee Woeltjen, who was the beautiful soloist at the wedding. Sweet Eulalie was accompanied by the talented pianist Dewey Tucker, of Fitzgerald and New York, whom people still remember to this day.

Southern weddings are definitely a family affair. My mother made the top layer of Jaye's wedding cake which was fruit cake. The cake designer from Macon, Georgia incorporated it into her beautifully designed cake. Jaye's cake was one very similar to my own wedding cake which featured grapes rather than flowers. My mother also had made a fruit cake topper when I married 25 years earlier, because fruitcake was the traditional wedding cake.

Southerners have a thirst to hold on to tradition as tightly as they can. On the wedding cake table was a Tatting tablecloth, made by my maternal grandmother Sally, for whom Jaye was named. My grandmother Sally made the cloth when she was a teenager as part of her own trousseau. Guest favors were small boxes of miniature fruit cakes, compiled by my dear cousins from Hawaii, Dotsy Milne and Quinton Adams. It was very special having the two of them here to help before and after the wedding and I will treasure the memories.

Jaye was fortunate to wear an exquisite Vera Wang wedding dress, encrusted with lace, sequins, and pearls, that had belonged to her second cousin, Susan Jay Lundren, of California. Her wedding veil was the wedding veil that I had purchased in Brussels while in college and had worn on my own wedding day. This is the same wedding veil that my younger brother's wife, Kerry Finlayson, along with both of their daughters, Kristy Wilson and Kelly Cross, wore at their weddings. The veil certainly holds special memories for me and I will always hold them dear to my heart.

Jaye carried a mother of pearl Bible brought to her by her maternal grandparents from Jerusalem. She also carried a handkerchief made by her paternal great grandmother, Two-Moms, and one made for my wedding by a family friend, Mrs. John Dorminy, Sr., or better known to me as "Malindy." Jaye wore a sixpence in her shoe and a guardian angel pin given to her by Susan Hogan and Susan's son, Cliff. What indescribable memories each of these treasures hold for her.

During the wedding ceremony, when the minister asked for the ring, the groom turned, stepped down into the congregation, and walked towards Jaye's maternal grandmother. Jaye's MeMa handed Jay the wedding ring that her late husband had given her on their 50th anniversary. When Jaye's grandfather, Pa, gave her MeMa the ring, it was with the understanding that when Jaye married, she was to give it to Jaye. I might also add that Jaye and I helped her grandfather pick out the ring in Atlanta and that is why he especially wanted it to become Jaye's ring one day.

Speaking of Jaye's wedding, I could not have pulled it off without the help of my dear friends, Charlotte Knight from Eatonton, Ethelyn Underwood from Midway, and Susan Singleton. They helped to select the music, run errands, and even had the tedious honor of pressing the wedding dress. How thankful I am that they wanted to be a part of this special day and the role that they played was indeed significant.

Let me add that I could not have hand-picked a better soul mate for my daughter than the one that she picked herself. As I mentioned earlier, Jaye met and fell in love with a "boy named Jay" while still in college. Jay supported her while she was still in college and was always available when she needed him. He is probably one of the best, most dependable men I know. He is a man who puts his God, family, ethics and morals first in everything that he does.

It was not always easy for me when I was "stuck at home" caring for my parents, especially after losing the best daddy ever. Once again, God sent an angel when Jay came into our lives and filled the void that was left for Jaye, my mother, and me. He provided us with so much love, happiness and patience. I will always be indebted to him for the laughter and dry wit that he brought back to the Jay household. On numerous occasions, my mother would literally wet her pants and get choked from laughing at Jay and his antics. Even though he enjoys giving me a hard time, I know that if I ever needed anything, he would be there for me.

When Jaye and Jay married, I suggested that as they entered their new home in Dublin, Georgia, that Jaye go by her birth name, Sally Jaye, since they were both named Jay. "Boy Jay" would have nothing to do with that and responded to me, "No, because when others meet us for the first time, it will be easy for them to remember us since we both have the same name."

I furthered asked, being the typical mother-in-law, what would happen if someone called their house and asked to speak to Jay. His response was simple. He explained that if it was a boy, then it was for him, and if it was a girl, then it was for Jaye. What wisdom he possessed. I am sure they might not have been remembered, since neither were from Dublin, if it hadn't been for them having the same first names. Let me also add they have the same initials, JSM!

After my parents died, and with the help of Jaye, I continued the tradition of sharing Christmas with my brothers and their families in my parents' home. There was always lots of family, boyfriends, girlfriends, and love that abounded in the house. It was a special celebration and a high point for me. For thirteen years, I spent weeks rearranging furniture and planning our Christmas celebration in Fitzgerald. It was held at my house, which was the old home place, known today as "The Jay House." There were fresh pine garlands wrapped in gold roping meandering up and down the banisters on the staircase and lots of candles burning in antique silver or crystal holders throughout the house.

The old home place was the natural setting and location for my brothers and our families to all come together. As the years passed though, the number of those attending began to dwindle. These times had always been so magical and reminiscent of our growing up in this beloved house that was filled with so much happiness and love. Often though, after polishing silver, cleaning the house, and managing a full-time job as a counselor, I would sit and wonder why I was still trying to do this task with so little help from the rest of my family.

Yes, with a job and with my accelerating age, I began to wonder if it was worth it and if it was what everyone wanted to do. I would then reminisce about Helen scurrying around in the kitchen, mother giving her orders to all of us, Ms. Dismuke bringing in her caramel cake, Mae bringing in clean linens, and then I felt that I had no choice but to continue the tradition. This is what my Christmas had been like for 67 years even though the event now emulated a different era and a different lifestyle.

With our families growing and some not attending, I decided a few years after that we would get together later to celebrate Christmas. We discussed dates and decided on the second week in January every year rather than in December. With so many families from out of town and with so many different itineraries, it appeared to be our only solution. We continued this tradition at "The Jay House" in Fitzgerald for a few years, but soon things began to change again.

In January 2012, I was beginning to have some major health issues and did not know how I could again host "The Jay Family Christmas." My devoted daughter Jaye stepped up to the plate and agreed to have the celebration in Dublin. Little did I realize that it would be the beginning of a new day when family Christmas celebrations would become fewer and fewer.

When 2013 arrived and The Jay House was rented for several months, I asked my two brothers if they would like to host the event since Jaye had done so the prior year. After some discussion but no resolution, I decided that the time had come to pass the mantle on to the next generation. Jaye and my two favorite nieces, Kristy and Kelly, agreed that they were ready to accept the challenge, and I felt adamant that these three would never cease this tradition.

The celebration has been dismantled during the past few years with fewer and fewer making the effort to attend. I will say, for those who do attend, it is a weekend filled with boisterous and lively conversations and it instills a tradition to be passed on to our children and grandchildren. My brothers and I definitely need to pay homage to our loving parents who were so precious to us. It is a grave disappointment to me, the lack of interest from those who my parents loved so dearly, but then I remember that is the way life is sometimes.

Jaye and I are similar in so many ways, but I have no recollection of ever being the mother that she has become. I was so blessed, like she, to have stayed home with my children until they were ready to head off to college. Yes, I worked one year, after getting my first Masters and had several part time jobs, but I am referring to having a full-time job. For nineteen years, I was a wife, ran carpools, baked cookies, was a grade mother, a team mother, and a community volunteer. I, like Jaye, loved every second of it even though the world was a different place then. In those days, I was blessed to have Eloise Shelton, who helped me at home, as well as my parents, who were also available when needed. With such wonderful assistance, I was able to help make this community a better place.

Today, Jaye has no one to help with these matters, and I believe that is another reason why I am in awe of all that she accomplishes. She is a wonderful Christian and knows from whence all her blessings come. I feel that God puts us on this earth to care for our own as well as for others and that He expects that from us. I honestly feel this is a trait I have passed on to my own daughter for she cares so deeply for others.

As mentioned earlier, my children were teenagers when their father unexpectedly announced one day that he was miserable and wanted to have a life of his own. We had been married for nineteen years, so I was certainly scared and confused about the life that awaited my children and me. Their father and I decided to legally separate and then two years later we divorced.

It was very challenging for all of us but especially for our two children. With my parents and the grace of God, we all made it successfully. As I began to map out my life, I told my children that I would not date anyone until they graduated from college. I wanted them to know first and foremost that I would be there for the two of them and that I did. There was never a doubt that they would not graduate from college, and once they did and began a life of their own, I redirected my life with plans for my future.

I would be remiss if I didn't mention Christmas on Roanoke Drive with Rob and Jaye. The first Christmas that the three of us were celebrating Christmas together without their daddy, I knew was going to be difficult for them. I pondered what I could do to make it easier for them. Christmas had always been such a spectacular time at the Sherrell house, and I wanted to keep it that way. I don't consider myself particularly garish, but if ever there is a time that I am, it is at Christmas.

We had always had a 9-10 foot Christmas tree in our den, but that year I decided to put another tree outside on the side porch. After the wind blew it down twice, I decided to bring it inside. That was the beginning of a tree in every downstairs window at the Sherrell house. I put the outside tree in our breakfast room, and that made the two rooms on the right of the front door have trees, while the left side had none. To keep the house from appearing to be off balance, I added two more trees, one in the dining room and one in the guest bedroom.

By the next year, I had added Christmas trees upstairs and ended up with 11 trees, all beautiful, live, handpicked trees! I had trees with the following themes: Victorian, Fairy, Children's, Angel, Blue and Silver, Hunter's, Sports, Doll, Blue and Green, Charles Dickens, Traditional, and a Proud to be an American tree. Every room upstairs and downstairs had a tree in one of its windows.

It was amazing to us how many people discovered our house and would stop to take pictures. Afterward, our house became known as the house with a tree in every window, according to the conversation around town. The next year, I put our house on the Tour of Homes so that others could view the trees from inside the house. We decorated all these trees for the next eight years. We only stopped after I sold the house and moved into my mother's house to care for her. By that time, I was getting older and tired of decorating so many trees!

My fervent prayer is that I have instilled in Rob and Jaye the traits that will help them both to be successful and loved by others. The following lessons were taught to me, and in turn, I have passed them on to my children. Some of the sayings, such as "Yes Ma'am or Yes Sir" does not imply that someone is older, but rather it is an expression of respect. There are other lessons of importance for them to remember and pass on to their children such as the following:

- If you can't say something nice, just don't say anything at all.
- Always have grace wherever life might take you.
- Don't forget to always be a blessing to others.
- Do remember that in the South, there is probably a rule for every occasion, so just think before you do any thing.

My Children's Favorite Recipes

Homemade Ice Cream

1 ¼ cups sugar	1 quart heavy cream
⅛ tsp salt	2 tsp vanilla

If you want to add peaches, you need to add 2 tsp lemon juice. Otherwise, you can add candy bars like Snicker or Milky Way or whatever you prefer. This is just a good basic ice cream.

Custard

4 eggs	4 cups milk
1 cup sugar	2 Tbs vanilla flavoring

Beat eggs just enough to mix yolks and whites together. Stir in sugar and cook until dissolved well. Add milk, dash of salt and cook slowly on top of stove, stirring constantly. Can serve or bake. If you bake, put 12 glass cups in a pan of water in oven, and bake at 350 for 35 minutes.

Marshmallow Creme

1 envelope Knox gelatin	4 egg whites
½ cup cold water	1 tsp vanilla
½ cup boiling water	1 ½ square chocolate or 4 Tbs cocoa
1 cup sugar	
¼ tsp salt	

Pour cold water in bowl and sprinkle gelatin on top of water. Add hot water, sugar and salt. Stir until dissolved. Let mixture cool and add to egg whites slowly. Divide quickly into 3 parts. Part one add vanilla and pink color. Part two add vanilla and blue color or melted chocolate. Part three is white or yellow with vanilla and lemon extract. Mold into layers. Can add nuts to pink or cherries to the white. Chill.

RED VELVET CAKE

3 cups flour
3 tsp baking powder
1 cup crisco
2 cups sugar
4 eggs
1 cup buttermilk
1 tsp Vanilla
2 Tbs Cocoa

Sift together flour and baking powder. Cream crisco and sugar and eggs together. Make a paste with food coloring and cocoa and add to flour and crisco mixture. Bake in 3 layer 9" pans, greased, at 350 for about 20 minutes.

Frosting:

8 oz cream cheese
1 box powdered sugar
1 stick margarine

Beat the cream cheese and margarine together and add the sugar. Ice between layers, sides and tops.

RITA PRYOR'S SIX WEEKS MUFFINS

1 box Raisin Bran, 15 oz
1 cup vegetable oil
3 cups sugar
4 eggs, beaten
1 quart buttermilk
5 cups flour
5 tsp baking soda
2 tbs salt

Mix dry ingredients. Add liquids. Store in refrigerator covered for up to six weeks. You can add additional raisins and pecans.

GREEN BEAN CASSEROLE

1 can cream of mushroom soup
½ cup milk
1 tsp soy sauce
1 dash pepper
4 cups green beans
1 can fried onions

Put all ingredients in casserole dish and stir together. Bake 350 for 25 minutes and add onion rings to top. Bake an additional 5 minutes to brown onions.

Ethelyn's Hot Cheese Olives

1 stick butter
2 cups cheese, extra sharp cheddar, grated
1 ½ cups flour
⅛ tsp salt
¼ tsp cayenne pepper
⅛ tsp worcestershire sauce
1 egg
50 pimento stuffed olives

Preheat oven to 350. Beat butter and then add cheese and mix well. Stir in next four ingredients until smooth. Beat egg with 2 Tbs water and add to dough and mix. Refrigerate about 45 minutes.

Remove dough and roll into a thin round flat ball. Put an olive on top and shape dough around it. Place on un-greased sheet and bake 15 minutes.

Chapter 9

My Career

I had always assumed that I would be married to the same man for my entire life, but God had other plans in store for me. When Jaye started the first grade with Kay Batten as her wonderful, caring teacher, I decided that the one thing missing in my life was a Masters degree. At the time, I did not understand why I wanted to go back to school. Later I understood that it was in God's master plan because one day I would be a single parent. I applied to Georgia Southwestern College, in Americus, Georgia, and returned to college where I earned my first of many post-graduate degrees.

I drove 65 miles one way several nights a week and two summers in order to complete this first masters at Georgia Southwestern in Americus, Georgia. It was an enlightening experience in early childhood education since my first degree had been in secondary education. After obtaining my masters, someone ask me what was I going to do with this degree now that I had it. My response was "Nothing at the moment except put it in my back pocket in case I ever need it." And, bless my heart, that is exactly what was in my future.

A month after earning my Masters in December, the local school system had an opening in kindergarten and desperately needed a preschool teacher to finish out the school year. After much pressure from the Superintendent and long time friend Gene Harper, I decided to work the half year. I felt that it would be a great opportunity to see how my family and I got along with me working full time.

My family did great that half a year, so I decided to accept a contract for the next school year. I do not know what happened that next year, but it became evident that my working and caring for my family was not going to work. At the end of that school year I resigned and returned home as a full time mother and wife. I thoroughly enjoyed my students, and still today, I cherish the fond memories of the time I spent with them.

If I had to select my favorite stage in my life, it would have to be the years that I spent rearing my children. I am most thankful that I was able to stay home with my children until they left for college. Yes, I did spend a year and a half as a kindergarten teacher at Ben Hill Primary and thoroughly enjoyed being at the school with my own children. I also spent eight years as First Baptist Church Preschool Director, but that was only three mornings a week. Even with these two jobs, there is little doubt that my calling in life was first and foremost to be a mother.

How blessed I was to be a homemaker, a tennis player, a bridge club member, a garden club member, a book review club member, a Sunday School teacher, a Mission Friends teacher, and a volunteer for numerous organizations. I volunteered for a jail ministry for young inmates, the American Heart Association, American Cancer Society, the Mothers' March of Dimes drive, and PTA Carnival Chairman.

Honestly, I did not realize the role leadership played in my life until a friend, Beverly Pool, commented to me that she loved being a co-chairman with me. When I asked her why, she announced all that she needed to do was just follow me around while I accomplished the mission. Later, in life, I realized that is not a sign of a good leader because a good leader involves everyone in the job. I now understand that and all these organizations and individuals involved helped mold me into the person I strived to become.

For the next few years, I enjoyed staying home and being a full time mom and wife again. After all, that was all I had ever wanted to be in life. I reverted to the carpool mom, the sports mom, the piano mom, the dance mom, the Doncaster mom, and the husband mom.

Everything was running smoothly when I received a call from one of my best friends, Quita Carswell. She called to tell me that they had a preschool teacher at First Baptist Church Preschool who would be leaving January 1st. She said that she thought of me and wondered if I would be interested in a three mornings a week job. After much discussion with my family, I agreed to fill in for the next four months which led to my being there for the next wonderful eight years.

Once there was a television program called "Kids Say the Darnedest Things." Being at First Baptist Preschool, did I ever live that statement! Let me indulge you with one of my favorite stories during those enlightening years there.

Halloween was coming and oh how the four year olds loved Halloween. I was reading the book, "*Gus the Friendly Ghost*" when one of my students, Andy Smith, told me that he was afraid of ghosts. I spent a few minutes trying to explain to him that there was no such thing as a ghost. Immediately this precocious little girl, Rachel Milligan Wynn, said aloud, "Oh, yes there is because my mommy told me so." Now, that did put a kink in my discussion. Over her arm waving and loud insistence, I finally said to her to please explain. Rachel stood up, put her hands on her hips, and said to me "Ain't you ever heard of the Holy Ghost?" Needless to say, I was at a loss of words for one of the few times in my life.

At the end of my first year, Quita Carswell left and I became Director of First Baptist Preschool. I, along with my friend, Susan Hogan, will avow that those eight years were the best years of employment either of us ever experienced. It was a dream job with dream co-workers and dream students. Being a preschool worker allowed me the opportunity to serve as an officer of the Georgia Preschool Association for several years. There, I formulated long lasting friendships with so many fine Christian and dedicated aides, teachers and directors.

One of the most significant relationship I forged at the state level was with Charlotte Knight from Eatonton, Georgia. Charlotte and I were assigned to be roommates at our board meetings for many years, and we were so much alike. While we were at a meeting, I mentioned that Jaye and I were planning a trip to Europe. On a whim, she announced before we left the meeting that she thought her daughter and she would join us and they did.

It was an entertaining and enjoyable two week trip to Europe. I am still awed that we were not part of a tour for the first few days as I drove the four of us through France with a limited French vocabulary. Later, my dear Charlotte is the same Charlotte that came several days before Jaye's wedding to help us get everything organized. She was also the person responsible for most of the beautiful music selections that were shared by Dewey Tucker, our pianist.

The year after I resigned from the preschool association, I was presented with the Georgia Preschool Advocate of the Year Award. This prestigious award was given that year to one other director and one teacher. Touchingly, I was nominated by my local constituents, Susan Hogan, Sally Mann and Carol Davis. What a humbling experience it was to receive this award, and it is an honor which I hold very dear to my heart.

During my employment at First Baptist Church, my husband came home one day and announced that he was no longer happy being married. I continued to stay at the preschool for another year understanding that one day I would need to work full time. I just did not realize how imminent it was.

In September 1988, I was at the church getting ready for the fall opening the next week when I received a call from my dear friend, Butch Frye. Mr. Frye was an administrator at Fitzgerald High School and called to ask if I would consider coming to Fitzgerald High School. He informed me that the school had a social studies teacher who had resigned during the first few weeks of school, and they were in desperate need of a teacher.

I knew in my heart of hearts that I needed to reap the benefits of insurance and full-time employment to help finance my children's college education. Also, a social studies opening is rare and had not occurred in many years. I agreed to come on board probably because of the smooth-talking Mr. Frye, who could sell me ski boots in South Georgia if he wanted. Regardless, he did allow me to get the Preschool up and running with Sally Mann at the helm. He also allowed me some time off in preparation for my new adventure at Fitzgerald High School. You are probably wondering why a preschool teacher would even be considered for a high school vacancy, but my BA degree was actually in social studies at the secondary level.

I began my tenure at Fitzgerald High School during the year that my daughter Jaye graduated. It was a busy but exciting year, where I taught World Geography and Georgia History to eighth and ninth graders. That summer, I returned to college again. This time I went to Valdosta State College, in Valdosta, Georgia, to obtain my re-certification in Social Studies. The gods were definitely with me for my second year, I was assigned to teach World History to tenth graders. My assignments kept getting better because the year after I was allowed to teach AP World History and Psychology, both of which I adored.

I thoroughly enjoyed my two years of teaching AP social studies classes at Fitzgerald High School. Growing up in a small town has numerous advantages, but it also has disadvantages of which I had not be so emphatically aware. It did not take me long to discover the limited horizon of many of my students.

The majority of my high school students had never been more than fifty miles from home and envisioned the world only as their little corner of Georgia. I spent months trying to explain to them that there was a world beyond Fitzgerald and life after Fitzgerald which became very daunting at times. For to fully comprehend what I am talking about, you must understand that my town is an impoverished, rural South Georgia community, where most parents possess only a high school education or less.

Realizing that it was up to me to make a difference in their lives, my very supportive principal, approved some marvelous field trips to the Atlanta area. Today, in education that is a rarity because of so many budget cuts. I was able to expose my AP students to the High Museum of Art, Jimmy Carter Library, Holy Spirit Monastery, Carlos Museum at Emory University, the Atlanta Historical Society, the Swan House, the Nutcracker Ballet, Lenox Square, and several excellent restaurants in the Atlanta area. It was an experience that is still in the minds of many of these young people, according to what they tell me when I encounter them today.

A former student, Jermaine Duffie, who was the former Dean of Students at the prestigious Spelman College, reminded me I taught him proper etiquette. I gave them some tips on eating in a fine restaurant so they would feel comfortable. Jermaine said he still remembers the following little ditty about eating soup, "As little boats go out to sea, I dip my spoon away from me." It is interesting what they do and do not remember!

Recently, several other former AP History students, Lynn Dalton, Karen Kelly, Tracy McKie, Stephanie Passmore, and Katie Harrison posted pictures of our Atlanta trip on Facebook. I cannot believe they still have pictures of our trip. They added the following comments on my Facebook page: "The fact we all remember this trip and your entire class so fondly, after nearly 25 years, would tell you how we feel about you." I don't have to tell you how warm and fuzzy a comment like that makes a teacher feel!

The next day, Jeff Maris followed their comment with "Ahh, the Pleasant Peasant Restaurant. Lydia Jay Mason certainly made sure we got our culture in." Good manners, a little culture, and a hunger for newfound experiences have taken all of these students to higher ground than they knew was possible back then. I can honestly say that my earnest desire for my students was met with such comments as these.

I have one former parent, Shirley Brooks, a member of the local Board of Education, who reminds me often that her two girls began their thirst for travel while in my class. Of that she is proud but also disappointed that they rarely return to Fitzgerald. My response to her always is "I am sorry to hear that, but aren't you proud that they have seen much more of the world than most of the people from our community?" Of course, you rightfully know her answer.

Another interesting adventure occurred, two years later, in 1992, when I discovered that a presidential candidate, Bill Clinton, was hosting a political rally in Tifton, Georgia. Not having sufficient time to arrange and get approval for a field trip, I shared the information with my students in hopes that they could attend. I was disappointed that very few were able to be a part of this event.

It was a rainy night in South Georgia when my colleague and dear friend, Susan Singleton, her daughters and their friend, Amy Johnson, and I left for the political rally. We went to hear Presidential candidate Bill Clinton and Vice Presidential candidate Al Gore. The huge red, white, and blue campaign buses pulled into the Agrirama plot, amidst the white cotton fields, while Alabama's song "High Cotton" was playing. I must admit, even though I wasn't a Democrat, it gave me cold chills.

Having gone to see the candidates, my friend from Illinois' daughter, Shannon, made a comment about the cotton fields. Immediately, I responded "This is what we mean by the expression 'livin in high cotton' in the South." That statement led to a discussion of the term "high cotton" which means complete success. My understanding is that when the cotton reaches the height necessary to be ready for harvest, then the work is done, and the farmer can sit back and wait to reap the benefits of his hard labor. This, along with

"Just hold on a cotton picking minute" are stellar examples of how the vernacular of the South is often based upon some significant part of an individual's life.

The following year, Mr. Frye, who had become my principal, walked into my classroom after school, and asked if I would consider going back to school to obtain a counseling degree. Mr. Frye felt that the time had come for our counseling program to be revamped. Again, I heeded the call, and returned to college.

I began my program at Columbus State University, in Columbus, Georgia, in 1994. It was their first year of a counseling program, so they were under the tutelage of Georgia State University, a college well-known for its counseling program. I will never forget leaving home every Saturday morning at 6:00 A.M., in order to be in class by 8:30. Our class let out at 5:00 P.M. and I would make the two and one-half hour trek home. This long but productive adventure lasted for a year and one half. After attending classes and an internship in school counseling, I finally completed my M.Ed in Counseling degree.

I was most fortunate that Mr. Frye asked Debbie Wilson, a business education teacher at the high school, to join me the next year as a counselor. Thus, the two of us began our counseling careers. Debbie and I were an excellent team. With our teamwork and dedication, we turned the counseling program around at Fitzgerald High School.

For the next eight years, we saw considerable success. The scholarships given to our students went from approximately $200,000 to over $800,000 during that time. We devised a plan which allowed every student to graduate with both a Technical Career Program diploma and College Preparatory diploma. In addition, we implemented dual degree programs from the high school and our own technical college. Those years turned out to be some of the most productive years of my life. The students and friends that touched me are still a significant part of my life and have definitely had an impact on me.

With an understanding that I would not be able to achieve my 30 years in education for retirement, I decided that the time had come for me to begin working on my doctorate degree. I was accepted into the doctoral program at Valdosta State College which consisted of a weekend program on Friday nights and all-day Saturdays. After only one quarter, I had to switch to the Nova Southeastern University program because the time had come when I was unable to leave my mother overnight. In comparison, the Nova program was taught only on Saturdays from 8:30-5:30, in Macon, Georgia, which accommodated me better.

For the next two years, I enjoyed my study group that consisted of Elaine Connell of Dublin, Georgia, Lynn Overstreet of Baxley, Georgia, and Greg Tanner of Douglas, Georgia. We met often on Sunday afternoons to mull over our assignments and class notes. You might be wondering why I did not participate in an on-line degree. Believe it or not, at that time, there were none available. I realize that sounds archaic today with on line courses every where and with colleges on almost every corner of the world. However, that was not the way it was for me.

While at Fitzgerald High School, I probably witnessed the most earth-shattering experience of my adult life when the planes hit the World Trade Towers in New York City. How well I remember where I was on that morning of September 11, 2001. I can still get goose bumps when I reflect on the moment and the after effects. The school announcements had just aired and the TV was still playing in the Career Center, outside of my office.

As the news commentators began to describe what had happened, Sylvia Ellis, our registrar and wife of our local sheriff, came running in to tell us to look at the TV. We were mesmerized and totally speechless as we saw another plane hit the second tower never realizing at that moment how this event would change our daily lives. A few minutes later, we learned that a third plane had hit the Pentagon and that a fourth plane had crashed in an open field in Pennsylvania.

How helpless, weak, and unsure we all felt that morning. Not long after the attack, we were informed that the pilots were affiliated with Al-Qaeda, a little known Iraq terrorist group. The group took full responsibility for flying the planes and attacking America. This life-changing event became the first ever act of terrorism against the United States on its mainland.

Within minutes of the World Trade Center attack, emotional parents began to enter the school wanting to check their children out, take them home, hold them tightly, and keep them well within their sights. All U.S. airports closed, our U.S. borders closed, and our government shut down as we embraced this incomprehensible event. Never in my wildest dreams did I believe that an incident such as this could happen on American soil! How thankful I was that my parents never lived to see such a horrific tragedy as I reflected upon this event.

With the influx of television, I spent every waking moment, when not at work, in front of the television trying to comprehend what had transpired. It was reminiscent of how I had felt thirty years earlier with the assassination of John F. Kennedy and Martin Luther King. I prayed that our parents would take this opportunity to hug their children tightly and tell them just how loved they were. I also prayed that if ever such a tragedy happened to these students as adults, they could comprehend the importance of loving their own family.

In 1999, I received my doctorate from Nova Southeastern University. A few years later, a new school superintendent arrived and decided to move me into another position at the Ben Hill Middle School. He and I discussed the fact that being an assistant principal and a counselor at the same time did not go hand in hand, and that I did not feel comfortable in such a position. He further stated he felt that with my leadership degree, the fit was perfect. Being determined to move me, he practiced nepotism at its best and placed his wife in my position at the high school. How did I know that he had planned this from the beginning of that school year? The superintendent's teenage daughter told several of her friends that her mother was coming to Fitzgerald High School as a counselor and one of them came to me to discuss the matter.

Even though parents, teachers, and students made their wishes known that I was needed more at the high school than the middle school, it was to no avail. I will never forget the support of my peers and students. It definitely helped to fill a hole left in my heart with my love for each of them.

It was not that I had an aversion to the middle school, it was that I had not achieved the goal I had set at Fitzgerald High School. The first year as a counselor at the high school, I had set a goal of reaching one million dollars worth of scholarships within ten years. During my ninth year, I had almost accomplished that goal and with one more year, it would have been a reality. I had to tell myself constantly that it just wasn't in God's plan and that He knew better than I.

I will tell you what was in God's plans and that was that I made some of the best friends I have ever had while at Fitzgerald High School. My first two years as a teacher, I was on the East end of first hall with Dianne Herndon, Pat Wilder, Kathy Tyree, John Owens, Ed Haile, Susan Singleton, Brenda Whitley, Anne Wynn and Sherry Haskins. They all had a compelling influence on me, whether it was good or bad, LOL. On the West end of the same hall was Beth McQuaig, Charles Lewis, Louellen Haile, Al Strom, and Patty Gordon, who also significantly impacted my life.

If I hadn't connected with these unique individuals, I would have never had the wild tales about going to the Shakespeare Festival in Montgomery, Alabama. Nor would I have gone to Hilton Head, South Carolina and Taos, New Mexico with my newfound friends. There were more trips than I can relate, along with parties together once a month, but the memories will never leave my mind. What an enjoyable time it was to bond together, socialize together, and collect their best assets as we each learned from one another.

The environment at Ben Hill Middle School was satisfying and enjoyable during the next four years. I am not sure whether I made a difference or not, but I will say that Karen Hewett and I gave it all we had. By the time that I left, I felt all that I had done was "put out fires." To this day, however, I am grateful for the friendships that I established with these teachers, administrators, and my counseling partners. If God had not sent me there, I would have never personally known some of the best people in Fitzgerald. They have certainly enriched my life and for that I am grateful. Sometimes, blessings come in strange packages!

God definitely had a plan for me because had I not transferred to the middle school, my life would have turned out differently. When I was at the high school because of the immense workload, I was spending ten to twelve-hour days at work. There was little or no time for anything or anyone else in my life except for my family. I understand that those hours are no longer necessary because some of the duties have been shifted to others which has led to more productivity for their counselors.

I have had young people ask me if I wished that I had worked early in life rather than staying home with my children. My answer has always been the same, No. I would not give anything for being able to be a part of my children's lives during their preschool, elementary, and high school years. I delighted that I was able to participate in every segment of their school years.

Yes, at a much older age, it was difficult going to work full time, going back to college, and earning multiple higher degrees, but I would not change a thing. I am so grateful that I was able to spend the majority of my life doing for my children. I feel fortunate that I did not have to work full time until Rob was in college and Jaye was a senior in high school. I will always cherish those years I spent with them at home.

On numerous occasions, I have been referred to, by students and peers, as a true "Southern Belle." It has always made me hold my head up a little higher like "Miss Scarlet," in the exalted *Gone with the Wind*. It is obvious that true Southern Belles know when they need to take off their white gloves and step up to the plate. We are not known to be crybabies, or even flakes, but rather we are known to pull ourselves up by the bootstraps and move forward, just like I did.

Speaking of Southern Belles and the ingenuity we possess, I am reminded of an incident while at the middle school. My principal and friend, Danny Young, asked me if I would speak with an irate parent. Mr. Young told me that the parent felt she had been wronged, and he could not seem to make anything right with her.

Mr. Young was in my office, when I called the parent in, and we discussed the issue at hand. When the parent left, he looked askance and said to me, "You told her exactly what I did, but when she left me, she was cussing at me, but when she left you, she was smiling and thanking you." I told Mr. Young that the difference was I never raised my voice nor looked exasperated. I just sat there, and listened to the parent pitifully, while nodding and smiling the entire time. After she finished, I had my say in a quiet and unobtrusive manner.

I asked Mr. Young, as he left my office, with a smile on my face, if he had ever heard the expression, "You catch more flies with honey than vinegar?" He just looked at me and shook his head. There is something to be said about the southern traits where ladies are taught to never raise their voice or try to intimidate others. Especially, when trying to win someone over to their side.

As I reflect upon my career as an educator, I cherish the time I spent getting to know my students and my coworkers. It has certainly provided me with a different perspective on life. There is little doubt that God placed me at Fitzgerald High School shortly after I divorced. I discovered that I could better understand teenagers and their parents who were experiencing divorce and/or grieving the loss of a parent or child. I am totally satisfied with living that part of His plan. I genuinely believe that I made a difference in the lives of many of my students and parents because of my life experiences.

When I was a child, life was all about me and my own little world. As I have grown older, I understand that life needs to be more about others and less about me. The world today has become more about self and immediate gratification. I wish I had an answer about what we could do as a society for this to change. As my mother taught me, I am often reminded when seeing those in need, "Except for the grace of God, there go I." Amen!

Everybody can take the time and try to make the world a kinder, gentler place by caring about others rather than concentrating on themselves. As only one individual, you might be wondering, "What can I do to make life better for others?" There is so much that you can do regardless of your age or station in life. Have you thought about taking a neighbor who just lost her dog of ten years a plate of cookies or a bottle of wine? What about inviting the little old lady down the street to your next church social or to come over for a glass of sweet tea? How about being a physician to others by helping to heal broken hearts even though you don't have a medical degree?

Yes, there is much you can do to change the direction of our world. You can be the intermediary for change by giving it your best and inviting others into your world. There is no doubt that as change agents, we can all make a significant difference in the lives of others. Go give it a try!

MY FAVORITE RECIPES

TIA MARIA

6 Tbs coffee, instant
4 cups sugar
2 cups boiling water
1 pint whisky

Dissolve coffee and sugar in boiling water. Add whiskey. Take 2 quart bottles and 2 vanilla beans in each quart. Mix good and turn bottles each week for 4 weeks.

CHAMPAGNE PUNCH

4 bottles champagne
4 glasses cognac or brandy
3 glasses curaco
2 bottles white wine
8 lemons
2 quarts club soda
2 bottles cherry juice
2 cans pineapple chunks (large)

Mix everything together except club soda. Serves 45 people.

JOYCE MASSEE'S CHINESE CHICKEN SALAD

4 chicken breasts
2 ginger roots, fresh and sliced
1 large lettuce, chopped
3 oz rice sticks
½ cup almonds, toasted
¼ cup sesame seed, toasted
2 onions, green, chopped

Dressing:
4 Tbs sugar
1 Tbs salt,
⅓ tsp pepper
½ cup salad oil
4 Tbs wine vinegar

Boil dressing ingredients until well dissolved. Add oil at the last minute. Add to salad. Cook chicken in water with ginger root. Wash and drain lettuce and chopped onion. Place almonds and sesame seeds in 400 oven until brown. Cook chicken. Fry rice sticks and drain on paper towel. Put in a paper bag with dressing and shake well.

Hot Shrimp Salad

2 cups shrimp, cooked
2 cups celery
½ cup bell pepper
½ cup almonds
½ cup mayonnaise
½ cup celery soup
1 jar pimento, small
2 tsp onion, grated
2 tsp lemon juice
½ tsp salt
3 cups potato chips, chipped
2 cups cheese, grated

Cut shrimp in half. Combine all other ingredients except chips and cheese. Mix well and pour into well greased ramekins. Bake 350 for 20 minutes. Combine chips and cheese and sprinkle over shrimp mixture. Return to oven and cook an additional 10 minutes.

Arnold Palmer (Tea)

3 quarts tea (2 large bags)
⅓ cup sugar
1 can lemonade, 12 oz
1 ginger ale, quart

Pepper Jelly

2 bottles Certo
3 bell peppers, large
12 hot peppers
5 lbs + 1 cup sugar
¼ cup water
3 cups vinegar

Cut up peppers, put in blender and add little water and little vinegar. Boil sugar and vinegar. Add vegetables and cook until it boils rapidly. Remove from heat and strain through cheese cloth. Add Certo and green food coloring. Makes 7 pints.

Rice Casserole

1 cup brown rice, uncooked
1 jar mushrooms, 4 oz, juice
½ onion soup, dry pkg
3 beef bouillon cubes, dissolved
¾ stick butter

Dissolve bouillon cubes in 3 cups Water. Pour into a casserole dish over ingredients. Cook at 325 for 45 minutes.

SPOTTED PIG'S LEMON ICE BOX PIE

Crust:

2 tubes Town House crackers, crushed	1 stick butter
	2 Tbs sugar

Melt butter and sugar together. Press into 2 pie plates to form crusts. Bake 350 for 10-15 minutes and cool.

Filling:

2 cans condensed milk	6 egg yolks
4 lemons, juice only	1 carton Cool Whip, 12 oz

Boil lemons in water before squeezing to get juice out. Save the 6 egg whites for meringue. Mix together and put in pie crusts.

Meringue:

2 Tbs corn starch	1 cup water
4 Tbs sugar	

Cook the above in a small boiler over medium heat until thick. Stir constantly. Remove from heat and set aside. Beat egg whites and dash of salt until stiff but not dry. Add 6 Tbs sugar, beat some more and then add corn starch mixture. Top two pies with meringue. Sprinkle a few cracker crumbs on top and bake at 350. Can refrigerate or freeze.

Chapter 10

My Grandchildren

No one can comprehend the feeling that a grandmother has when she falls in love with her very first grandchild. Almost every waking hour, you find yourself wanting to be there for him or her as well as for yourself. As you look into that newborn's face, it is as if you are looking at your own child again. Then surprisedly, you begin to wonder if you could love this baby even more than you do your own child.

I could not help but think about my mother and wish she could have been there to see this little bundle of newfound joy. She once told me that if I didn't stop kissing on my own babies that they would not have any skin left to protect themselves. I sat there holding my precious new grandchild, wondering what her response would have been, when she saw the love and joyful tears on my face.

On a Friday night, January 14, 2000 I received a call from Jaye that she felt the time was near for her to give birth. I immediately grabbed my suitcase, which had been packed for weeks, and left for Dublin. Jay, Jaye, and I sat around all day on Saturday and nothing happened. Then Sunday morning arrived and still nothing. The phone rang and Jaye began talking to her lifelong friends, Amy Smith Parrish and Danna Smith. After a few minutes, Amy informed Jaye that it sounded to her that she was beginning labor. There was Jaye's kindred soul once again instructing her as to what she needed to do next!

Jaye, Jay and I left for the hospital. Within hours, a beautiful baby boy entered our life and it has not been the same since. My first grandchild was Whitaker Clayton Mason born on January 16, 2000, in Dublin, Georgia. It was a year that was entered with much anticipation because it was the emergence of a new millennium. A new millennium brings forth excitement as well as concern for our world. Prices were significantly higher with the cost of gas at $1.23 a gallon, a loaf of bread at $1.72, and a postage stamp was .33, according to Wikipedia. Within the reach of this newborn was a world in which he would become an integral part and could help to make it better than he found it.

We made calls to family and friends with the exciting news. Before I had finished my calls, in walked my dear friends, Johnny and Ethelyn Underwood. When I called them, they immediately drove the 45 miles, as the bluebird of happiness shined down on all of us. I will never forget the feeling as I held my precious first grandchild. My day now would begin with prayer for another person as I began my own day.

Being a single grandparent, I told my daughter and son-in-law that I would have to be the grandparent that baked cookies and bought cute outfits. Financially, I knew I would not be able to make large monetary contributions to them or help send them to college. I did know I had seen a miracle when Whitaker was born and that I could help to mold him into a viable human being.

"Boy Jay," as we call him to differentiate him from my daughter, "Girl Jaye," and I had a conversation later about money. He informed me that if I saved all the money that I spent on clothes and items for his children, I could send them both to college. My response to him was, "I am doing just what I want to do for them and enjoying every minute!" I comprehended that it might not be practical but then I have never been the most practical person in the world, so why would I change now?

My dear friend and preacher, Gene Wilder, once asked me if I did my grocery shopping in Dublin or did I just schedule doctor appointments there. Living 85 miles away, I did everything possible there so that I could be with my Whitaker. Needless to say, Gene did not have grandchildren when he asked me that question. Once his grandchildren arrived, it did not take him long to understand why I used every excuse I could to get to Dublin.

Jay has always been known for his quiet wit and ingenuity. When Whit was only 16 months old, Jay decided I needed to fence in my back yard in Fitzgerald. I called my dear friend Jim Parrott at Standard Supply Company and he sent out what I needed for Jay to build the fence. After Jay finished, he posted a sign in my yard which he had made which read: "Fence constructed by Suckered Son-in-Laws, a non-profit organization. Call 1-800-IMA-FOOL, if you need a fence. Don't call me. Get your own son-in-law." I promise that is only one of the hilarious antics of my son-in-law.

Whit is my most serious thinking and probably the most compassionate grandchild I have. He is an outstanding athlete and can tell you any fact you want to know about sports, much like his Uncle Rob. Whit has enjoyed playing little league sports but when he was 10 he began to enjoy a sport that was new to me called "travel ball." I was totally unfamiliar with it and later felt that there was too much competition and travel. Another factor was they played baseball on Sunday mornings, and I certainly did not approve of that.

I would like to share the following story that appeared in several area newspapers about Whit when he was 14 years old and playing travel baseball in Cochran, Georgia. Let me begin by explaining a few things to you. Whit was asked by his baseball coach, if he would be willing to forego his batting average, to let a young man who was going blind from the opposing team, pitch to him. Without hesitation, Whit said, "Yes, Sir."

Whit stepped up to the plate and waited for the opponent to throw the first ball. When he did, Whit played the part of the batter perfectly. The young pitcher threw three pitches that barely made it to the plate. However, Whit struck at all three and struck out. The fans went wild with jubilation. Now, the spine-tingling part to me is that Whit had just hit a home run out of the park. Actually, it was the first one out of the park since the baseball field had been built three years earlier. A comment from a Cochran newspaper reporter was as follows:

> *The same young man, that crushed the first in game home run on our field in three years, humbled himself to strikeout to a young man that will never forget and always talk about the time he was able to pitch in an 8th grade ball game.*

Yes, my grandson Whit is an outstanding athlete. More importantly, he possesses godly principles and compassion which his parents have taught him. Best of all, Whit understands how to apply these principles in situations which arise.

As a tenth grader, Whit was moved from the position he had always played in football to quarterback to help out the team. Whit had never even thought about playing that position. He learned it quickly, enjoyed this position, and there is evidence that it definitely helped to enhance his self-esteem. When moved to this new position as quarterback, Whit comprehended he had a leadership role to assume and that others were counting on him to do his best. His first year wasn't what he had hoped for but his second year he helped to lead the team to the playoffs.

During Whit's senior year, he broke a Trinity Christian School record that had been in place since was 1999. He had 2,378 passing yards by the first game of his senior year. At the end of Whit's senior year in football, the new coach wanted him to play a defensive position and he did so without question. It is quite obvious that whatever Whit is doing, whether it is in football, track, basketball or baseball, he is definitely giving it one hundred percent of his time and talent. Whit continues to love sports, even though now he is in college, and he is strictly playing intramural sports.

Whit's junior and senior year, he was fortunate to spend his spring vacation doing mission work in the Dominican Republic. He prayed and played ball with the children every day when they were not working on a project. Whit also was afforded the opportunity to play baseball, and do additional mission work in the DR, during the summer after graduation.

During Whit's high school years at Trinity Christian School, he maintained an overall A average and belonged to several school clubs. Whit was selected to participate on the Laurens County Youth Leadership Team as a tenth grader. As an eleventh grader, he was selected to the Morris State Bank Youth Board. At the end of his eleventh grade year, Whit was chosen to participate in an all-expense paid EMC's Youth Leadership Conference in Washington, D.C. I believe this was most definitely a highlight of his high school career.

I asked Whit, during his junior year in high school, where he would like to go for his graduation gift from me. First, he said that he would like to go to the islands and swim with the pigs. A few weeks later, Whit called and said that he had a better idea. He suggested that I use that money so that we all, the Sherrells and the Masons, could go on a Disney Cruise. Why a Disney Cruise? He said that his own family loved it when they went years ago and that he thought Robert would love it as well.

On Thanksgiving Day, during Whit's senior year, we all left for Port Canaveral. The next morning, we left on a cruise to the Caribbean. Words cannot express the enjoyable trip we had. I am not really sure who enjoyed it the most, my teenage grandchildren or my three year old grandson. I do know that we all had the time of our lives. The fact that Whit is the person he is, allowed us to make memories that will stay in our hearts forever. With this kind act, he truly exemplified the meaning of unselfishness and love of family.

Whit has been afforded many opportunities and for that I am thankful to God and his parents. Every year since Whit was eight-years old, his father and another father-son duo, have spent a weekend at a major league baseball stadium somewhere in the United States. What a tremendous opportunity for travel and exposure that has been for Whit. Most of all, it has taught him the importance of family and specifically of spending time with his daddy and friends.

In the fall 2018, Whit began his college career at Georgia College and State University, in Milledgeville, Georgia, where his mother graduated. His plans are to major in business and possibly to continue pursuing a law degree. Thus far, Whit has enjoyed college and I know that whatever he decides to do, he will be a success. As we are told in Jeremiah 29:11, God has definite plans for us and I can't wait to see what he has in store for Whit as well as my other grandchildren.

Whatever Whit attempts to do, he is successful. Even though Whit is in college, whenever he is home, he is still an active member of Pine Forest Methodist Church. In fact, he just returned from this church's winter vacation trip. At Georgia College, Whit attends Bible Study every Thursday night of which I am most proud. I hate to admit it but it never entered my mind when I was a college freshman to attend bible study.

Indeed, I am proud of Whit's honors but above all, I can say that his manners are impeccable. I once heard a teacher say that Whit never ended his texts without thanking him and saying yes sir. He is definitely on the road to becoming a true Southern gentleman. Of course, high on my agenda, is that he always takes the time to tell his MeMa that he loves her!

My only granddaughter is Laura Elizabeth Mason. She was born on April 2, 2002, in Dublin, Georgia. Laura Elizabeth was named "Laura" for her paternal grandmother and "Elizabeth" for her maternal grandmother. How proud both of us were to share our names with her.

Laura Elizabeth's birth was the most miraculous event of which I have ever been a part. Right before Jaye was wheeled into the birthing room, Jay invited me to be in there when Jaye gave birth. It had never entered my mind that I would be a witness to such an extraordinary event. I must admit that it was definitely a momentous time in my life. It was even more meaningful because the two doctors delivering the baby were a couple married to one another which is rare indeed.

I was ecstatic, needless to say, to observe Laura Elizabeth's birth but there were parameters on which Jay insisted. Jay told me that I would not be allowed to express my feelings openly with my typical "ohs, ahs, and thank you Lord." The second perimeter was that I was not to become too emotional and sob. Now, if you know me, you know that was an almost impossible task. But, if you know my son-in-law, you would understand that comment because he is a man of few words. I can reflect now on how joyful an experience it was and how wonderful God was to give us that beautiful baby girl. Gottacha, Jay!

Laura Elizabeth, who is often referred to as Laura Beth or L. B., came into the world as her own little beautiful self and with her own distinct personality. When she was almost two years old, Gene and I went to Dublin for him to meet my grandchildren and son-in-law. We were all sitting around conversing when Laura Beth, walked over to her daddy and said, "Shake your booty, Shake your booty."

We were all dismayed as she demonstrated how to shake a booty. Jaye asked her who in the world had taught her such a thing. Incredulously, she looked her mother straight in the eye and said, "Mr. Gene." Now, let me remind you that she had only know him for about 30 minutes when she made this accusation. It was an accusation that was not true and one that she had concocted on her own.

After the "Shake your booty" episode, Whit and Laura Beth were visiting with me in Fitzgerald when they saw Mr. Gene drive up to my house. They were outside playing, when Whit came running to me and said, "MeMa, Mr. Gene has half a car." Confused, I followed him to the car. It turned out to be a SSR by Chevrolet, which was actually a convertible truck, strange looking even to me.

The next day when Mr. Gene came over to my house, he drove up in a typical convertible with the top now. Laura Beth was standing inside, at my kitchen window, looking out. She looked at him and then at me and said, "There's Mr. Gene, MeMa. Can I ride in his car that doesn't have a top on it?" Out of the mouths of babes!

My daughter is rearing her children much as I did and as well as my mother before me. Jaye and I were both taught and firmly believe that children are to mind their parents and always be respectful of adults. Jaye truly expected her children to follow the rules and rituals that she had followed many years before when she was their age.

When Laura Beth was going to four-year old preschool at Pine Forest Church, my daughter Jaye would put her clothes out for her to wear each day. One day, Laura Beth told her mother that she did not want to wear her little "frog dress" to preschool. Jaye looked at her askance and told her that it was not an option. Finally, Laura Beth put the dress on, came down the stairs, and walked to the car with her hands over the frog. When Jaye asked her why she was doing that and why she didn't want to wear the dress, Laura Beth looked at her and answered "Because I am tired of looking precious." It turned out that her teachers were always telling her that she looked "precious" in her clothes.

When Jaye put Laura Beth out at preschool that morning, Laura Beth still had her hands over her chest covering the frog. Jaye went back to pick her up at noon, and she came dancing out as if the world was beautiful. Jaye inquired if she had a good morning and asked her what made her so cheerful now. Her response was "Mama, I walked into the bathroom, looked in the mirror, and said, 'Laura Beth, just get over it'." Truthfully, that was not the answer that Jaye expected, but it was a typical Laura Beth answer. I am afraid that my husband has adopted that saying "just get over it" and uses it more often than I like with me!

Gene has noted numerous times that Laura Beth was a child wise beyond her years and I am frequently reminded of that thought. I remember Jaye, Whit, Laura Beth and I were riding down the road before either of them were in school. Jaye and I were firing rhyming words at them as fast as we could. Laura Beth, who was only two, was quickly answering before Whit had time to answer. Whit turned to me solemnly and said, "MeMa, how can she do that so fast?" How many times have I thought the same thing. Thus far, life has been a little too effortless for Laura Beth, and I often wonder just when will she hit that brick wall.

Laura Beth was about six years old and was returning to school after her summer break. I asked her if she was ready to start school again. Her answer was "Of course. I need to go back to school because I am sure everybody missed me this summer." Shocked at such confidence, my response was "Oh, really, L.B.?" She looked at me straight in the eyes and said, "Yes, MeMa, because everybody loves Laura Beth." It is admirable that she has so much confidence, is her own person, sees others in a different perspective, and does not care whether she emulates the crowd or not.

Another delightful story about Laura Beth is when the two of us went to Evergreen Cemetery in Fitzgerald. I was telling her one day about my mother, daddy, and my baby sister, and we had a memorial to them out at the cemetery. After a lengthy discussion, I asked Laura Beth if she would like to go to the cemetery to visit with them. "Sure," she said, so we went out there for a visit. After meeting the three of them, talking about their graves and the flowers we had brought, Laura Beth turned to me and asked, "MeMa, do you know anybody else out here?"

Of course, being in my late 60s, I knew a myriad of people at Evergreen Cemetery. As we went down the lane, I introduced her to my husband's first wife, Carole, who had earlier died of cancer. Laura Beth asked me inquisitively if we could sit on the bench by Carole's grave and talk to her, which we did.

When we got home, Laura Beth's serious brother, Whit, asked her where we had been. She answered, "We have been at the cemetery visiting and talking to some of MeMa's friends." Whit looked at her and said "Laura Beth, those folks are dead, they can't talk." Laura Beth looked at him and replied, "I know that, Whit, but they still like to have visitors." Now, what a lovely thought that was for me, at this twilight time of my life. I love thinking that someone might come by and talk with me one day when I am settled in at Evergreen Cemetery.

There was another time that I was reminded of how exceptional Laura Beth's thought process worked. Jaye and I were keeping Rob and Amy's precious new baby Robert. As we drove down the road, Laura Beth said to me that she did not have on her seat belt. When I inquired as to why not, she stated: "In case of an accident, MeMa! I need to be ready to throw myself on top of Robert to save him. I have already lived 12 years, but he has only lived for seven months." Now, I ask you, "How did she come up with that unconventional analogy at 12 years of age?"

Another afternoon in Dublin, Laura Beth and I were riding on the golf cart, down a country lane in search of wildflowers for a table arrangement for her mom. What a learning experience that turned out to be for this 12-year old female. Laura Beth and I would stop, pick a few wildflowers, and then discuss how we would arrange them once we got back home.

When we finally arrived home, the two of us arranged the wildflowers just like we wanted. What did Laura Beth learn from our little sojourn while her brother was at baseball practice? Evidently, a lot. Three weeks later I returned to her home to help her mother get ready to host a Sunday School party. Just guess who had arranged the flowers for the party? None other than Laura Beth!

Probably one of the most treasured moments of my life with Laura Beth was when I said to her that one of her friends, Julia King, had asked me to be her friend on Facebook. I told her how touched I was that she had asked. Laura Beth looked at me and responded, "Well, MeMa, why wouldn't she? You are just so lovable to everybody." Wow, what a compliment to me and I will carry it with me as long as my mind allows me to do so.

When Laura Beth was just five years old, one of Whit's friends called her "smoking hot" and that was humorous to him. Now that she is sixteen, I understand that some of his friends are referring to her in that same matter, but he no longer finds it funny. What a difference it makes now that Laura Beth is a teenager. I hear that Whit becomes very uncomfortable when his friends began to discuss his little sister, and he lets them know that she is off limits to them.

Laura Beth was in the ninth grade when she was selected by her class to be their representative on Trinity Christian School's homecoming court. We were all so excited and could hardly wait for the night to come. About thirty minutes before it was time for her to leave, the back door bell rung and there stood baby Robert in his daddy's arms, holding a bouquet of flowers. I do not think that if Thomas Rhett, her favorite country singer had been standing there, she could have been more elated.

The first time that Laura Beth was invited to the Jr.-Sr. Prom, Whit had to give his approval on her date. He had a definite say so about who could and could not take her to prom. There is something to be said about a girl having an older brother to protect and take care of her. There is a definite connection between the two of them. They can relive the family joys and sorrows and are always there as two against the world.

Laura Beth is an A student at Trinity Christian School and is active in swimming, competitive cheer, track, and soccer. She has also won numerous awards in these sports. Outside of her school life, her youth group at Pine Forest Methodist Church is a significant part of her life. Laura Beth also participates in art classes and a community choir.

When Laura Beth was fourteen years old, she exhibited her artwork, at Fitzgerald's Arts Center, at the invitation of an Arts Council member. Since that time, she has been commissioned to paint several pictures for other people beside her family. Laura Beth has donated her artwork for charitable auctions but normally she gives her work to others rather than keeping it for herself. When it came time for me to design a cover for this book, to whom do you think I went? None other than the illustrious Laura Beth Mason!

During the past four years, Laura Beth has sung the National Anthem at Football and Basketball games as a soloist. As a sophomore, she was invited to participate in Laurens County Youth Leadership and to serve on the Morris State Bank Youth Board. This past summer, she was selected by a panel from the state of Georgia to attend the HOBY Youth Leadership program at Georgia State College and University. She continues to enjoy the wonderful friends that she met while at HOBY and keeps up with them through Twitter and visits.

Laura Beth, during her tenth grade year, was able to go on a mission trip to the Dominican Republic during her spring break. Upon her return, she immediately said to me, "MeMa, if I could go back today, I would." She is anxiously awaiting spring break this year, so she can return and serve as a youth missionary. Her summer plans are for her to go on a mission trip to Uganda for a few weeks in July.

Laura Beth has very deep religious beliefs and convictions. When you go into her bedroom suite, you will see Bible verses posted everywhere on her wall. It is obvious that she does not mind sharing her beliefs with others because I have seen her Bible verses show up on Instagram. If Laura Beth is aware of a family member or friend having a difficult time, she will share a bible verse with them to help them get through their difficult days.

I have told Laura Beth on numerous occasions that God gave her a multitude of talents, and wisely she must cultivate them. When she arrives in heaven, God will either be happy or sad with her, dependent upon how she utilized them on earth. I honestly believe that she will use them to her fullest ability and she will continue to put God first in her life and share His love with others.

Indeed, I am proud of Whit's and Laura Beth's religious beliefs, and the foundation given to them by their parents, their school, and their church. I strongly believe that one of the best opportunities provided them was when Jaye kept her daily devotional book in her car, before either of them could drive. As she drove them to school each day, Whit and Laura Beth would take turns reading the devotional for that day. What a sense of grounding that had to be for them as they began each day at school.

I have given much praise to Whit and Laura Beth, but I must acknowledge their parents as well. Just about everything that is done in their family is done together as a family. Jaye and Jay built an outdoor covered area where friends can come over after football games for parties, and other celebrations. It encompasses a fire pit, kitchen, television, and plenty of seating. Yes, my Jaye would have loved a swimming pool, but she realized what this outdoor area could provide for her children. Truthfully, I can say that Whit and Laura Beth's parents, more often than not, put the two of them ahead of their own desires and wishes, and it has substantially paid off.

Robert Steele Sherrell brought joy and life into our world on June 24, 2014 at Piedmont Hospital where Rob was born 45 years earlier. It evoked all kind of memories for me as I walked through the front door and reflected on the birth of my firstborn Robert Ashley Sherrell.

Upon entering Piedmont Hospital on June 24, 2014, there was a handsome portrait of Carter Smith, a dear friend of my parents, hanging on the front wall of the hospital. Dr. Carter Smith was one of the leading pioneers at Piedmont Hospital and a well-known, prominent Atlanta physician. When I saw the portrait, I felt that it was a sign from my mother and daddy that they were there with us on that special day when Robert Steele Sherrell was born.

What a beautiful blessing for the two families and friends present in that elegant birthing lounge. I do not believe there could be many birthing suites as beautiful, and most importantly, as comfortable.

What jubilation it was that we were all together to enjoy this special occasion. I will never forget the wonder and love on Rob's face when he walked out of Amy's room into the lounge with Robert in his arms. Laura Beth would be most upset if I did not add that Rob handed baby Robert to her; therefore, making her the first one to hold that special little boy. What a celebration that was!

I would be remiss not to mention the lovely note that I received from Amy's sister, Lisa Steele, a few days later. It began with the well-acclaimed quote "All grandchildren are brilliant and beautiful and obviously take after their grandmothers." Lisa continued in the note to her mother and me the following:

> *Robert doesn't yet know how lucky he is to have you two as his Grandmothers. I can't imagine the feelings and emotions you felt this week, watching your children become parents for the first time. I saw sides of both Amy and Rob that I've never seen before and this baby is going to grow up in a world with lots of love and guidance from those two who will keep him safe, healthy, and happy. Why? Because both of you raised such amazing children who are now one hundred percent ready for this journey. Sleep tight!*

Words are inadequate to express the jubilation I felt upon receiving such a special note from Amy's sister. Yes, Rob and Amy had been through so much to get where they were in life, but every trial and tribulation had undoubtedly paid off; not only for them, but for their families as well.

Rob and Amy began the brainwashing of Robert very early. He had not even arrived before one could see there was UGA clothing and UGA balls in every nook and cranny of his house. Sprinkled throughout were also a few articles from UNC where Amy graduated, but truly everywhere you looked, there were signs of "Go Dawgs" and UGA clothing in infant sizes.

Eight weeks later, I went up to spend a few days with Robert and I thoroughly enjoyed every second of it. Amy was most generous, especially for a first time mom, and allowed me to have full rein of him. Boy, did I ever enjoy that opportunity. I will admit, during those few days that I counted my many blessing, but getting to see Amy and Rob as first-time parents was the biggest treat.

Before Robert was born, his parents thought that they would send him to a day care program when he was three months old. Once he arrived, they immediately decided against that option. At that time, Amy started the interview process for a Nanny. I felt so thankful that I was there and could be a part of that process.

After interviewing three nannies, Amy and Rob decided on Evelyn Kummerow. Evelyn speaks fluent Spanish and asked them if she could share her language with Robert. What an incredible opportunity for him to learn a second language so early in life! She devised a rather strenuous schedule to make sure that Robert's day was filled with play, exercise, reading, cuddling, and sleeping. Evelyn has certainly been a blessing to the three of them and was God sent.

Two weeks after my memorable visit with Robert, I had a detached retina and a detached macular while driving in Fitzgerald. I immediately went to my local ophthalmologist, Dr. Henry Schneider, who called a retina specialist in Tallahassee, Florida. I had the first appointment the next morning, and the next day the doctor performed surgery.

During the next six months, I had a total of four eye surgeries. Afterward, I was not able to regain much sight in that eye and felt I could no longer drive to Atlanta. Interestingly, when I told my surgeon that all I wanted was to be able to drive to Atlanta, she looked at me with a quizzical expression and said, "Now, why would anyone want to do that?" Words are inadequate to express how dejected I was knowing that I could not spend as much time as I wanted with our precious new baby. I had to constantly remind myself how blessed I was to have spent the time with him the past few weeks.

Robert has been as good a baby as his daddy was and has brought so much love and joy to all of us. As a friend of my daughter's said, "Looking at Facebook and all the pictures of Robert, you can tell it's been a long time since ya'll have had a baby in the family." How correct she was!

The exuberance was indescribable when Amy called and said that Jaye and I were welcome to keep Robert at any time. I immediately hung up the phone, called Jaye, but was too late. She had already called Amy and was told that she could get Robert whenever it was convenient. Before I was able to even get my calendar to check available dates, Jaye had already arranged his first visit to Dublin. I must admit though that she has been most generous to allow me to spend time with them whenever Robert is there.

The first time Robert went to visit the Dublin Masons, Gene took me to Jaye's house to participate in his arrival and what joys ensued that week. Jaye, Laura Beth, and I were up by 7:00 AM every morning because Robert was first come, first serve. Obviously, we all wanted to be the first one to hold him when he awoke. The three of us girls spent the weekend taking turns holding and talking with Robert. I must add that Whit and Boy Jay weren't far behind us for I believe they enjoyed him as much as we did. This was the beginning of Camp Mason which henceforth now occurs every summer.

In the spring of Robert's first year, we planned a trip to Fernandina for all of us. The selected date fell during his birthday week and what a celebration that was. When Rob and Amy arrived at our condo, before they even unpacked, Rob rushed down to the beach with Robert in his arms. He could hardly wait to see Robert's face when he saw the ocean for the first time. All of us followed quickly behind them because we wanted to see his reaction as well. We immensely enjoyed that short week together with one another. The trip to the beach has now become an annual event.

Robert is a precocious and inquisitive child. We never know what he is going to do or say, especially at bedtime. I remember the first night that Gene and I kept him at the beach, he had just turned two years old. After playing for a while, it was time to put him to bed. Everything went well until Robert got into the crib and then it began. He kept calling out to me, over and over, saying, "MeMa, I love you. Mema, I love you." Gene begged me to go get him out of the bed, but I was proud of myself. I just sat by his bedroom door, listened to his sweet little voice, and left him in the bed.

In May 2016, the final performances occurred for the Ringling Brothers' Greatest Show on Earth. What a sign of the times that people no longer wanted the entertainment of a live circus because they felt the animals were being mistreated. Really, now! As a child, Rob and Jaye went to the Ringling Brother's Circus as I had done many years earlier and enjoyed it tremendously.

When I saw that the circus was coming to Atlanta for one of its finalities, I secured tickets for Robert's parents and Gene and me to take Robert to see this legendary circus. Of course, when Jaye and Laura Beth discovered I had tickets, they immediately secured tickets, which luckily were near us. They wanted to be a part of as many of his experiences as possible.

What an exhilarating time we had watching the performance, but none compared to seeing our two-year old's face light up with excitement. Certainly, it broke my heart to think that the circus would no longer be available for children to enjoy. There were very few animals in the show for it consisted mostly of acrobatic feats. The only disappointment was that Amy did not get to join us. Of all times, it was moving day for the Sherrells and Amy felt that she needed to stayed home to direct the movers.

Rob told me that one night, when Robert was three, he was holding him, and Robert looked up, and said, "Daddy, let's cuddle again." Rob responded "We will, son, but just one more time. You know what one more time means, right, Robert?" Robert looked up at him and said, "Yes, Daddy, three more times" as he held up three little fingers. That precious boy has already learned that the number one can easily turn into the number three with those who love him so dearly and value every moment with him.

The enjoyment that Robert has brought into our lives is insurmountable. He always seems to know the right thing to say at the right time. For instance, when you give him a gift, his response is always "Oh, this is just what I have always wanted." When you ask Robert whose boy he is, his response is "I'm MeMa's boy" and you know how that makes my heart sing!

Amy said that one day she took Robert to Publix and the cashier gave him some stickers. He kept putting them on himself and saying to the cashier, "I am the sticker man." A few minutes later, in the car, he responded, "Mama, I'm MeMa's sticker man." Robert certainly has a way of making you feel special even when you aren't around and his mother is kind to share his experiences with me.

Our family normally spends Thanksgiving in Milledgeville, Georgia at Jay and Jaye's lake house. Boy Jay's family has always celebrated Thanksgiving day together at their parents' house, thirty miles away, so the lake is convenient for them. It also works out well because the lake house has enough bedrooms to accommodate all of us and is about half way between Atlanta and Fitzgerald.

In 2017, our families decided that we did not need to continue giving Christmas gifts to one another. It seemed that all of us had what we wanted and if we needed any thing, we usually went out and bought it. I suggested that we take the money that we would spend on one another, put it in a pot, and save it for a memorable trip each year. Of course, we still give each child a small Christmas gift but nothing extravagant as in times pass.

Our first big trip was a Disney Cruise in November 2017. We scheduled it so that we could spend our Thanksgiving holidays together in the Caribbean. I don't believe any of us will ever forget the expression of Robert's face when he saw Mickey and Minnie Mouse. Once we were on the ship, he could not believe all the Disney characters. His favorite was Captain Jack Sparrow and I'm not really sure what that says about him! Robert loved the pool, the musicals, the games, and of course, the free ice cream.

This past May, my sweet daughter-in-law brought Robert to visit me in Fitzgerald. When he walked in my house, he looked up at me and said, "MeMa, I thought you lived in Dublin." I can unquestionably understand why he thought that since every time he has been to Dublin, I have been there.

On our third beach trip to Fernandina, Robert was turning four the next week. This trip was even more enjoyable than the others. My son Rob, who often feels that he can't be out of the office except for a few days, certainly did not want to leave his little fella. He informed us that next summer, he would be there for the entire week, so as not to miss anything. It is nostalgic for me to think that now a third generation is enjoying the same condominium that my parents gave to my brothers and me thirty-two years ago. Maybe we need to do a commercial that says this is a trust that never dies but just keeps on giving!

In August, I returned from another week of Camp Mason hosted once again by the Dublin Masons. We had a glorious time. One afternoon we took Robert swimming, and he thought he was as big as Whit and Laura Beth. When Whit jumped off the diving board, Robert said that he could do that. We cautiously watched him as he jumped off the diving board. It was the first time that he had ever done that, which we did not know at the time, and he did so without a swimmie.

Laura Beth proceeded to do a backward flip off the diving board, and Robert responded to her the same way that he had to Whit. This time however, his backward flip consisted of jumping off the diving board backwards. When you think about it, that was pretty original. When Robert got home, he told his mom that he wished summer would last forever so he could stay at Camp Mason.

Gene and I have enjoyed having a little one again as much as the Dublin Masons have. We are storing up memories from beach trips, camp trips, day trips, Circus trips, sports activities, and a Disney cruise. Amy and Rob have been so thoughtful about sending us pictures almost every week and allowing us to FaceTime with Robert often. It has been exhilarating for us. Our constant prayer is that God will allow us more time to be with Robert as we approach the twilight of our life.

Rearing children today is indeed different from our day and from the day of our parents. There was no such thing, back in the day, as having a planned "playdate". All we had to do was to walk down the street until we found someone to play with on that particular day. It breaks my heart to realize that my grandchildren will never have the carefree life that their parents had. Their parents and grandparents could ride their bikes wherever they wanted and could walk home from school unattended. They could play outside, roam the neighborhood for hours, and could always come home to an unlocked house.

My grandchildren's generation will never be able to comprehend that to make a phone call, one had to dial a rotary phone or could only talk while standing or sitting next to the phone. This reminds me of when my children were young. If ever I talked on the phone and they were nearby, they always seemed to need me. You must realize that during those days, the telephone cord would only reach so far. It always appeared that when I was on the phone, it became a time for them to play "Discover" because they knew they were out of my arm's reach or rather the cord's reach.

Yes, it is totally unimaginable to them the progression of phones from earlier to what is available today. Technology is convenient but it has also brought about the lack of verbal communication and interaction among people. It is of grave concern to me as to whether my grandchildren will be able to converse face to face with others when needed.

When used appropriately, technology has made life easier to stay in contact with each other. It is wonderful to be able to visit with children and grandchildren via FaceTime or Skype. I am also grateful for an exceptional daughter and daughter in law, who allow me to share in their children's lives through technology. Yes, technology is often overused and abused, but like everything in life there is a time and a place for it. My wish is however that children would spend less time inside their house and more time outside playing and using their imaginations.

What joy grandchildren are to their grandparents and what delightful stories they provide us. It literally breaks my heart to think that these children will not be products of the world in which their parents were reared. Life was far more simpler and people were definitely more tolerant of one another.

One can easily tell that I am pleased with the adults that my two children have become and the families that they are rearing. I am reminded of the little boy who looked at me inquisitively and said: "Mama, if you take that necklace off, will your head fall off?" Being very observant, Rob knew that I never took off the diamond pendant that my daddy gave me upon high school graduation. Today, Rob is a caring husband and father. My petite little girl Jaye, who entered this world at only 5 lbs, 4 ozs, after being two weeks late, was timidly shy, but if her newfound friends heard that, they would not believe it. Today, she is one of the best at being a mother, a wife, and an assertive young adult.

Yes, I am proud of my children and the parents that they have become. My greatest fear, as a mother, was that my children would grow up to be lazy and not hit a lick at a snake. I realize that I grew up with more than most people of my generation and I acknowledge that. I also grew up knowing that people had to earn certain rights and that laziness was totally unacceptable. To me, there is no excuse for laziness and as my daddy use to say, "Idleness is the devil's workshop." I firmly believe that to be true.

The joy and satisfaction that my children and grandchildren continue to bring into my life is indescribable. I sincerely appreciate their love and the fact that they constantly find time for me. Of everything that I can bequeath to my children and grandchildren, I want them to always remember that the greatest contribution to the kingdom of God is not necessarily what they accomplish in life but rather how they treat others, as well as their own families. Hopefully they will always focus on investing in those things which are permanent and remember that material things will pass and fade away. To God be the glory, amen!

My Grandchildren's Favorite Recipes

Rice Krispies Treat

3 tablespoons butter or margarine
1 package-about 40 marshmallows
2 tsp vanilla
6 cups Rice Krispies cereal

Butter pan and set aside. Melt butter over low heat, add marshmallows and stir until completely melted. Remove from heat. Stir in vanilla and desired food coloring. Add cereal and stir until well coated. Last, decorate with frosting or candies according to seasonal decor.

Symphony Brownies

1 box brownie mix
2 Symphony candy bars

Follow directions on brownie mix box. After mixing together, pour half of batter into a square pan. On top of batter, place 2 Symphony candy bars, and then pour rest of batter on top of them. Bake according to mix.

Danna's Chicken

2 cups green beans
3-4 medium potatoes
2-3 large chicken breasts
1 pkg Italian dressing mix
½ cup butter (1 stick)
Salt and pepper

Preheat the oven to 350 degrees. Rub casserole dish with butter. Wash the chicken, green beans and red potatoes. Peel the potatoes and cut into small cubes. Line one side of a 9x13 baking dish with green beans and line the other with the chunks of potato. Place the chicken breast or fingers between the green beans and potatoes. Cut up butter and place over dish. Sprinkle it with Italian seasoning, salt and pepper. Cover with foil and bake for 1 hour.

LASAGNA

1 pound sweet Italian sausage
¾ pound lean ground beef
½ cup minced onion
2 cloves garlic, crushed
1 (28 ounce) can crushed tomatoes
2 (6 ounce) cans tomato paste
2 (6.5 ounce) cans tomato sauce
½ cup water
1 ½ tsp dried basil leaves
1 tsp Italian seasoning
2 Tbs sugar
1 Tbs salt
¼ tsp black pepper
4 Tbs chopped fresh parsley
12 lasagna noodles
16 ounces ricotta cheese
1 egg
¾ lb mozzarella cheese, sliced
¾ cup grated Parmesan cheese

In a large pot, cook sausage, ground beef, onion, and garlic over medium heat until well browned. Stir in crushed tomatoes, tomato paste, tomato sauce, and water. Season with sugar, basil, fennel seeds, Italian seasoning, 1 tablespoon salt, pepper, and 2 tablespoons parsley. Simmer, covered, for about 1 1/2 hours, stirring occasionally.

Bring a large pot of lightly salted water to a boil. Cook lasagna noodles in boiling water for 8-10 minutes. Drain noodles, and rinse with cold water. In a mixing bowl, combine ricotta cheese with egg, remaining parsley, and 1/2 tsp salt. Preheat oven to 375.

Spread 1 1/2 cups of me at sauce in the bottom of a 9x13 inch baking dish. Place 6 noodles lengthwise over meat sauce, spread with half of the ricotta cheese mixture and top with one-third of mozzarella cheese slices. Repeat layers, and top with remaining mozzarella and Parmesan cheese. (Sometimes I substitute cottage cheese for the Ricotta cheese.)

Cover with foil and bake in preheated oven for 25 minutes. Remove foil and bake an additional 25 minutes. Cool for 15 minutes before serving.

Butter Bean Soup

This was a third generation recipe when my mother gave it to me. She always made this soup, whenever I was sick, and I have passed this down to my children and grandchildren.

1 can butter beans	3 cups milk
3 Tbs butter	1 cup Half and Half
1 small onion	salt and pepper

Take 1/3 can of Butter Beans and mash up and add chopped onion. Pour in milk and half and half and add butter. Last, add seasoning, and cook about 15 minutes.

Chapter 11

My Golden Years

A Southern daddy often sets the stage for the future of his daughters and shapes them into who they become. There are few things in the world comparable to that of being a "daddy's girl." It is like having another heart of your own where you learn the true meaning of unconditional love and understand a father's role is to provide and protect his little girl. I was always a "daddy's girl" and cannot imagine what my life would have been like without him there for me.

Once, when my daddy was interviewed by a Macon newspaper about his life, the interviewer said it was obvious he had a special fondness for his little girl. She quoted him as saying, "Those little ole boys of mine, I don't care anything about them-now don't you put that in the paper, you know I'm just kidding." But, it did not take her long to know where his heart truly laid. The love that my daddy had for me is indescribable. Not only was I my daddy's little girl, but he had lost a baby girl one year before I was born; therefore, making me "an extra special Daddy's little girl."

Every now and then, someone appears on the scene who is so different he stands out from all the rest. To me, that was my daddy. To him, life was a real challenge that he faced daily without fear because of his Christian beliefs and foundation. His presence was like oil on troubled waters. My daddy never spoke unless he knew what he was talking about and felt it would add meaning to the conversation. He was always a good listener. He was empathic and trustworthy. My daddy had a tenacious sense of fair play that was only excelled by his love and concern for his church and his family.

My daddy taught me one's family comes first, even before one's own self. He exemplified that belief when on his own birthdays, he always gave his family monetary presents, based on the number of his years he had spent on earth. He was forever scolding all of us for giving gifts to him. My daddy was a basic human being who never personally wanted a whole lot materially in his entire life. He was a completely satisfied person and how rare is that?

One of the many tributes to my daddy was given only a few days ago, from my 48-year-old daughter, Jaye. She stated that she would always treasure the way she felt when she walked into a room where he was because his face would light up. She further exclaimed that my daddy made her feel like she was the only person alive. Jaye adored his impish smile and his love for her always shone brightly. I do not know how many times I have heard her say how blessed she was to call him "Pa."

And, not to leave out my son, Rob. I well remember him writing an essay, while in Mr. Butch Frye's eighth grade social studies class. He stated his grandfather had never missed a single Sunday going to Sunday School and church. Of course, his Pa had missed some Sundays, but in the eyes of Rob, his grandfather was just that perfect. Even today, Rob will tell you that his Pa was the greatest man who ever lived, and he believes that with all his being. Of all the material items that Rob could have selected from his grandparent's home, the only thing he wanted was a framed American Flag. This encased flag flew over the White House, in commendation of his grandfather's 80th birthday. I understand both of my children's feelings about this giant of a man because I, too, felt the very same way.

By far, the most intelligent person I ever knew was my daddy. He possessed wonderful verbiage and taught me the importance of reading and a good vocabulary. Daddy instilled in me the importance of both and often would repeat this quote from Mark Twain: "The man who doesn't read good books has no advantage over the man who can't read them." Today, I am reminded of how many books from my past have shaped me into the person I am and how my fascination with words has led me to desire a better vocabulary. My husband once asked me how I became a "wordsmith," and my response was, "I didn't know I was, but if you really wanted to see a true wordsmith, it was my daddy."

When other children went on vacation, they were taught to count cows, horses, or cars, but my daddy taught us new words. If we did not know their meanings, he told us to write the word down and look it up when we got home. This is the kind of wisdom that he taught us as we traveled down the highway of life. What a wise man he was.

Yes, being Southern is definitely a birthright and was passed down to me from my parents and grandparents. As a Southern woman, I was taught by both of my parents not to be fragile but rather to be "bulldog tough." I am thankful that they felt the need to mold me into a strong person. As I entered my golden years of life, I have once again realized the importance of being resilient.

During the past 10 years, I have broken both wrists, had arthroscopic surgery on both knees, gallbladder surgery, two total hip replacements, a broken calcareous with six fractures, hospitalized with Sepsis, back surgery, and recently carpal tunnel surgery. Now that might not sound like a lot to you, but it was to me. Through the years, the only time that I was sick was when I had bronchitis. As my daddy used to lament, "Getting older is not for sissies" and I agree wholeheartedly.

Yes, the past years have been eventful, but overall my life has been one filled with so many blessings. I have always felt my lifetime goal was to give back to others in some small way. As I was taught, by my parents, all my life "To whom much is given, much is expected." Yes, the past is gone forever, and there is no need to rehash mistakes made or have regrets. There were definitely times I would have liked to have had a "say so" in God's plans, but that did not happen. At a later time, I will discuss these debacles, of which I am reminded with Him, when I get to Heaven.

My fervent prayer has always been that my children and my grandchildren would live Christ-like lives and be there for others. As a caregiver for my parents, I realize now the valuable lesson it taught my children we are to be caregivers. I pray that when I ask them to take my hand and help me to walk as I did for them many years ago, they will be just as receptive. I also pray that when I forget what I want to say or do, they will be patient with me because all I ever wanted was to be there for them and with them.

Oh, how I cherish the memories of being there as my children took their first steps as well as the first time each grandchild called me "MeMa." The only thing that I ask of them now is to lend me a helping hand when needed, as I enter this final stage of my life. True Southerners who are taught well, learn early in life that to help ladies is of utmost importance, especially older ladies. I hope that belief will live on with my own family and that I can be an enduring legacy to them.

When I was just a child, Fitzgerald was a "stop over" for tourists. Traveling south, many tourists spend the night in a local "mom and pop" motel while traveling from the North to sunny Florida. Fitzgerald was a place where church bells chimed from Central Methodist Church to denote the hour of the day. In my childhood days, the factory whistles would blow, so the workers would know it was lunch time.

Fitzgerald was a hamlet where children walked down the street smelling and sometimes picking the gardenia bushes or the honeysuckle vines, blissfully. It might sound somewhat idyllic and to me growing up in Fitzgerald was that and more. It is a more subdued town today, as in many small communities. Fitzgerald has given way to many abandoned buildings and factories but it is still my home that I love and, it will always have a special place in my heart.

My community, along with many other small towns, is recognized by our county more often than our town. Have I ever had grandeur illusions of living somewhere else besides a small community? Of course, I have. There were many years, after my children left home, I dreamed of moving to faraway places. I was never able to do so because I had parents who needed a family member close by for them.

Certainly, my life could have been more glamorous. I might have been afforded different opportunities, but I have no regrets. No one can take away the memories I have of being able to stay home and care for my parents. Being a part of their "golden years" was something that neither of my brothers were able to enjoy nor do they understand what they missed. You do not comprehend what life is like unless you have been there. No, it was not always easy. I was more often than not, unable to leave home for long weekends because of my parents. I certainly have no regrets and sacrificially understand that it was all part of God's plan.

I am thankful I have been able to preserve the home where my brothers and I grew up. Today, it is known as "The Jay House," a guest house in Fitzgerald. It is a stately home, designed as Georgian, by local architect and family friend, Lauren Parrott. It was built by him in 1934 and is located on one of the two main streets, Central and Main. These two streets have beautiful parks running down the middle of each of these streets. This layout has special meaning to me because it was designed by my grandfather when he was Mayor of Fitzgerald.

Our house originally had five fireplaces and was built with exquisite molding, hardwood floors, and eleven foot ceilings. However, no longer is a fireplace necessary in the kitchen; now the home only has four operative fireplaces. These fireplaces are located in three of the four bedrooms, in the living room, and also in the dining room. In 1950, my mother sold her farm in Crisp County and used her money to add on a great room or as some called it back then, a den. My daddy thought she was being frivolous and that it was not necessary. According to him, we had a small den, located next to the screened porch, and that should be sufficient for anyone. If only I had inherited his practicality.

The only other adjustment to the original home place was in 1997. I sold the house my children had grown up in and moved into there to better care for my mother. I contracted with Lee Hogan to add an upstairs to her garage which he did. This addition allowed me to have additional storage for my furniture and items from my previous home.

I did not want to disrupt the lifestyle of my mother and felt that it would be best for me to store my furniture. In the central upstairs window, over the garage, I placed a beautiful stained glass window from the old First Baptist Church. What a tribute the window was to my family who were original members of that church. In addition to the upstairs, I added a covered patio and re-landscaped the back yard to give the house a more updated feeling.

During my adult life, several friends invited me to join the Fitzgerald Rotary Club, but I always declined. After the death of my daddy, who had been a charter member of the club, I decided it was time for me to join the Rotary Club. Gene Wilder, my dear friend and pastor, inducted me into Rotary. At that time, I had become a high school counselor and my principal, Mr. Butch Frye, felt that it was advantageous for me join. Mr. Frye was a big believer in his administration and teachers being a viable part of the community, and I must agree.

I thoroughly enjoyed the fellowship at the weekly Rotary Club meetings especially with the following members who usually shared my table: Cecelia Campbell, Tommie Dampier, Van Waters, Gene Mason, and Debra Weil. We discussed the stock market, education, community interests, and some of our favorite foods such as barbecue and seafood.

One day, when we were discussing barbecue, Gene Mason spoke up. He said that the best barbecue he ever had was from the White Diamond Grill in Bonaire, Georgia. Before he could finish his sentence, Debra and I piped in that we loved their barbecue as well. He looked at us peculiarly and stated that his family went there often when he was growing up in Warner Robins. Gene asked me how I knew about it. I then told him that my sister-in-law's family owned the restaurant. Debra, as well as several others at the table, had also bought barbecue from there.

In the fall of 2003, I was having a party at my house and decided I needed to mop my kitchen floor before I left for school that morning. After I finished mopping, I walked back into the kitchen, slipped on the wet floor, fell, and broke my arm. I wasn't sure it was broken, so I went on to school. Around noon I began to hurt and decided that I needed to see the doctor. Yes, my arm was broken. The doctor was able to put it in a cast, and I was able to continue my life without having surgery.

While my arm was still in a cast, I arrived at the Fitzgerald Rotary Club one day to have Gene Mason offer to assist me with my lunch tray. Being single for so many years, I had become very independent. I thanked him, but told him that I could handle it by myself. He insisted with a response of "I once broke my arm and someone offered to help me. I am just doing the same thing by passing it on." With that response, I agreed.

The next week when I arrived at Rotary, Gene was waiting to assist me with my tray which I let him do without any debate. When we sat down at our table, he saw that I had a piece of fried chicken. Being the gentleman that he was, he offered to cut it up for me. Well, needless to say, that did it! No one since I was a wee little tot had offered to cut up my meat for me.

I realized at that moment, even though I had known Gene casually for 30 plus years, what an exemplary person he was. I had often heard during the past year about how kind and loving Gene had been to

Carol, his first wife of 39 years. Carol had died of cancer earlier that year and the fact that he had been so caring to her truly made an impression on me.

A few weeks after Gene's kindness to me, my sister-in-law, Kerry Jay, brought me some barbecue from the White Diamond Grill. Having some of it leftover, I decided to offer it to none other than my Rotarian friend, Gene Mason. I felt since he had spent the past month, assisting me at the Rotary Club, that was the least I could do. Little did either of us know that gift would be the beginning of a two-year courtship. As Gene likes to bemoan to others, a broken arm and a piece of chicken, got him into a lot of trouble.

When Gene and I decided to marry, we casually mentioned it to Gary Smith, president of the Fitzgerald Rotary Club. Gary invited us to the front of the club to make the announcement we were engaged. "As far as I know," Gary said to the club, "This is the first 'legit' love affair that we have had between two of our own Rotarians. I am happy to announce their upcoming marriage." Everyone clapped and then my special cousin, the notorious and controversial Philip Jay, said aloud, "Welcome to the family, Gene!" I don't think I will say what Gene's response to Philip was after that comment.

During our whirlwind courtship of two years, Gene purchased a condominium at Fernandina. In no time, much like me, he fell in love with the sleepy little village of Fernandina. Knowing how much I loved the beach, he decided that the perfect place to propose to me was at Fernandina. On that particular night, on the beach, the stars aligned, and I said yes.

Being sentimental, Gene proposed to me on the same spot that he first told me he loved me, after only a few months of dating. I must admit the first time was more emotional because I was not ready for a commitment. However, this time, the moon was shining brightly on the water as the tide danced across the ocean, and everything was perfect. I have never regretted one moment of our being together. Three months after our engagement, we were married.

I feel that I must add I was totally contented with my life before Gene became a part of it. I spent every waking hour caring for my children, my mother, building a new career, and enjoying my delightful grandchildren. In the beginning, it was difficult for me to imagine that the time had arrived when God sent me His choice for a husband.

I had not seriously thought about someone with whom to share my life. After numerous conversations with my inner being, I reminded myself, "It is His time and His way."

After 17 years of being divorced, I had gone to Dublin one day to visit with my grandchildren. As we were playing, I told my grandson, Whit, that Mr. Gene and I were going to get married. Whit, being my serious grandchild looked at me and asked me why. I told him that I had waited for years until I could find a man with the same last name as his because I wanted us to have the same last name. Whit just looked at me bewildered, smiled, and said, "O.K., MeMa, I understand now."

I must admit that my grandchildren and I having the same last name, Mason, has certainly led to many interesting and problematical moments. A few months after Gene and I married, my daughter had gone out of town and asked me to get her children from school.

I walked into the front office of Trinity Christian School, wrote my name down on the sign out sheet, and asked for Whit Mason and Laura Beth Mason. The secretary saw my name, mistook me for "Boy Jay's" mama who had been seriously ill and said, "Oh, Mrs. Mason, you look good to have been so very sick." I smiled and said with amusement, "Oh, you must think that I am Boy Jay's mom, but actually I am Girl Jaye's mom." She looked at me, then at the sign-out sheet, and looked over at the other office lady. After a few minutes, she said, "You know, I'm from the North, and up there, we just don't do things like this." As you can imagine, many a laugh has been garnered from that conversation.

As Gene and I have often said to the other one, it is obvious that we were born to be soulmates. What is a soulmate? To us, it is someone who is your perfect fit and can show you what you are capable of becoming in life and who helps you to become that person. Yes, neither of us would have probably selected the other when we were young, because we searched for different things at that time in our lives. We both agree there is no doubt that God definitely brought us together during a time when we each needed the other. It is obvious Jesus showed up and showed out!

Gene and I felt that we wanted a small, private wedding. We originally discussed a destination wedding but we felt church had become such a part of our lives that we should marry there. Neither of us had spouses who attended church regularly and we rejoiced that church had become a vital part of our new life together. We invited our families and a few friends who had been a part of our lives during those past two years to the ceremony. Kelly Brown, our minister at First Baptist Church, married us in the church's chapel on the morning of December 17, 2005.

My precious aunt, Rosa Lee, along with her daughter-in-law, Marion Jay Curry, her granddaughter, Jenny Jay, Ethelyn Underwood, and Ron and Susan Singleton, hosted a wedding luncheon at her home. We enjoyed toasts from Van Waters, on behalf of our friends; Jay Mason and Charles Jay, on behalf of my family, and from my uncle, Clayton Jay, on behalf of the host and hostess. This was the beginning of the merging of our two families and together, we now had four children and four grandchildren.

After our wedding luncheon, we left Fitzgerald. It was a rainy afternoon as we headed down to Longboat Key for our honeymoon. We both had always vacationed on the East Coast and the Panhandle, but neither of us had spent any time on the southwestern side of Florida. We spent a week at Longboat Key and enjoyed every minute of little mini trips to Naples, Sarasota, Venice, Siesta Key, and St. Armands. We absolutely fell in love with Longboat Key and would love to definitely spend more time there than we do. Since it is a six-hour drive from Fitzgerald, we seldom return there.

Yes, during the past 15 years, we have had some health problems and other issues, but I truly believe that God's plan was for Gene and me to be together during our golden years. As the Bible states, in Ecclesiastes 3, "There is a time for everything……a time to tear and a time to mend, a time to be silent and a time to speak, a time to love…"

In our early 20s, Gene and I both married the first time for young love. This second time around, not only did we marry for love, but we also married for companionship as well. We both believe that God definitely had a hand in this marriage. I cannot express the joy that we share because we both love having the other one in our pew on Sundays. I am thankful He sent me a Southern gentleman who honors Him, is interested in learning and exploration, has impeccable manners, and a kind heart. We know that God is on His throne, this is His world, and we are His children.

How blessed that God is a part of every plan and decision that we make in our lives. Our day always begins with prayer. Every meal throughout the day, regardless of whether we are at home or at a restaurant, is begun with a blessing of thanksgiving. As good as God has been to us, how could we do otherwise?

Today, Gene and I are blessed to continue our love affair, after 13 years of marriage, as we continue to enjoy our life together. With both of us having condos at the beach, we consider it to be one of our happy places. In our early years together and before all our surgeries, Gene would even help me pick up sharks teeth and seashells amidst children asking him why. They could not seem to comprehend why a grown man was carrying a sand bucket and picking up ocean debris. Gene always seemed to have an interesting response to their questions, with no two ever being the same. This adventure led to my beginning a small craft business called "She sells seashells."

Gene has always been my biggest supporter and has encouraged me to follow my dreams whatever they might be. By spending so much time at the beach, I decided to fulfill my dream of making and selling seashell mirrors. Being my advocate, he helped me by making mirror frames and also the display ladders that we used. Those years were definitely enjoyable adventures as we traveled, met interesting people, and discovered new places. Later, due to health issues, we stop entering craft shows and sold the mirrors at Mason's Home Furnishings in Fitzgerald.

Writing about the beach also reminds me of the dinners, dancing and fireworks celebration at the elegant Ritz Carlton and other places on Amelia Island. This year will be the 10th year that we have enjoyed celebrating New Year's Eve with friends. We have been blessed to have places at Fernandina Beach, so we could invite friends down to celebrate. Our dear friends, Jim and Connie Parrott, Johnny and Ethelyn Underwood, and Van and Patricia Waters have spent New Year's Eve with us there numerous times. We are always joined on New Years' Day by Ron and Susan Singleton and Gene and Pat Wilder to watch the bowl games and enjoy the camaraderie.

Last year was a different New Year's Eve celebration. There were only two couples, Connie and Jim and Gene and I, who were able to celebrate together. We no longer can accommodate everyone at Fernandina, so the four of us decided on a different venue. We spent our time on St. Simons Island at the King and Prince. We had an enjoyable time until the ice storm hit. There was no electricity; therefore, there was no food or warmth. We were lucky that we were four of the last people to get off the island before they closed the bridge.

What delightful memories, unforgettable one-liners and comments, we shared during those first years together. One of the most entertaining escapades was when Connie, Ethelyn, Patricia and I went to Chico's shopping. We all bought matching outfits at a greatly reduced price. When we left the condo, where our husbands were watching football, we all had on our own clothes. When we returned, we were all dressed alike in exact matching outfits. You should have seen the beguiling looks on the men's faces and heard the enigmatic comments from them, when we walked in. The four of us ladies were ecstatic, because we had finally discovered a way to get our husbands' attention during a football game.

This year, our New Year's celebration returned to Amelia Island where it all began. We are now down to just three couples, but we still have a delightful time. Gene and I went down a little earlier for me to meet with a real estate agent to put my condominium on the market. I have enjoyed it, along with my family, for the past 36 years, but it is time to close that chapter in my life. Our celebratory group was delighted to change our venue and stay at Amelia Island Plantation. We have found during the last ten years together that it doesn't really matter where we stay, as long as we are all together.

My precious mother loved to entertain and taught me the art of entertaining. Even though New Year's Eve was a big celebration at the beach, I still had to discover something special for our guests. As a memento through the years, our guests have received champagne flutes with the year etched on them. This has become a collectable gift for all of us to admire and reflect upon our delightful memories when we return home.

Obviously, the beach is the place where I can always go and rediscover myself. Whether I am besieged with joys or disappointments, marriages or divorces, reunions or sorrows, the beach is my heart beat. It is a noncompliant place sometimes, but it is the one place where I can understand life when I can no longer make sense of any thing else. It is my place of contentment.

Certainly, it is an enigma to me why everyone doesn't love the beach like I do. Unequivocally, it holds a special place for me. It is also the place where I decided, with Gene's urging, to write this book. Gene went with me to my first meeting of "Writers By the Sea" in

Fernandina. It is a delightful writers group that meets monthly to discuss the craft of writing. I have also found it to be an unbelievable support group.

Gene and I attended several writing sessions with Marla McDaniel leading the group discussions on creativity. It was here Gene discovered that he had a yearning to write as well. Gene loves writing short stories, but he never failed to concentrate first and foremost on my writing. I believe that last sentence displays the love and support that I have babbled about, concerning my husband.

When I remarried in 2005, Gene and I lived for three months in my family home. We both desired to find our own house as we began our new life together. Wanting to downsize, we searched for a smaller house. Each of us had certain wishes that we desired in a house. Gene wanted a swimming pool, a bedroom with a his and hers bath, and a screened porch. My only wishes were to live on a lake again and have a screened porch.

If you have never lived on a lake, you cannot imagine the peaceful, brown water as it slowly flows by or the sound of a flock of geese while landing and taking off. One can see a mirror image of the houses across the way and hear the voices echo. It is the morning sun rising or maybe it is the afternoon sun as it slowly sinks into oblivion. Oh, to be a part of that once again was my number one desire as Gene and I searched for a new home together.

Several months after we married, Gene came home and said he thought he had found us a house. The house actually encompassed all of the expressed wishes that we both desired. We went to look at the house, which was located on the outskirts of town, that very same afternoon. When I saw where the house was located, it was almost mystical. If someone had walked straight out of the front door of the house that my children lived in for 25 years, he would be at the front door of this new house in which we were interested.

When we drove up to the house, I wasn't as sure about the house as Gene. The house was built in the 1970s and was terribly outdated. However, he assured me that we could gut the inside and make it just like we wanted it to be. Well, I should say almost like we wanted it. I am not sure if you can ever make a house exactly the way you want it, but I will say that we did come close.

Gene and I bought the house and renovations began. While we were in that process, I must relate an amusing discussion that Whit and Laura Beth had when they saw the new house. Things were a wreck. There was wallpaper half off the walls and the carpet was torn up for new wooden floors to be installed. Gene and I overheard them ask the other what they thought about MeMa's new house. They both looked questionably. Within a few seconds, we heard Whit say, "Laura Beth, I liked their old house better. This one doesn't look very nice to me." And, Laura Beth nodded in agreement.

As we were giving Whit and Laura Beth a tour of the house, we giggled at the amusing discussions that the two continued to have with one another. Gene and I took them out to the pool house. As we showed them the disarray of it, he told the two that he was considering putting bunk beds in it. They looked at us and Gene told them that when they came to visit, they would have their own little space where they could camp out. Immediately, Whit got this distraught look on his face. He looked at us and said, "Mr. Gene, do we have to?"

When Gene and I moved out of my childhood home, I left every piece of my furniture there and Gene did the same in his house. We each agreed that we would bring one piece of furniture that was special to us for our new home. I brought a red painted oriental armoire that we placed at the front entrance. Gene brought a three-tier table that is presently in our guest bedroom. We both love our small, new home and feel that it is a part of each of us. Certainly, there are days that we definitely miss having a larger home to entertain but then we remember why we downsized.

Gene thoroughly enjoys entertaining our friends and always looks forward to seeing what elaborate decorations will come forth. He takes pleasure in seeing me scurry around to make the dazzling flower centerpiece and/or an unique and compatible table setting. Gene's favorite is always the resourceful goodie bag I make as a favor for our guests. Please note this is not as I see it, but this is strictly as he sees it when he describes it to others. Why do I go to the trouble of making our celebration so special? Because Gene encourages me to do it and who better to do it for, than your dear friends?

Knowing that you are not going to be criticized or put down for new thoughts and opportunities gives you the freedom to experiment with divergent ideas. My heart aches for those who never experience this because of the fear of intimidation by their spouse. How blessed I am that Gene came into my life for he is my number one fan and has helped me to come into my own. Studies show us that trying something new when you are older and breaking from the old routine is healthy and productive. I know now that is exactly what I am striving for at this stage in life. Gene has taught me it is okay to fail but that I must not be afraid to try. He is my biggest cheerleader and loves me unconditionally. What more could a spouse desire?

Getting older has its advantages and disadvantages much like the aches, pains, and joys that accompany it. I grew up with a peacemaker mentality wanting to appease everyone while being somewhat compliant to their wishes. Today, I find myself entertaining what I would call "discerning thoughts," something I would never have done when I was younger. Why, I don't really know, but I guess I feel that I have earned that right. I am not referring to negative thoughts because they will bring about negativity, but rather more candid and outspoken thoughts. I believe this often occurs with getting older much like Jenny Joseph describes in her poem "When I am Old, I shall wear purple."

On the plus side of getting older, it is nice being able to invite friends over and never even fret about the condition of your house. It no longer matters that the cake you are serving came from the bakery and is not homemade. I no longer desire to be wonder woman who has to have everything perfect. I wonder if I feel this way now because there are less consequences for not following the rules and going strictly by the book. My biggest regret is that I did not learn this earlier in life. If only I could impart this to the younger generation, what a more pleasant and less stressful life they would have.

A wonderful example of how my life and thoughts have changed with getting older is how I reacted several years ago. I was in the kitchen when I heard a shelf in my dining room fall from the wall, breaking all my inherited, as well as my own crystal stemware. Did I cry? Heavens, no! I just carefully picked up the pieces of glass, as not to cut myself, and reminded myself that those elegant glasses were only "things."

As my dear friend Ethelyn said when I related the fiasco to her, "It's ok. Nobody's hurt, nobody's sick, and nobody's dead." I wholeheartedly agree. It doesn't matter what you have in your life, but rather who you have in your life that truly matters. Doesn't that speak volumes, regardless of your age or whether you live in the North, the South, the East or the West? If only the younger generation could adopt that philosophy, how much easier their lives would be.

The years have flowed by like a flooded river, sometimes pushing me under as I struggled to catch my breath. Overall, it has been an exceptional, gratifying life. Weeks have become days, and days have become years, as I enter this final phase of my life. There is little "high cotton" left and not much work to be done. The living is no longer as easy, as in the Porgy and Bess "Summertime" song. I am now in the fall of my life and I wonder often where the time has gone? Of that I am not sure. The one thing that I am sure of is that I no longer dream of recapturing the days of my youth. Those days are done and will never be again.

As Gene and I drove in from the beach a few weeks ago, I was reminded that my time on earth is rapidly coming to an end. The storefronts in my small hometown, that I once was a part of, are now dilapidated; weeds are knee high in my old neighborhood; my old school is no longer a school but rather a Christian Kitchen for those less blessed. It appears that those are not the only changes I see. My mind is slowly eroding so many of my memories.

Feeling a little despondent, I realized that the beautiful red roses on Meadowlark Boulevard that have led us into our neighborhood all spring and summer are now beginning to fade. Just as the leaves are beginning to turn rust, along with a multitude of other changes, it is definitely the autumn of our lives. I am not complaining for I have been blessed with the American dream. I have had a wonderful life, but I must be realistic.

The grass has been mowed. The lawn is glistening with a touch of moisture from the rain, and the swath of fading yellow Lantana is welcoming us into our driveway. It is fall, a new day, and a new beginning for almost everyone but not for us. Even reflecting as I enter our home, I discover that the "humming" sound of the attic fan has been long gone and has now been replaced by the "humming" sound of the central air conditioning.

Someone once told me that old age is one of the hardest stages of life because you realize what lies ahead of you. That just might be true. It is not that we are not Christians and know where we are heading, it is just that we want to enjoy our family and friends a little bit longer. The time has arrived where Gene and I must devise our own plan of coping with this stage of life. We must utilize this time as we plot to adjust to our final years together.

Yes, life is different and so are we but we must learn to acclimate ourselves to the changing times. Gene likes to remind me often that we are no longer of this new generation. Truthfully, it is probably best for us to move on rather than be discouraged and question so much of the happenings in our world today. Don't get me wrong. I am thankful to still be part of this world and am grateful for every day. I am most thankful for every opportunity that Gene and I have to share our love with one another and with others as well.

The end is fast approaching as I find myself reflecting on my life and I pray that I have never tried to stifle anyone's happiness or their creativity. The time has come where I want to grab hold of everything and the goodie out of whatever is available to me. As I think about it that is exactly what I am doing. I had never ridden a jet ski, but now I can say I have owned one the past few years and enjoyed it. I had never painted a picture but I began a little painting three years ago. I had never written a book, but now I am finishing my first one.

These coming years, I am committed to filling my life with indescribable joy. I constantly am asking myself, as our dear friend, Howard Jordan says, "Are you having a large time or are you living life large?" I hope that I am living life large for this life is too fragile to be anything but happy. I want my life to be filled with much laughter for that is the best medicine ever and helps to keep my stress level low.

Don't wait until you are older like I, to focus more on your own life, but begin today. Surround yourself with good people, especially people who make you happy. Be sure that you concentrate on those individuals who are void of any drama, and know how to make the most of every day.

Gene and my life's journey is almost through, but what memories we can share with others around us. We have had an abundant life, complete and full of happiness. God has allowed us to move mountains of trials and tribulations, mountains of doubt and confusion, and mountains of worries and anxieties. We are beginning to get weary and realize again that the time is almost here. It is without much sorrow because we know that we will be with our Lord in a mansion, not made with hands, but eternal in the heavens.

As stated in a beautiful poem titled *The Train of Life* by Richard Gray. Our lives are filled with joy and sadness as we travel the journey we call life. People get on and off our train at different times in our lives. This poem states it so much better than I. It tells us that when our time comes, and we must step off the train, our lives should be so that they will spark memories for those left behind. This is the purpose of this book. I pray that all the passengers on my train of life have benefited in some small way, as they have traveled with me on my life's journey. God speed!

THE TRAIN OF LIFE

At birth we board a train and meet our parents. We believe they will always travel by our side. However, at some station, our parents will step down from the train, leaving us on this journey alone. As time goes by, other people will board the train and they will be significant-siblings, friends, the love of your life, children, and many others.

Some will step down and leave a permanent vacuum. Others will go so unnoticed that we won't realize they vacated their seats. The train ride will be full of joy, sorrow, fantasy, expectations, hellos, good-byes, and farewells. A successful ride requires having a good relationship with all passengers. We must give the best of ourselves.

The mystery to everyone is that we do not know at which station we ourselves will step down. So, we must live in the best way, love, forgive, and offer the best of who we are. It is important to do this because when the time comes for us to step down and leave our seat empty we should leave behind beautiful memories for those who will continue to travel on the train of life.

I wish you a joyful journey on the train of life. Reap success and give lots of love. More importantly, thank God for the journey and I thank you for being one of the passengers on my train.

Richard Gray's *The Train of life* is an edited version of an earlier poem written by an unknown author.

Photographs

Grandmother Sally Wheeler Coney,
age 18, Cordele, GA (1906)

My mother, Lydia Coney, Age 20,
Martha Washington College (1926)

My father, Harvey Jay, Age 21,
Mercer University (1927)

Four Generation of Jays,
the baby being my daddy, age 2 (1908)

1922 Fitzgerald High School Football team, my father, age 16, holding the football

Dr. Will S. Haile is shown with little Lydia Jay, daughter of Solicitor General Harvey L. Jay and Miss Louise Smith, librarian at the ceremonies of the ground-breaking of the children's building at the Carnegie Library, which is now under construction.—Photo by John Carter, Herald Staff Photographer.

Dr. Haile, Ms. Louise Smith and me, age 5, dedication of children's library annex (1948)

Me, age 10, (1953)

Me, Charles, Mother, Daddy, and Harvey (1950)

My parents, siblings and me (1981)

Daddy, age 68 (1974)

Mother, age 87,
Jaye Sherrell's wedding (1995)

My brother Harvey and wife Barbara Jay (1997)

My brother Charles and wife Kerry Jay (2007)

Lydia Jay, age 20, Brenau College, (1963)

My first year teaching, First Baptist Church Preschool (1981)

Lydia Jay Sherrell, age 23, Wedding Day (1967)

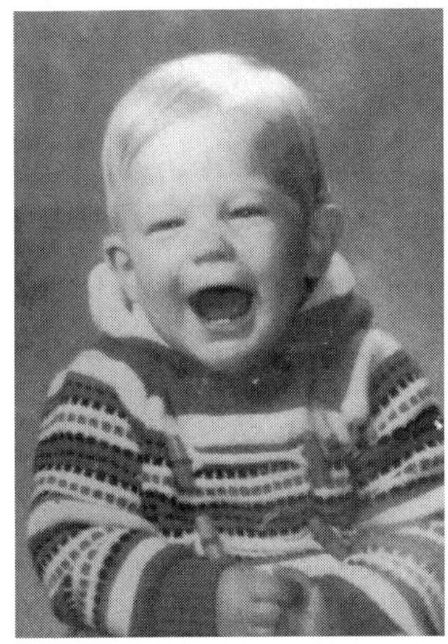

Rob Sherrell, age 6 months, (1969)

Jaye Sherrell, age 4, (1974)

Jaye Sherrell Mason's Wedding (1995)

Jaye and Jay Mason (2015)

Laura Beth Mason, age 4, and
Whit Mason, age 6 (2007)

Laura Beth Mason, age 16 (2017)

Amy Steele Sherrell's Wedding (2005)

Rob and Amy Sherrell (2018)

Rob, Jaye, and Robert (2014)

Robert Sherrell, age 4 (2018)

Whit Mason and Robert Sherrell, Disney Cruise (2017)

Fitzgerald's Woman of the Year,
Lydia Sherrell and Gene Mason (2004)

Lydia and Gene Mason's Wedding (2005)

Gene and Lydia Mason, Hawaii (2010)

Grandchildren,Laura Beth Mason, Robert Sherrell, Whit Mason (2018)

Our annual Fernandina Beach Trip (2018)

Made in the USA
Columbia, SC
03 November 2019

82600051R00167